# A Fundamental Basalt Flake Analysis

## Based on experimentally-produced and used flakes as well as the prehistoric Waikalua material

## Boris Deunert

BAR International Series 614
1995

Published in 2019 by
BAR Publishing, Oxford

BAR International Series 614

*A Fundamental Basalt Flake Analysis*

ISBN 9780860547952 paperback
ISBN 9781407349190 e-book

DOI https://doi.org/10.30861/9780860547952

A catalogue record for this book is available from the British Library

This book is available at www.barpublishing.com


BAR Publishing is the trading name of British Archaeological Reports (Oxford) Ltd.
British Archaeological Reports was first incorporated in 1974 to publish the BAR
Series, International and British. In 1992 Hadrian Books Ltd became part of the BAR
group. This volume was originally published by Tempvs Reparatvm in conjunction
with British Archaeological Reports (Oxford) Ltd / Hadrian Books Ltd, the Series
principal publisher, in 1995. This present volume is published by BAR Publishing,
2019.

# BAR
PUBLISHING

BAR titles are available from:

        BAR Publishing
        122 Banbury Rd, Oxford, OX2 7BP, UK
EMAIL   info@barpublishing.com
PHONE  +44 (0)1865 310431
FAX     +44 (0)1865 316916
        www.barpublishing.com

To Shawn

## LIST OF ILLUSTRATIONS

# ACKNOWLEDGMENTS

I am particularly indebted to Shawn Buchanan, Robert Borofsky, and Helmut Ziegert.

Shawn ( Archaeological assistant at the Bishop Museum ) postponed her personal career to help me through a phase of administrative difficulties and disputes about competence. She also helped me search for literature and did most of the correction of the manuscript. Without her, I would have given up.

Robert Borofsky (Associate professor at the Hawaii Loa College) was my supportive advisor and eloquent teacher in Hawaii. He always encouraged me to go on, even if everything seemed to be against me. Rob was challenging and provocative every second we spent together and helped me develop creative ideas.

Helmut Ziegert ( Professor for pre- and early history at the University of Hamburg ) supported me as best as he could several thousand kilometers away. He provided me with literature, as well as, helpful and critical advice. Prof. Ziegert also awoke my interest for the earliest remains of human history.
                    These three people never gave up believing in me.

I am grateful to Paul Cleghorn ( Leader of the Applied Research Group at the Bishop Museum ) for having introduced me in the high art of Hawaiian adze manufacturing and helpful advice since then.

I wish to thank Dr. Mary Schramm-Coberly for the careful recording of the tool use experiments and helpful suggestions. She has been a real friend. Dr. Terry Hunt provided me with the necessary appliances for the basalt flake analysis and MA Jo Lynn Gunness supported me with aiding advice and unconventional help. Dr. Yoshi Sinoto, Dr. Mary Riford, and Dr. Stephan Dane Clark made it possible that I could use the Waikalua material and the partly unpublished survey and excavation reports.

I also wish to credit the Botany Department, the Department of Geophysics, both at the University of Hawaii, as well as the Honolulu Police Department for the use of their facilities and for the sacrifice of their valuable time.

Special thanks to Mike the butcher for giving me the opportunity to cut up a 1/2 year old pig. MA Scott Medbury from the Foster Botanical Gardens provided me with the wood I needed for the experiments and Myrna, Brandon, and Alex were the Guinea Pigs for the blind tests.

I would also like to thank my parents, as they always supported my education. Without them, I would not have come so far.

Financial support was provided by a Government Grant of the Federal Republic of Germany and my parents.

Failings that may appear are my own responsibility and do not reflect the helpful advice of the above mentioned people.

# TABLE OF CONTENTS

## 1.1 OBJECT ORIENTED PROBLEM

I searched through the archaeological reports of the Bishop Museum with the intention of finding an assemblage or at least a subassemblage of stone tools, in order to answer the following questions:
A) Is it possible to find special manufactural techniques through the analysis of the edges of the stone tools ?
B) Are there any scratches or notches on the stone tools which could give a hint of their usage ?
C) Are earlier reports of assemblages analytical, and if so are they appropriate ?
D) Does my developing model fit the common artifact analytical models or do I have to add some points to prove special hypothesis ?
E) Is artifact analysis helpful and useful in solving prehistoric questions ?
F) Finally, do I have the possibility to synthesize cultural behavior of ancient Hawaiians based on the archaeological remains ?

After I finished searching through the material from the last 28 years, I had to face the fact that there was no appropriate stone tool assemblage that would be useful for my analysis. An artifact analysis with 53 different artifacts varying in appearance, and presumable use, is of little or no profit. By searching through these reports my attention was drawn to the thousands of basalt flakes that had been found on nearly every extensive excavation. Fortunately, no one had analyzed these flakes, leaving me with the opportunity to select one of the more recent excavations at Waikalua in Kaneohe. More then 12.000 flakes were found, waiting to be analyzed under the following questions:

See questions A to F.
G) Is it possible to recognize a manufacturing place or was the material pretreated at another location ?
H) Were flakes used for cutting, scraping, etc. in agri- or aquacultural use ?

## 1.2 THEME DELIMINATION AND DEFINITION

### a) factual

In order to answer these questions, methods had to be worked out that would be useful to support the hypothesis.to which the questions are related. Because of the unfamiliarity of basalt and its flaking attributes it was necessary to conduct several basalt modification experiments to show the usefulness of flakes for cutting and/or scraping purposes. A second step was the application of these flakes to material of different hardness or softness to investigate possible edge damage and use-wear. To make the experimentally produced flakes comparable to the Waikalua flakes, similar conditions had to be created. Assuming that most of the present flakes were waste flakes, resulted in the tool manufacturing process, the quantity of the produced flakes in relation to the finished worked stone tools had to be investigated. The determination of the most convenient angel of use for scraping and or cut-

ting should explore the necessary retouchment of the flakes to make them useful for this purpose. Decisive for the determination were factors like vulnerability during use versus sharpness. Who would use a flake for cutting when it hurts the user him/herself ? He/she will produce a flake with a convenient angle of use that will not hurt him/her while using. If this convenient angle of use would influence the sharpness of the flake so that it would be rendered useless he/she would find possibilities to cover or haft this flake. Because of theses reflections the resulting hypothesis concerning the Waikalua flakes would be the following. If the angle of use of the Waikalua flakes is not convenient ( considering the vulnerability ), but the botanical-chemical analysis shows plant and/or animal residues, or the flakes show use-wear or edge damage associated with cutting or scraping, these flakes were probably covered or hafted.

A last consideration in this experimental part was a comparison of waste flakes and especially produced cutting and/or scraping flakes to examine the hypothesis that simply retouched or unretouched waste flakes were used as easy to handle cutting and/or scraping tools.

The next main methodical part was the measurement of the Waikalua flakes in order to prove the above mentioned hypothesis. If there appears a clearly recognizable pattern in the edge angle measurements then it would support the theory about the most convenient angle of use. A clearly recognizable pattern in the dimensions would speak against the thesis that simply retouched or unretouched waste flakes were used for cutting and/or scraping purposes. Other measurements established the criteria for the selection of the flakes that should be considered for low and high power magnification.

The low power magnification shows recognizable use-wear, edge damage, and retouchment that clearly indicates the use of these flakes as tools. The obtained results should be compared with the investigated edge damage and use-wear of the flakes in the experimental part to relate these typical damage patterns to possible cut or scraped material.

The high power magnification can confirm or deny the results that are to be obtained in the low power magnification. If the botanical-chemical examinations show different plant or animal residues than assumed in the earlier experiments, we can conclude other cutting and/or scraping purposes of the flakes. If the results of both experiments correspond, the previous hypothesis seems to be very likely. A comparison of the botanical-chemical results with the faunal and floral analysis of the Waikalua site shall provide a further line of positively confirmatory evidence.

### b) spatial

The present basalt flake analysis is a continuous study of the archaeological salvage excavation at site 50-Oa-G5-101 Waikalua-Loko Kane'ohe conducted in 1986. On sixteen nonconsecutive days between 20. August and 3. October 1986 fieldwork was carried out in two phases: " (1) 14 days of controlled excavations in selected test areas to obtain samples of the archaeological deposits; (2) 2 days of monitored backhoe trench excavations. " ( Riford,Clark 1986:2 )

Under several other artifacts about 12.000 basalt flakes were found, 11.000 of them in provenience. The sorting criteria were diagnostic flakes, flake fragments, flakes with polish, awls, and modified/utilized flakes. The given definition of diagnostic flakes is: " Byproduct of tool manufacture and core reduction, termed debitage, having a ventral surface and complete proximal ( striking platform ) and distal (termination ) ends. The lateral edges may be complete or broken." Flake fragments are " debitage having a ventral surface and one or both ends broken. " Flakes with polish are described as " distinctive byproduct of tool ( usually adz use) resharpening and/or reworking, exhibiting one or more polished surfaces from the original tool. " In his 1979 work Clark defined awls as " nonhafted basalt flake or core tool on which one or more points were formed by modification (reduction) of one or two adjacent edges. "Modified/Utilized flakes are seen as " flakes and fragments of basalt which display macroscopic marginal scattering. The scars of purposeful modification prior to utilization are generally larger than utilization scarring on an unmodified edge." ( Riford/Clark 1986:46-47 ) Only the diagnostic flakes and flake fragments combined are 98,8% of the total basalt artifacts from controlled excavations. 56% of these flakes were recovered from the units 9-1, 9-5, and 13-4. 639 flakes and fragments were recovered from a posthole filling ( Feature 1a ), that was situated adjacent to sample area 9. During the presorting process, that included an examination under the microscope at 10x, twenty-four modified flakes and twenty-three awls were identified comprising thirty-two respectively thirty-one of the total number of recognized tools. Edge damage in the form of rounding, polish, and crushing was determined, but a detailed analysis was never made.

An additional macroscopic sorting which was based on the visual texture was made after studying several basalt samples from all over the Island of O'ahu. The basalt material was sorted into three categories of observed surface texture: medium, medium fine, and fine. These categories relate to the density of the visually examined basalt flakes. Four probable basalt sources were found. Ko'olau Caldera, Waiahole Quarry, Kailua Adz Quarry, and the Kane'ohe region. The nomenclature of this presorting will not be taken over in the present basalt flake analysis even though this might lead to confusion. ( See section II. ) Another objection to this previous nomenclature is the often hasty decision about the probable use of a tool and even, perhaps, the decision about weather it is a tool and the resulting classification thereafter. (See also 1.4 about computer application )

## c) temporal

Chronometric data of layer II indicate the occurrence of first settlement around AD 1070. This early date was established from the feature 1 pit that was dated AD 1070-1390. The duration of occupation was about 340 years until AD 1405. As all of the investigated basalt flakes ( in provenience ) were recovered either from the base of layer Ib or from layer II, these flakes must fall into this time frame.

## 1.3 RESEARCH LEVEL AND HISTORY

The study of the earliest remains of human history fascinated generations of scientists and hobby researchers. Their studies were characterized by their field of interest and/or experience they gained in their respective occupations. Innumerable theories and hypothesis were derived only for the possible use and manufacture of stone tools, however, their enumeration is outside the scope of this overview. The aim here is restricted to the description of the broader research concepts and theories developed over the past four decades, concerning the systematic analysis of stone tools under special consideration of flakes. Still influenced from earlier work " researchers " started to diversify and refine attribute classes with the purpose to obtain better typologie according to which they could classify and date lithic material. John Evens with his book " The ancient stone implements, weapons, and ornaments of Great Britain " was probably authoritative for the later American research ( Evens 1872 ). Even if Evens approach was a functionally oriented classification, that used a few use-wear features, the further research was more concerned to develop attribute classes derived from measurements of the stone tools. This approach culminated in the typological studies of the Upper Paleolithic period from D. Sonneville-Bordes and J. Perot ( 1954, 1955, 1956 ), Escalon de Fonton and de Lumley ( 1955 ), Boamers (1956), de Heinzelin ( 1962 ), and G. Laplace (1964 ). The purpose of these type-lists was to make a synthesis of the characteristics that the material may represent so that the lithic component of an archaeological assemblage can be understood. Over the years these studies were used to assign lithic material to the respective time outlined in the type-lists. Refined dating and working methods, and the improvement of those typologies through several blind tests indicated that different ways of classification led to different conclusions, so that the whole typologically derived interpretations are highly suspect. ( Minzoni- Deroche 1985 )

Several relicts from this speculative approach to stone tool classification are representative i.e. in the writings of Sieveking ( 1958 ), Tugby ( 1958 ), Sacket ( 1966 ), Shutler and Kess ( 1969 ), and Hole, Flannery, and Neeley ( 1969 ). In 1969 Sabloff and Smith tried to rescue the typological method through changing its nomenclature to type-variety system in order to obtain attribute variations. In this analytic and taxonomic classification a type represented " an aggrate of visually distinct... attributes already objectified within one or ( generally ) several varieties which, when taken as a whole, are identitive of a particular class... produced during a specific time interval within a specific region. " A variety would be the " minor, but significant variations within a type, either intrasite or intersite. " ( Sabloff/Smith 1969:278) This " new " system that was also used by Parson ( 1967 ), Wallrath ( 1967 ), and Culbert ( 1965 ) for ceramic classification is in general the same subjective classification model as the old " typologies ". Both research methods rely on a high degree of predefined attributes in order to establish a chronological sequence. In the sixties statistical methods were applied to master the large amount of data received through necessary measurements in typological systems. In 1963 Dempsey and Baumhoff i.e. tried to convince the reader that „ a purely statistical method of establishing dependable sequences is possible, but also that contextual analysis is a sufficiently sensitive technique to solve the archaeological problem. „ ( Dempsey/Baumhoff 1963:496 ) For further reading to the application of statistical-mathematical seriation methods of archaeological material it is recommended to consider an article of Allan Gelfand published in 1971. With the introduction of the computer, and the subsequent description of archaeological data in computer language, an even larger amount of data could be processed. The application of these new techniques in the concern of typologies, stretched only a misery carried over years from the archaeological discipline.

and weapons commonly used in their own culture. The ethnoarchaeological approach considers stone implements belonging to still existing preindustrial societies such as the Inuit, Australian Aboriginies, African tribes, and Native American . Through comparison of the stone tools used from these societies with the excavated prehistoric assemblages scientists try to explore function and manufacturing methods of these remains. Reports from Heider ( 1969 ) and Thomson ( 1964) can be exemplary for this kind of research design.

The step from pure observational ethnoarchaeology to behavioral archaeology was first done by Binford in 1969. He attempted to explore the relations which occur between prehistoric cultural behavior and the material record of that behavior. Gould, who became a representative of this method

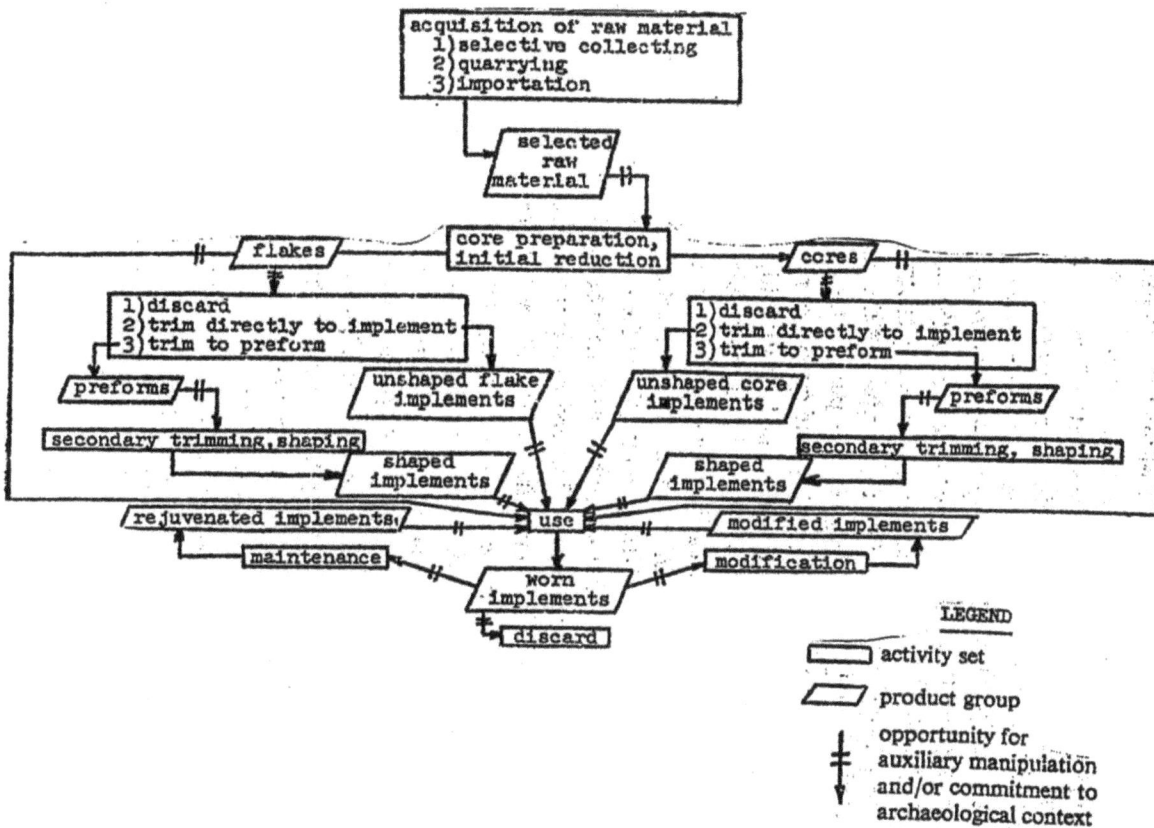

(Figure 1 Collins, in Swanson, Lithic Technology 1975:18)

Archaeology in the sixties also experienced a boom in different methodological research concepts. As they all arose at nearly the same time, it is impossible to stay in a chronological sequence with this historical overview. They will be handled in the succession: a) ethnoarchaeology and behavioral archaeology, b) experimentation, and c) use-wear.

## a) Ethnoarchaeology and behavioral archaeology

For a number of decades scientists sought to discover the true identify of prehistoric tools through analogy with metal tools

expressed the new design as follows: " Since discard behavior and residue formation, like language are universal human characteristics, their patterning can be studied in a manner akin to grammar in language. Consistent observed relationships between human behavior and material residues in contemporary societies may posited as proportions for cross cultural testing and comparison with prehistoric human residues. " ( Gould 1978:815 ) In Earl Swansons 1975 published lithic technology we get acquainted with a generalized flow model of the population of chipped stone tools. ( Collins 1975:18 ) He considers the three main criteria that influence the use-life of tools, the manufacturing process, the use and possible recycling phase and the discard of the emaciated tools. ( Figure 1 )

Further development and refinement of the use-life model was done just recently by Kelly ( 1988 ), Grimes and Grimes ( 1985 ), and Shott ( 1989 ). " Use-life is the straightforward concept that denotes the length of service of tool classes in systematic context ". ( Schiffer 1976:60 ) It can be measured on a variety of scales, including the number of strokes for which a tool is employed and the number of specific uses. Factors other than the length, width, and thickness of a tool must be considered to make use-life measurable. Determinants of use-life are : 1) The breakage in production, which implies immediate discard or purpose unrelated use to the original function, 2) abandonment during or after production, which means that even intact tools may be abandoned, if proved unsuitable for their intended purpose, 3) loss or breakage in use, that could lead either to discard or to 4) recycling, a process that could change the original function of a tool, 5) rejection and abandonment of tools that are still functional ( stylistic change ), 6) depletion before or after possible rejuvenation, 7) labor investment or manufacturing cost are an indicator of quick or late discard, as it seems not plausible to abandon a tool in which a lot of labor was invested, 8) curation or maintenance technology are indicators for high use-life, as it seems reasonable that the more curated items are longer lasting. ( Free after Shott 1989:18-23 ) A further try in behavioral archaeology to relate mobility to the organization of a technology was shown to be unrealistic. (Bramford 1986 )

**b) Experimentation**

As could be seen in the behavioral, archaeological approach, experimentation was a necessity to improve tool function related hypothesis. In the past thirty years archaeological investigations into human history have increasingly employed the concepts of model- building in the attempt to predict and understand ancient activities. To lead these often highly theoretical models into the higher ranks of probability they had to be tested in some way. This testing could be done through observation of contemporary societies, the enforcement of experiments or, even better the combination of both. Experimental archaeology imitates past cultural behavior though the carrying-out of experiments. The text book to learn for example, stone tool manufacturing techniques are the ancient stone tools, flakes, and debitage themselves. The aim is to reproduce these tools, flakes, and their arrangements as found in the archaeological excavation. Nowadays, experiments are quite common in archaeological investigations and are drawn near to several archaeological problems derived because of the lack of background information. Particularly Denmark, i.e. the Lejre center carries out noticeable research in this direction. ( Hansen 1974,1975 ) Several scientists (Ascher, 1961; Callahan, 1976; Coles 1973, 1979; Ingersoll et al. 1977; Knudson 1978; Reynolds 1977,1978 ) have refined this approach that finds its application also in use-wear analysis.

**c) Use-wear**

Use-wear analysis led to a new avenue of research, as it enables the scientist to examine striae and edge damage that were caused by natural or human forces. Because of experiments the analyst is able to assign special patterns on the tool surface (arrangement of groves, notches, etc..) to tool functions and as such to state the field of activity of ancient man. Lithic use-wear analysis, the systematic study of the distribution of traces of use in relation to overall shape of the implement, started out worldwide with the translation of Semenovs 1957 published book " Lithic Technology " in 1964. Sonnenfeld who wrote a paper about " The function of primitive implements " ( Sonnenfeld 1962 ) without prior knowledge of Semenovs results can be put in one line with the founders of the low power magnification approach. In general use-wear analysis can be devided into two groups: 1) One group focusing on traces of " edge damage ", microscopic fracturing, and abrasion visible at relatively low magnification. ( Wilmsen 1968, Crabtree 1973, Nissen and Dittemore 1974, Trigham et al. 1974, Odell 1977, 1979, Odell and Odell-Vereecken 1980 ) The other group deals with striation and polishes ( microwear ), at relatively high magnification ( up to 700x ) under direct lighting. The second approach was developed by Keeley (1980 ) and was further applied by Moss ( 1983), Vaughan (1985 ), Toth (1985), and Yerkes ( 1987 ). Ilkjaer lamented the lack of easy access to high power magnification devices that will lead to a decrease in observational accuracy and delays in documentation and classification of use-wear. (Ilkjaer 1979:345 ) Because of this deficit, the high power approach was over the years seen as less important, and single works in this field were little noticed. The more about this research method was published the clearer it became that this approach could not be denied, especially after the proof of its accuracy through several blind tests. ( Keeley 1980, Bamford 1986. Shea 1987 ) Proportional to the justification of the high power approach, the critique towards low power, especially the edge damage approach grew. In particular the attempt to relate tool edge angles to specific tool functions. Wilmsen ( 1970 ) asserts that tools with edge angles of 40 degrees to 55 degrees are probably associated with hide scraping while tools with edge angles ranging from 66 degrees to 75 degrees are better suited for scraping wood and bone. Siegel showed proof that there is no significant relationship between particular working activities and the corresponding tool edge angle. " It may be suggested that tool edge angle is related to gross categories of activities. In other words, tools whose edge angle falls into the lower range ( i.e. 26 degrees to 35 degrees ) may be considered likely to have been used in activities based upon longitudinal motion. These would include cutting, sawing, whittling, and carving. Tools with edge angles in the higher ranges may be considered as having been used in activities based upon transverse motion, as scraping planing and adzing." ( Siegel 1985:93 ) Several edge damage influencing factors that were not considered from the researchers dealing with edge damage investigation are listed by Donahue: " 1) Different worked material cause different rates of microwear development and rounding. 2) Different kinds of flint ( and silica in general ) also vary in their rate of rounding and microwear development. 3) Inclusions of foreign matter, such as dirt, in materials being worked can greatly affect the rate of microwear. 4) Edge-angle, edge-length, and fracturing rates affect the rate of rounding and microwear development. 5) The rejuvenation of worn edges by retouch can confound estimates on the amount an edge was used." (Donahue 1984:365, see also Lawrence 1979:117 ) In addition the analyst must also consider the complicating factor of damage done to an edge after the tool was abandoned. (Sheets 1973 ) In the knowledge of this, Keeley examined the discriminant factors between traces resulting from natural processes and those humanly produced. ( Keeley 1980:28-62 ) He also noted the necessity of experiments carried out in the natural environment rather then in a laboratory, as the flake falling on the ground receives its first use-wear. ( Keeley 1980:16 ) Especially Jelinek et al. (1970) and Keeley ( 1980:8,15,25,26 ) criticized experiments carried-out under constant conditions in a laboratory like Speth's hard-hammer-percussion experimentation. ( Speth 1971:74-75 ) Speth's mechanical droppings of steel balls on to massive glass prisms at an impact angle of 45 degrees should determine the effects of oblique impact on several attributes of flake size and flake shape.

Regardless of the numerous critiques " edge damage researchers" went on to develop attribute classes of edge damage patterns and in the end a " logical and consistent system " ( Odell 1979:329 ) to record the produced amount of data. This attribute defining system strongly resembles a typological method to sort tools after a type-list and this, in general was attempted to do. Speth's comment to this kind of attribute classification is that " it will produce a massive quantity of redundant information with little or no improvement in its explanatory value. " ( Speth 1972:56 ) Another problem is that researchers working largely in geographic and academic isolation will vary in the quality of recording and experimental design that would lead to different attribute classifications. That even this is the main discrepancy show blind tests from Mc Guire ( 1986 ) and Siegel ( 1985 ). Both researchers state that there are differences between individuals using use-wear analysis. Shea, who did the same test concludes that " the results of six blind test results, show apparently equal abilities of individuals using microwear and edge damage techniques to determine stone tool uses. " ( Shea 1987:44 ) Mc Guire argues that experience apparently plays a part to receive quite comparable results. ( Mc Guire 1986:62 ) That Mc Guire's concluding statements are right show case studies obtaining different results on the same object, while using the same method. Nance concludes in a microwear study about so called " central Californian projectile points ", that these artifacts were rather used for cutting purposes ( Nance 1971), while Sheets ( 1973 ) clearly states their use as projectile points. Comparing Keller's ( 1966:303 ) developed model of edge damage patterns on stone tools in several stages of use with Tomenchuks ( 1979:124 ) developed model of the same kind, one becomes aware that there seems to be a discrepancy in the results, even if we consider the fact that Keller's experiments were carried-out in a natural environment through strokes with the hand versus Tomenchuk' mechanical approach. For the future it seems advisable, to be more accurate in investigating use-wear, to compare results and not to rely only on one kind of approach. ( Siegel 1985:90 ) Low power as well as high power magnification has its advantages, as Keeley ( 1980:12-14 ) states. A stereomicroscopic low power examination enables the observation of a three-dimensional image. The binocular microscope can be used to investigate larger objects, while the stage areas of a SEM are mostly to small to hold them. Therefore the higher magnification of an electron scanning microscope allows a closer examination of polishes and striation.

Cleaning of the examining tools is necessary in any case. Semenov suggested cleaning with " spirit or benzene and washing in hot water with a light application of soap " (Semenov 1964:24 ) Keeley immersed the tools in warm HCI ( 10% solution ) and NaOH ( 20% to 30% solution ), which removes lime, minerals, and organic deposits. After this treatment he immersed the tools in an ultrasonic cleaning tank to remove small particles such as sand, silt, or dirt. (Keeley 1980:11 ) Donahue used as a first step hydrochloric acid and acetone, afterwards non abrasive soap and water. The latter showed him that a chemical bath was unnecessary ( Donahue 1984:363 ) All researchers pointed out that it is essential to examine the tools before washing to detect possible residues that could give a hint of the tool's usage. As such it is beneficial to use the " new technique for the measurements of artifact angles " developed from Burgess and Kwamme in 1978 after the examination of the residues.

Subsequent research showed that it is indeed important to investigate plant and animal residues on tool surfaces. The founder of the plant and animal residue examination was Briuer in 1972. He identified through microscopic analysis morphologically distinct plant parts. These results were supported through the use of standard botanical-chemical reagents. He applied Ploroglucin and Hydrochloric Acid, Iodine Potassium Iodide, and Sudan III on tool surfaces to determine residues as outlined by Mc Lean and Cook (1941:73-76) All these reagents react in a typical way with the cell wall substance of the plant or animal. The indicator is mostly a visible color change. To exclude the possibility that the botanical-chemical examination of the flakes show only the plants that overgrew the artifacts when they were exposed at the surface, Briuer did additional research of randomly chosen samples of rocks and macrofloral remains from the same layer. Briuer's research was disregarded for a long time and was not taken seriously until 1979 in a study of Shafer and Holloway about organic residues. Contrary to Briuer's research they were able to scrape sufficient amounts of organic material from the tools to examine them under the microscope. Under consideration of use-wear, the amazing result of their study was, that a flake with a sharp edge was selected for cutting of every kind of material, rather than a flake that was produced for a specific task. Along with the examination of the plant and animal residues went the investigation of an observed " sickle sheen " on tools. The appearance of this sickle sheen has been explained through silica particles spreading over the tool surface while cutting organic material, especially wheat. " Opal phytoliths are created from a hydrated silica dissolved in groundwater that is absorbed through a plants root and carried through the vascular system..... Production of phytolith silica bodies is generally heaviest in the epidermal tissue of the stems and leaves in herbaceous plants, especially in monocotyledonous groups..... Silica body production is continuous during the growth of a plant, with silification being greatest in mature or senescent plant portions. " ( Rovner 1983:226-227 ) Rovner also gives an overview of the diverse methods of phytolith extraction and determination. ( Rovner 1983:238-240 ) Del Bene, Newcomber, and Kamminga ( in Hayden 1979 ) presented papers at the Simon Fraser Lithic Use-wear Conference about the built up, observation, and tool alteration caused by phytolith. Brown ( 1984 ) and Piperno ( 1984 ) published phytolith keys for the comparison and identification of phytolith groups. Studies of Anderson (1980 ) and Hurcombe ( 1986 ) draw a dark perspective for the analysis of plant and animal residues. Anderson states that only a small percentage of the tool residues will be adherent, and that the amount is mostly insufficient for qualified analysis. Hurcombe sees a very unfavorable relationship to the invested time and the outcome of those experiments, but is generally convinced from the validity of those investigations.

In 1980 Burton ( 1980 ) and Newcomber/Sieveking ( 1980 ) developed methods to analyze " waste flakes ", that would later be called debitage analysis. While Newcomber and Sieveking tried to figure out the relation between tool manufacturing and the resulting flake scatter patterns, Burton tried to relate flake groups to knapping activities and assigned them key attributes through dimension measurements. Fish wrote in 1981 about debitage analysis -- the systematic study of chipped stone artifacts that are not cores or tools -- " it provides important information for reconstructing prehistoric, lithic technology and patterns of human behavior. " (Fish 1981:374 ) Indeed his study illustrates how complex interaction of functional, occupational, and organizational factors differentially influences debitage assemblage variations. Stall and Dunn examined the size distribution of waste flakes resulting from the manufacture of bifacial stone tools. They found out that "the size of waste flakes from the manufacture of bifacial projectile points, knives, or large handaxes will systematically decrease from the initial to final stages of manufacture as the emerging tool is suduced, thinned, and shaped."( Stall and Dunn 1982:85-86) Therefore they advised excavators to be more cautious when screening in archaeological excavations as a particular flake size distribution represents the unbiased remains of bifacial manufacture. Sullivan and Rosen conclude in their 1985 paper that the assignment of key attributes observed on individual specimens is a non-reliable way to infer technological origins of debitage. Manufacture of chipped stone artifacts should rather be viewed as a continuum. ( Sullivan and Rosen 1985:755 ) They also criticize non-tool stage typologies as they clearly rely on subjective definitions which, for example, should be considered as a secondary or as a tertiary flake.

The Hawaiian research shows only little application of experimental archaeology concerning basalt flakes and their probable usage in prehistoric Hawaii. Patric Vinton Kirch (1985:194 ) as well as Jane Allen ( 1981:65 ) pointed out that little attention has been given to basalt flakes at all. Emphasis earlier was on those artifacts that could be seriated. ( Bonk 1954, Emory and Sinoto 1961, Sinoto 1962, Tuohy 1965, Soehren 1966, Kirch and Kelly 1975, Sinoto 1979, Chapman and Kirch 1979, Kirch 1979 ) The only extensive work about basalt flakes was done by Mc Coy and in continuation by Cleghorn. ( Mc Coy 1976, 1978, Cleghorn

1982) Mc Coy and Cleghorn selected 19 debitage flakes for thin sectioning as part of their research at the Mauna Kea Adze Quarry to examine the range of geographical and observable macroscopic variations in quarry rock. In 1982 Cleghorn experimented with the edge-holding and compressive strength properties of Mauna Kea Adz basalt. His debitage assemblage analysis, which also included the quantitative analysis of flakes resulting from the adz manufacturing process, should primarily enlighten adz manufacturing techniques and reduction strategies, rather than investigate the possible use of those "waste" flakes. (Cleghorn 1982) Beggerly examined edge damage on experimentally used scrapers of Hawaiian basalt in 1976. She developed the theory that the hardness or softness of the wood worked does not affect the edge damage patterns of the stone tools. She originally intended to use stroke variables of 1000 to 2000 strokes, however she altered her experiments to lower stroke variables such as 250 to 500, even though she noted that the tool was blunted after 200 strokes. (Beggerly 1976:23)

Clark (1979) who conducted a replication and use-wear study of Hawaiian basalt awls indicates the usage of these tools for delicate woodworking. Kirch (1979:169) suggested a possible usage of basalt flakes in fishhook manufacturing, fish cleaning, general fishing and marine exploitation tasks, or as Allen ( 1981:66 ) proposed for food preparation, like cutting taro corms for vegetative reproduction, harvesting leaves and corms, mounting earth for traditional taro cultivation, and cleaning small channels around the mounds for irrigation waters and drainage. Research about flakes, made of material other then basalt, was done with volcanic-glass flakes. Cleghorn ( 1974, 1975 ) investigated the technological and edge-damage attributes of an assemblage of some 1912 volcanic-glass flakes from the Wailea site at the Island of Maui. He provided a detailed non-metrical attribute analysis and examined unmistakably utilized flakes under the microscope. He concluded that " volcanic-glass flakes were probably used for minor cutting or scraping tasks. " (Cleghorn 1975:47 ) Kirch ( 1979:169-171 ) obtains a similar solution. Because of the fairly sharp edges of the flakes and their easy usage, simply modified flakes could have been used as a kind of multipurpose scraping and/or cutting implement. Barrera and Kirch ( 1973:185-186 ) saw a similarity to our " pocket knife " that fulfills the same purpose. The reconstruction of core reduction sequences through the analysis of volcanic-glass flakes was done by Schousboe, Riford, and Kirch in 1983. They developed a procedure for the description and analysis both non-metrical and metrical attributes and proposed a model for hand-held and bipolar techniques of core reductions.

In 1989 Williams conducted a debitage analysis of material from Ko'oho'olau Rockshelter No. 1 at the Mauna Kea Adze Quarry. He developed a reduction stage model that enables the excavator to assign specific debitage occurrences to stages in the reduction model.

The most recent study about microwear patterns on experimental basalt tools was done by Richards ( 1988 ) based on material from Cache Creek, British Columbia. He and his team conducted several experiments using Cache Creek basalt mainly for slicing, sawing, scraping. whittling, graving, and boring of different material with varying degrees of quality ( dry, wet, gritty, old or fresh ) Other variables were the tool angle, the prehension of the tool, the applied pressure, the duration of the experiment, and the number of strokes. Especially under high magnification Richards was able to detect use-wear in form of striation, polish, and rounding and assign those definite traits to special activities. Blind tests confirmed his statements. He did not however, examine if prehistoric Cache Creek stone tools show the same use-wear patterns or if they are detectable at all.

## 1.4 EVALUATION OF SOURCES AND TECHNIQUES USED

### a) Literature

America, the land of unlimited opportunities, finds its limits in the presence of European literature. While publications from England, France, and Spain are quite common and easily accessible in the libraries, the writings done in the countries on and eastward the line Sweden, Denmark, Germany, Switzerland, and Italy are hardly detectable. Supposing, that the exponation of the Hawaiian Islands towards the Mainland was the decisive factor for the lack of this literature, I assumed studies in Berkeley and Stanford would close this gap. The overwhelmingly sophisticated system of these libraries did help in gaining deeper insights in the English and American literature, especially dissertation manuscripts, but did not provide the above mentioned literature. The possibility to order literature lists, books and articles from the respective countries was not taken into consideration because of the restriction in research time. ( Three weeks ) Supported by the archaeological Institute in Hamburg it was possible to look into small parts of the recently published German literature. Confronted with these perspectives, a decision had to be made weather to restrict the research to the American, English, and French literature or to do further research in Europe. The limitations in time and financial budget forced the first possibility.

The archaeological literature is, similar to other countries, a child of its time. The financial shortenings in the social sciences affect the carefulness and conceptual feasibility of the archaeological research. Even if someone realizes the effectiveness of electron scanning microscopy and the valence of botanical-chemical experiments, he/she is restricted to the use of a binocular microscope or a few chemical tests to determine residues, while other science branches are reverse discriminated concerning accessibility of expensive appliances and money support. The " research level and history " ( part 1.3 ) shows the reliance on typological concepts up to the seventies, while innovative ideas, like Briuers plant and animal residue research were neglected for a long time. The fruitless typological approach is explainable as the attempt to keep research costs as low as possible, and indeed, the most expensive factor in this system is the capacity for work. This capacity is already paid, as the scientist is hired from the educational institute for teaching and research. Both, teaching and research are hardly combinable and lead to abridgments in free time. The generally positive try to publish the research results ends in overhasty written manuscripts, which are only partially presented ( abstract/summary ) or totally altered from the respective publisher. ( In this concern it was very useful to have the possibility to read the original manuscripts ) A few scientists have the opportunity to research and publish exclusively, supported through a grant or personal savings. These workings are in general more carefully performed and independent from prevailing research concepts.

The literature used in the present study can be seen as balanced, critical, and of high academic level, although it would be desirable to have a greater variety of research concepts.

### b) In what degree is the computer useful for archaeological questions in consideration of basalt flake analysis ?

" Computer archaeology ? You don't
dig up very many of those, do
you ? "
(Chenhall 1967:161)

The most visionary predictions have tended to underestimate grossly the rapid growth in the use of computers in all areas of our society. A computer is able to do sorting and selecting, processes that would involve a great deal of manual work for a single researcher. To meet these requirements one has to feed the computer with the appropriate input. An input is appropriate when converted into analogous symbols that adequately represent the real world of physical and cultural reality. Artifacts have to be described in the framework of models, to be made meaningful and convertible into machine language. Chenhall's proposed model seems to be a sufficient approach. He gives every archaeological object special attributes which he described as perpetual, inferential, and relational. In summary he described these attributes as follows:

**A: Empirical attributes:**
1. Spatial relations: Provenience -- site location, unit, room, level, etc.
2. Quantity
3. Chemo-physical specifications: Material(s), form, surface treatment and design, dimensions -- length, width, thickness, height, diameter

**B: Inferences**
1. Apparent function or use
2. Technique of manufacture
3. Apparently significant associations
( Chenhall 1967:162-163 )

This kind of theoretical structure may seem to be almost naively oversimplified in view of the kind of archaeological research being carried on today, but his system is sufficiently expandable. It shows a high degree of accuracy, especially in part A:, However, it has its weaknesses. These same basic weaknesses can be seen in every simple or complicated research project,( as will be explained further below ). Part B is based on subjective observations and personal or scholarly opinions. Number one and three especially, set limitations on further research. Once an opinion about the function, use, or significant associations of an artifact is entered into the computer, the artifact gets a lifelong stamp. Further research will not be uninfluenced, by this classification. If, for example, the associated function of an archaeological object is defined as an arrowhead in the opinion of researcher x, while researcher y, defines a similar looking object as an abrader, these objects will never be comparable to the computer. The computer's treatment is based on the input and can only work with that. It can not see a new classification based on the solution to some problem, unless programmed with that specific problem, Although the computer permits many things that were previously impossible, it can not perform miracles on its own.

Archaeology, more than many other sciences, has accumulated vast quantities of data over the years and continues to do so at an ever increasing rate. In the seventies many scientists wanted to create a data bank for storage and retrieval of archaeological data, if possible all over the world or at least for Europe and/or the United States. Most archaeologists agreed that it would be worth while to install such a system with some minimal level of information ( such as that represented in Part A of Chenhalls's proposed model ) on all archaeological sites and artifacts. A hot discussion kindled about the addition of evaluation data as, for example, the possible use of an artifact in a doubtful chronological arrangement of sites. Some archaeologists pointed out the uselessness of such a data bank system that would not contain all of the data about one artifact, feature or site. Others were skeptical about its value to future research designs, since possible research designs are extremely numerous and diverse, and to attempt to record data for all possible analytic contingencies would be impossible. Another crucial factor was the level of archaeological training and knowledge of concepts and terminology that would be needed by the classifiers to deal with this amount of material in a finite time. Scholtz and Chenhall explained that a periodic review of the instructions is desirable to prevent observers " from straying from what was thought to be a well defined path, and to insure that different observers have not given different interpretations to the instructions." (Scholtz/Chenhall 1976:94 ) This closed, self-monitoring system would not allow the innovative ideas that are so important in archaeological research.

Classical archaeology refused to accept the computerization of their branch of science for a long time. Computer scientists smiled at them and sarcastically commented that classical archaeologists still preferred to rely on intuition, feel, etc. What those scientists meant by " feel " and intuition was perhaps the refusal to accept a system that excluded further innovative ideas.

Scholtz's and Chenhall's prediction about a data bank that" has to be created to satisfy realistic and precisely defined needs " ( Scholtz/Chenhall 1976:96 ) is a variable with three unknown elements. What is realistic, how can this be precisely defined, and what are the needs ? Data banks have to be compatible, that implies an overall typological definition for Chenhall's Part B, to make reanalysis possible. This ar-

chaeological classification would have to question the nature of the data, the nature of the attributes used to describe or characterize the data, and the nature and supposed meaning of the desired classification. However, there would never be enough information that reading the data base would take the place of going back to look at the original artifacts.

The data bank is clearly concentrated on an extremely high level of detailed attribute definition. This particular level of long-term, fixed taxonomic hierarchy that would define overall types is simply " not flexible enough a priori for progressive archaeological research. " ( Whallon 1972:106 ) The status of every artifact is ascribed and as such not certain. If we rely on this ascribed status, we create at the same time true or false, but in any case uncertain history. (Borofsky 1987)

It can be seen from the above that even if we use the same criteria for identifying artifacts and their use, all over the world, and we use the same coding system for the computer, we will not obtain more valuable results. The problem will still be that the computer, (respectively programmer), thinks or functions in today's logical- mathematical way. In archaeological terms the broad aim of this logical-mathematical way is to assign each artifact to a defined type, and then to describe any assemblage quantitatively by the count or percentage of each type found. The question arises now, if "prehistoric people" thought in the same logical-mathematical way in which we try to explore them. Thomas Gladwin did research in this direction. As he worked anthropologically in Pulawat, a small island among the Caroline Islands, he found out that the conceptual model of thinking is basically different from our westernized one. He showed that the Pulawatans are unable to solve problems as they are defined in our IQ testing program. These people react with a lack of understanding to these examinations as we often do towards their society. He also found that Pulawatans who were educated in the western model had difficulties learning and accepting the old traditional values of Pulawat society. Gladwin asked the question: " What are the significant dimensions of intelligence, innovation, or abstraction to which we should be addressing ourselves when we make comparisons across cultural lines, whether these are between social classes or between the United States and Pulawat? " (Gladwin 1970:221) Indeed, although we do make comparisons between prehistoric society and our own, we probably do not begin to imagine how different prehistoric life may have been. The reason for this is the unfamiliarity of modern man with methods of manufacturing and even more of using flaked stone tools, and his remoteness in all ways from prehistoric groups that used such tools.

Nowadays archaeology is gradually adopting the computer as one of its major tools for research, because the computer permits more complex manipulation and statistical calculation than could be achieved in any ways. This adopting process is not unique in the history of archaeology. Adoption of techniques from physics, geology, biology, etc.. has been done years before. Mostly this adoption resulted in selfish borrowing of methods and theories to apply to archaeological problems and data. In most cases there was an active interplay between the borrowed method and the resulting thinking and the direction of research. Almost all of the recent and extensive work in the field of statistical or computer classification archaeology has consisted simply of borrowing methods, applying them to some body of data and considering the results. Sometimes data are processed by a computer program with out a very clearly stated purpose, although presumably it is hoped to discover at least something that can be used for further research. (If the predicted something never materializes, then the whole thing becomes a white elephant.) This unfortunate situation has resulted from the fact that many archaeologists are so overwhelmed by the enormous capacity and abilities of the computer that they forget , in this admiring phase, their own research concept. One has the feeling, for instance, that Gains and Gaines, (Chenhall 1968: 20/ Gaines and Gaines 1980:463-466) in their article about " Future Trends In Computer Application", admire the computer so much that they have forgotten the basic purpose of archaeology to get knowledge about prehistoric societies. Another problem is that the extensive unfamiliarity with the computer and its functions. Robert Chenhall asks " how many archaeologist are there , for example , who understand the difference between factor analysis and cluster analysis, or, for that matter even such elementary concepts as how and when to use the chi square?" (Chenhall 1968:23) Even today, computer applications are not often required for the study of archaeology, and also the author has to admit to having only insufficient knowledge about the vast facilities of computers. Today there are a lot of computer programs on the market. Archaeologists buy them and use them without asking the basic fundamental question if these adopted research tools fit their own research design. Wallon enumerates some of the computer abilities: "simple descriptive statistics, sorting, counting, cross-plots , parameters of distribution, frequency distributions , associations, and correlations " (Whallon 1972:40) but also nonstatisical tasks ranging from initial research planing, through field and laboratory work, to final report writing and archival storage of information. These functions make the computer in a high degree useful for archaeological cluster analysis, factor analysis, tabulation, horizontal and vertical artifact plots, simulation, regression, discriminant analysis, sampling, and pollen analysis. Today's analysis of artifacts could be described as the examination of micro settlement level, as this research explores only a small part of the prehistoric society. Many researchers overlook the necessary level of abstraction, since they can not determine modes of behavior through the analysis of artifacts without relating them to broader settlement patterns.

After all, basalt flake analysis will not be doable without the use of the computer. Desirable is a small, specialized data bank for basic measurements of edge angle, dimensions, etc... These measurements should not lead into a typology and should not be used to explain prehistoric cultures. The author uses them only in relation to data received though experiments in stone tool production. Both debitages will be quantitative analyzed through the computer to solve the problem about a possible manufacturing place.

In conclusion I am extremely doubtful that the computer can be used as a medium to solve archaeological questions. We should ask ourselves if the direction we take in the computerization of archaeology should not be rethought and shortened, as for instance in storing only data that are unchangeable. Maybe we should see the computer more as a tool for research rather than as a new research design.

## c) The use of sampling

In the last twenty years of archaeological research, sampling techniques have come to be used as a matter of course. Archaeologists realized that the methods of statistics and mathematics could be applied to archaeological research, especially to survey and to establish artifact attribute classes. This led to a wide range of suggested sampling techniques, which were often applied, more or less successfully. In the 70's "archaeological statisticians" contrived highly complicated statistical analyses applying to every problem archaeologists had regarding the selection of excavation units or the sampling of huge artifact assemblages. These statistical analysis were so complicated that it needed an expert to assign them to the proper task. In the end, archaeological sampling got its own nomenclature, like sample unit, sample frame , and stratum, while other terms, like target- or sampled population, were taken over from other fields. In the case of ( simple ) random sampling versus probability sampling this nomenclature led to fierce discussions. In general there are three ways of sampling, which will be at this point summarily presented:
> 1) statistical
> 2) archaeo-statistical
> 3) archaeological

## 1) Statistical Method

The aim of the statistical sampling method is to find a representative sample, eliminate bias through statistical methods and obtain reliable data that can be used to explain and reconstruct extinct cultures and past human behavior. The statistical approach needs to use clearly mathematically defined criteria to select subdivisions for investigation. This sampling method claims to be more sophisticated than the biased-choice method of the pure archaeological approach. In order to avoid the human bias of conscious selection, this sampling method was developed which was in a high degree static and simultaneously produces similar research designs for all basic questions, from the selection of excavation units to artifact analysis. ( See also the section about computer application in this thesis )

## 2) Archaeo-statistical Method

The archaeo-statistical approach takes into account both the archaeological problem, ( respectively research object ) and the statistical methods of obtaining representative samples. This combination allows the archaeologist to modify statistically valid sampling methods because of the archaeological data.

## 3. Archaeological Method

The archaeological or problem oriented method determines which subdivisions are selected depending on the research design. The main characteristic of this approach is that the sampling may be biased in a manner that can not be measured. Assuming that the research concept determines the selected objects, then there will be in reality as many solutions to selecting subdivisions as there are practicing field archaeologists. This implies at the same time many new research designs, questions, and innovative ideas that could solve broader settlement problems. A precondition for this approach

variables for the analysis. Often the spacial extent of a site is unknown, so that the archaeologlist considers only a sample of the site. The fact that the extent of the site is unknown implies that the cultural content also is unknown, and as such has to be sampled. The duration of occupation is known through stratigraphic excavation if the excavated units are not too shallow, as happens at some salvage excavations.

This model already includes three of the eight sampling factors that influence the present basalt flake analysis. The fourth previous sampling factor is the selection by the field workers of basalt flakes and flaked stone tools that were thought to be

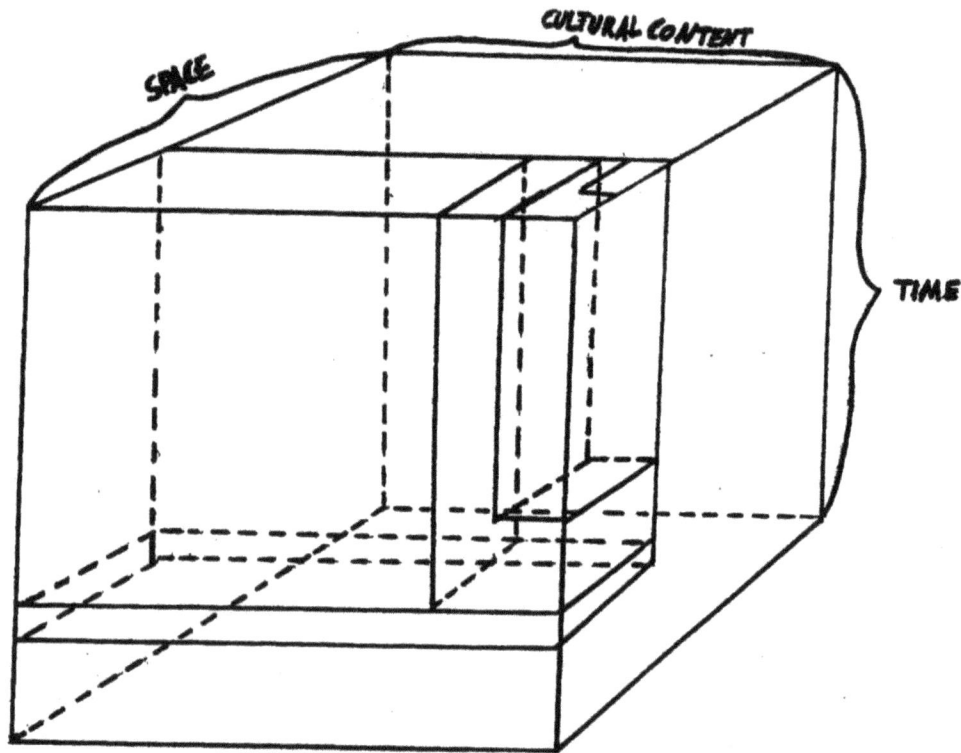

( Chenhall 1975:7 )

is that the methods, sampling criteria and research objectives are explicitly stated.

In many cases the archaeologist is not in a position to work exclusively on one site from the beginning survey phase up to the last analysis of the artifacts, faunal, and animal residues etc. This is the case in the present analysis of basalt flakes. In such cases, we can infer that sampling has already been done when the archaeologist begin their work. Many archaeologists recognize that this previous sampling influences their work immensely. The author counted for his work four levels of previous sampling and four levels of own sampling. Before the brief summary of these eight levels of sampling it may be opportune to make the reader acquainted with Chenhall's hierarchy of an archaeological population-universe. Chenhall presented this archaeological population-universe in his paper, " A Rationale For Archaeological Sampling ", as a cube. There is in each case one axis for time, space, and cultural content. All factors are limiting

significant in terms of the current theory. Those recognized artifacts were kept while others were thrown away. Some of these so-called ecofacts might have been identified as artifacts by some other more technical methods ( for example microscopic investigation of edge damage, use-wear etc. ). Assuming that this natural selection process occurred both in the field and in the laboratory, these flakes represent a strongly pre-sampled population.

Additional sampling will be done in that only basalt flakes that were found in provenience will be considered. The choice to analyze only the basalt flakes out of the artifact assemblage is also a sampling of the material culture. Limitations of time, money, and equipment restrict the number of basalt flakes that can be analyzed under the Electron Scanning Microscope. Most modification and highest possibility of plant and animal residues will be the criteria. The last and often underestimated sampling factor is the educational background of the author; the motto being: " You only see what you know and what you want to see! ", his willingly or unwillingly selected literature and his way of thinking. (see computer section)

Faced with these preconditions it seems to be impossible to see the sampled population of the basalt flakes as an expressive sample of the target population ( the original number of flakes at a certain time and place, of a certain culture). In statistical terms it is not valid to make any statements about "the target population in a relative-frequency-probability sense unless the target population is also the sampled population ". ( Chenhall 1975:4 ) In the special case of Waikalua the target population on the other hand is unpredictable as we are not able to exclude the possibility that "prehistoric people" did not sample the "waste flakes" in post hole fillings. In general, it is doubtful that all original implements are preserved until the archaeologist detects them, and those which do survive are not 100% exposed by the archaeologist. Hence the basic problem is that we are not able to state that the sampled population is representative to the target population.

The only possibility to solve this dilemma is to imply that the sampled population is a 100% sample of the target population so that the new precondition would be that the sampled population is equal to the target population. We could then draw a random sample of at least 30% out of the whole population. A 30% sample is the minimum requirement in statistical-mathematical terms to make any relative-frequency-probability statement. Even the least critical reader will observe the inadequacy of this procedure, although it is still often followed in archaeological research. Most of the authors did not acquaint the reader with these weaknesses. This could result either from their subliminal fear of the possibility that their work could be investigated or that they simply were not aware of this weakness.

Lewis R. Binford has criticized " the naive notion " many archaeologist have " that the archaeological research is directly observable as meaningful information about the past." His remark to those "ignorant archaeologists" is that the observed archaeological information is " not, never has been, and never will be " meaningful. ( Binford 1975:251 ) To maximize the meaningfulness of the archaeological information we have to ask the right questions, have to have a clearly defined, problem oriented research design, and have to make our statements testable for further research. If we do so, random sampling becomes important to archaeologists, for it establishes a framework within which to evaluate the reasonableness of samples whether or not that reasonableness can be properly stated in relatively-frequency-probability terms. The often sampled sample receives authorization with a clearly stated research purpose and becomes valid to support a special hypothesis.

This sample can not be evaluated using the chi square test. Chi square is a quantive, nominal-level statistic that determines whether the empirical results differ significantly of non-significantly from the expected results. What this implies is that we cannot test a thesis that is not established in statistical-mathematical terms with statistical methods.

In conclusion, it is questionable if it is of importance that we sample in a statistical-mathematical way rather than in an intuitive-subjective way, if we lack basic information like the extent of the site, the cultural contents and in some cases also the duration of occupation. All these limiting factors represent a sampling process itself and influence our ability to make exact archaeological statements. In other words reliance only on statistics is of little use as it narrows the mind and hinders us from seeing new research concepts. It is important to remember that we give the past meaning and try to evaluate our theories through facts ( statistical methods, physics etc. ) that are also created by us.

## 1.5 INQUIRY METHOD; CONSTRUCTION OF THE TEXT

After several discussions with scientific colleagues in America, who tried to convince the author of the " more interesting " and " publicly effective " writing style in American scientific publications, the author is still not satisfied with their arguments and chose for this thesis the problem oriented working method. The author can not deny the fact that he is influence by the Hamburgian school, specifically by Prof. Dr. Ziegert, who is a vehement representative of this research design, ( see H. Ziegert " Objektorientierte und problemorientierte Forschungsansätze in der Archäologie ", in: Hephaistos 2, 1980:53-65 ) The precondition for this problem oriented working method is one or several clearly stated problem(s). The concise definition of the problem(s) enables the researcher to establish criteria for a carefully directed search of information. The division of the problem(s) in several sub-problems is an important step in the problem analysis. Each of the investigations undertaken to solve these sub-problems, becomes a separate section in the outline of the final report of the study. With every step (the solution of one sub-problem ) the researcher is able to establish a hypothesis that can be tested with the next step. If a solution of a sub-problem can not be obtained, the reason for this must be questioned and a critical review of the research methods is a necessity to derive better results. After the solution of every sub-problem and the testing of every hypothesis, the solution of the basic problem(s) can be concluded.

The common critique of this method is that it would be "excessively methodical" and as such boring and uninteresting to read. Contrary to those persuasions, the author is of the opinion that the reading of severely problem oriented and methodical publications can be exciting in that moment when the reader starts to evaluate the methods and their effectiveness. Only this kind of research design offers the reader the possibility to be critical as it shows the possible weaknesses and restrictions as well as rational working techniques. Other methods give the reader preconceived solutions that are not testable. These methods can not challenge the reader to think about the work, but maybe this is one of the aims of those writings.

## II. MEASUREMENTS OF WAIKALUA FLAKES

The former intention to use the already presorted Waikalua material in its present categories had to be revised, as it proved to be useless for the purpose of this work. The author was unable to find that many diagnostic flakes, as mentioned and defined in Riford's analysis (see 1.2 b). A complete striking platform could seldomly be found. Even under a 10x hand lens the vast majority of flakes under 10 cm in size were either flake fragments or debris rather than diagnostic. In Riford's classification, the bulb of percussion was not taken into consideration. As the author was unable to assign his experimentally produced flakes to Riford's categories, it was unavoidable to establish his own classification in order to obtain comparable data.

Each collection unit was sorted into four debitage categories plus one nondebitage category. The sorting followed the new approach to debitage analysis proposed by Sullivan and Rozen in 1985. This system was found useful to derive interpretation-free categories, again measurable by every individual with some lithic knowledge. The debitage categories were complete flake, broken flake, flake fragment, and debris, while the nondebitage category was core. All flakes that have a single interior surface, that is indicated by positive percussion features such as ripple marks, force lines, or bulb of percussion are at least flake fragments. Flakes where these features are not discernible were assigned to the debris category. If the flakes with single interior surface also show the point of applied force, indicated by an intact striking platform intersected by the bulb of percussion, they are either classified as complete or broken flakes. If the point of applied force is absent, they fall under flake fragment category. The distinction between complete and broken flakes is made over the margins. In case where the margins are intact displaying a hinge or feather termination and at the same time

scribed above. In the case the distal end was broken, they were assigned to the broken flake category.

Every flake under 1 cm in size was examined under a 10x hand lens to discover possible percussion features. The flakes were counted, weighed, and classified by units. The decision to weigh and count the flakes again was made after the detection of huge discrepancies at the spot check of one unit. The discrepancies in the number of the flakes exceeded mostly the rate of possible increase through crushing and breakage in the bags, they where commonly stored in, so that they have to be explained in counting errors. Likewise the different weight measurements have to be explained in weighing errors. The counting method used in this study, was to count flakes up to 100, put them aside and count afterwards the heaps together. That the weight measurements in each category have to be accurate, shows a comparison to the total weight of each unit. In the previous study, the same amount of flakes, counted from both parties, resulted in different weight measurements. This leads to the ascertation that in the present study no flakes were missing that could have resulted in the often higher weight measurements of the previous study.

An OHAUS E 120 scale as well as an OHAUS Tripple Beam Balance was used for the weight measurements, a caliper and a ruler for the dimension measurements. Each flake was carefully examined for retouch; no intentional retouch was found. After each category was sorted out, it was counted and weighted separately and the size distribution was established. Flakes with cortex and polish were mentioned separately. The platform thickness of each complete and broken flake was ascertained and the thickness range was added into the chart. ( Table A ) The purpose of these measurements was to establish possible criteria of comparison towards the experimentally produced flakes. The comparative analysis was done in section 3.5.

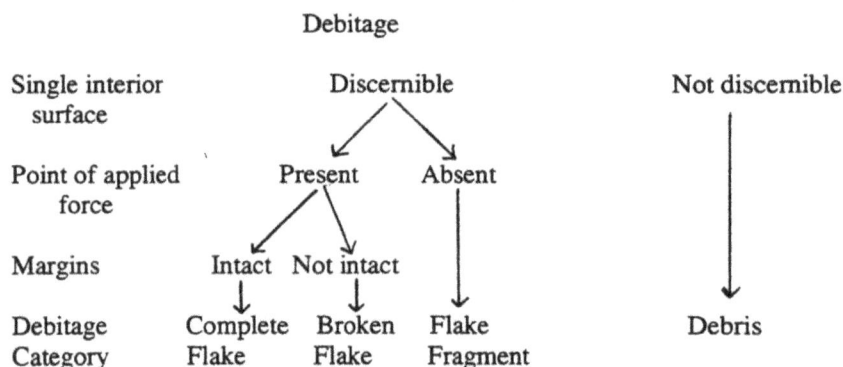

Debitage

| | | | |
|---|---|---|---|
| Single interior surface | Discernible | | Not discernible |
| Point of applied force | Present | Absent | |
| Margins | Intact   Not intact | | |
| Debitage Category | Complete Flake   Broken Flake | Flake Fragment | Debris |

(Fig 2: Technological attribute key; Sullivan/Rozen 1985:759)

no lateral breaks interfere with accurate width measurements, we speak of a complete flake. This technological attribute key is schematically shown in figure 2:

In the special case of the Hawaiian flakes that arose while on-anvil bipolar flaking, flakes with disturbed unbroken distal ends (flat, crushed) were also considered to be complete, if they displayed all the other characteristic features, de-

In a second step, flakes that were to be examined under low and high power magnification, were sorted out. Flakes were selected that either were meant to show obvious use-wear or meant to be suitable for cutting, scraping, etc. tasks. The length was measured from the proximal end to the distal end. If a flake fragment did not show the point of applied force and it could not be inferred, the most distant points were taken for the length measurements. The width was measured from the most distant points of the lateral margins. The thickness was gauged at the thickest part of the cross-section. These measurements were taken to determine the size range of flakes possibly used for diverse purposes in prehistoric times and to classify the flakes. Edge angle measurements were under taken, in the course of which the relative as well as the absolute edge angles were taken into account. ( see Nowatzyk 1988:10 ) These angle measurements were necessary in order to comply to the research design which investigated the most convenient and suitable angle of use and to classify the flakes. The edge curvature and the edge morphology was also noted to figure out the most suitable curvature and morphology for diverse purposes and to classify the flakes. ( see appendix A)

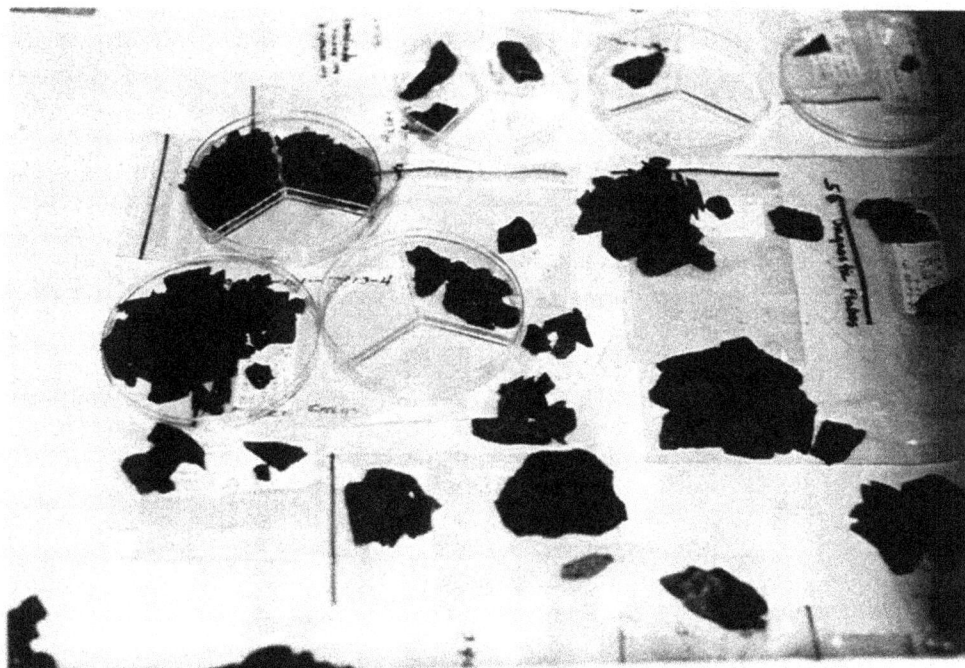

( Photo 23: Sorting into debitage categories )

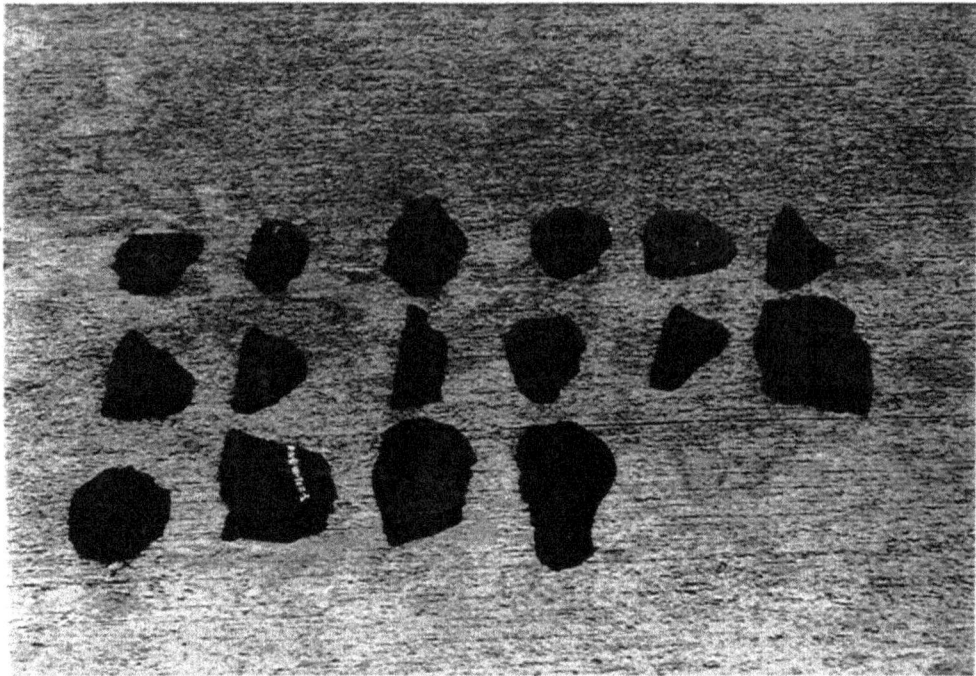

( Photo 24: 16 Waikalua flakes )

( Photo 25: 18 Waikalua flakes )

| Provenience | Weight | CompleteFlake | Broken Flake | Flake Fragment | Debris | Core | Total No. | Size Class | Cortex |
|---|---|---|---|---|---|---|---|---|---|
| TP 13-6 | 515.98 gr | 108.3 gr 21% 12 Pieces 4.6% — 1-3 cm = 3, 3-6 cm = 8, 6-9 cm = 1 — 2 with cortex Platform Thckn 0.4-0.8 cm | 31.9 gr 6.2% 38 Pieces 14.5% — 0-1 cm = 13, 1-3 cm = 17, 3-6 cm = 8 — Platform Thckn 0.3-0.7 cm | 198.1 gr 38.4% 166 Pieces 63.3% — 0-1 cm = 92, 1-3 cm = 53, 3-6 cm = 21 — 4 with cortex 11 polished | 66.28 gr 12.8% 45 Pieces 17.2% — 0-1 cm = 27, 1-3 cm = 12, 3-6 cm = 6 — 6 with cortex | 114.4 gr (21.6%) 1 Piece (0.4%) 1 Piece 5.4 x 5 x 3.2 111.4 gr | 262 | 0-1 cm = 132 1-3 cm = 85 3-6 cm = 43 6-9 cm = 1 | 12 — Polished 11 |
| Without Core | 404.58 gr | Pieces 4.6% Grams 26.7% | Pieces 14.6% Grams 7.9% | Pieces 63.6% Grams 49% | Pieces 17.2% Grams 16.4% | | | | |
| TP 9-2 | 63.7 gr | | 0.5 gr 0.8% 1 Piece 9% — 1-3 cm = 1 — 1 with cortex Platform Thckn 0.3 cm | 61 gr 95.7% 5 Pieces 45.5% — 1-3 cm = 4, 6-9 cm = 1 | 2.2 gr 3.5% 5 Pieces 45.5% — 0-1 cm = 2, 1-3 cm = 3 | | 11 | 0-1 cm = 2 1-3 cm = 8 6-9 cm = 1 | 1 |
| TP 9-3 | 21.9 gr | | 9.3 gr 42.5% 2 Pieces 18.2% — 3-6 cm = 2 — Platform Thckn 0.5-0.7 cm | 7.2 gr 32.9% 5 Pieces 45.4% — 1-3 cm = 5 | 4.5 gr 24.6% 4 Pieces 36.4% — 1-3 cm = 4 | | 11 | 1-3 cm = 9 3-6 cm = 2 | |

Table A: Measurements of the basalt flakes from the Waikalua excavation

| Provenience | Weight | Complete Flake | Broken Flake | Flake Fragment | Debris | Core | Total No. | Size Class | Cortex |
|---|---|---|---|---|---|---|---|---|---|
| TP 9 - 5 | 1686.4 gr | 80.9 gr<br>4.8 %<br>10 Pieces<br>0.4 %<br><br>1 - 3 cm = 5<br>3 - 6 cm = 5<br><br>Platform Thckn<br>0.5 - 1.0 cm<br>Pieces 0.4 %<br>Grams 4.9 % | 190.3 gr<br>11.3 %<br>70 Pieces<br>3 %<br>0 - 1 cm = 1<br>1 - 3 cm = 53<br>3 - 6 cm = 16<br>4 with cortex<br>5 polished<br>Platform Thckn<br>0.2 - 0.9 cm<br>Pieces 3 %<br>Grams 11.5 % | 1298.8 gr<br>77 %<br>2040 Pieces<br>87 %<br>0 - 1 cm = 1172<br>1 - 3 cm = 824<br>3 - 6 cm = 42<br>6 - 9 cm = 1<br>9 -12 cm = 1<br>56 with cortex<br>14 polished<br>Pieces 87.1 %<br>Grams 78.6 % | 82.15 gr<br>4.9 %<br>223 Pieces<br>9.5 %<br>0 - 1 cm = 181<br>1 - 3 cm = 41<br>3 - 6 cm = 1<br>18 with cortex<br><br>Pieces 9.5 %<br>Grams 5 % | 34.3 gr<br>2.0 %<br>2 Pieces<br>0.1 %<br>1 Piece 3.5 x 3 x 2.3<br>23.4 gr<br>1 Piece 3.1 x 2.2 x 1.7<br>10.9 gr | 2345 | 0 - 1 cm = 1354<br>1 - 3 cm = 923<br>3 - 6 cm = 64<br>6 - 9 cm = 1<br>9 -12 cm = 1 | 78<br><br>Polished<br>19 |
| Without Core | 1652.1 gr | | | | | | | | |
| Fe 9b  Fill | 2170.8 gr | 300.4 gr<br>13.8 %<br>17 Pieces<br>1.5 %<br><br>1 - 3 cm = 2<br>3 - 6 cm = 12<br>6 - 9 cm = 3<br>3 with cortex<br>Platform Thckn<br>0.7 - 1.1 cm | 354 gr<br>16.3 %<br>62 Pieces<br>5.7 %<br><br>1 - 3 cm = 30<br>3 - 6 cm = 30<br>6 - 9 cm = 2<br>7 with cortex<br>1 polished<br>Platform Thckn<br>0.6 - 0.9 cm | 969.2 gr<br>44.7 %<br>399 Pieces<br>36.4 %<br>0 - 1 cm = 98<br>1 - 3 cm = 205<br>3 - 6 cm = 89<br>6 - 9 cm = 7<br>27 with cortex<br>5 polished | 547.2 gr<br>25.2 %<br>619 Pieces<br>56.4 %<br>0 - 1 cm = 274<br>1 - 3 cm = 313<br>3 - 6 cm = 30<br>6 - 9 cm = 2<br>18 with cortex | | 1097 | 0 - 1 cm = 372<br>1 - 3 cm = 550<br>3 - 6 cm = 161<br>6 - 9 cm = 14 | 55<br><br>Polished<br>6 |
| Fe 9a  Fill | 720.9 gr | 72.2 gr<br>10 %<br>5 Pieces<br>1.4 %<br><br>1 - 3 cm = 2<br>3 - 6 cm = 2<br>6 - 9 cm = 1<br>1 with cortex<br>Platform Thckn<br>0.5 - 1.0 cm | 156 gr<br>21.7 %<br>22 Pieces<br>6.1 %<br><br>1 - 3 cm = 10<br>3 - 6 cm = 12<br>6 with cortex<br>Platform Thckn<br>0.5 - 0.8 cm | 262.5 gr<br>36.4 %<br>138 Pieces<br>38.2 %<br>0 - 1 cm = 61<br>1 - 3 cm = 59<br>3 - 6 cm = 18<br>8 with cortex | 230 gr<br>31.9 %<br>196 Pieces<br>54.3 %<br>0 - 1 cm = 110<br>1 - 3 cm = 72<br>3 - 6 cm = 13<br>6 - 9 cm = 1<br>5 with cortex | | 361 | 0 - 1 cm = 171<br>1 - 3 cm = 143<br>3 - 6 cm = 45<br>6 - 9 cm = 2 | 20 |

Table A: Continued

(Page 16)

| Provenience | Weight | Complete Flake | Broken Flake | Flake Fragment | Debris | Core | Total No. | Size Class | Cortex |
|---|---|---|---|---|---|---|---|---|---|
| TR 11 | 507.2 gr | 61.5 gr 12.1% 2 Pieces 0.8%; 3-6 cm = 1, 6-9 cm = 1; 1 with cortex; Platform Thckn 0.7-1.1 cm | 106.3 gr 21% 6 Pieces 2.5%; 1-3 cm = 1, 3-6 cm = 4, 6-9 cm = 1; 1 with cortex; Platform Thckn 0.6-0.9 cm | 180.3 gr 35.5% 85 Pieces 35.6%; 0-1 cm = 24, 1-3 cm = 47, 3-6 cm = 13, 6-9 cm = 1; 11 with cortex 2 polished | 159.1 gr 31.4% 146 Pieces 61.1%; 0-1 cm = 77, 1-3 cm = 54, 3-6 cm = 15; 7 with cortex | | 239 | 0-1 cm = 101, 1-3 cm = 103, 3-6 cm = 33, 6-9 cm = 2 | 20; Polished 2 |
| TP 11-1 | 1940.4 gr | 199 gr 10.3% 12 Pieces 1.2%; 1-3 cm = 4, 3-6 cm = 8; 1 with cortex 2 polished; Platform Thckn 0.5-0.8 cm; Pieces 1.2% Grams 12.7% | 285.4 gr 14.7% 53 Pieces 5.4%; 1-3 cm = 18, 3-6 cm = 35; 8 with cortex 2 polished; Platform Thckn 0.3-0.8 cm; Pieces 5.4% Grams 18.1% | 849.1 gr 43.8% 454 Pieces 46.7%; 0-1 cm = 200, 1-3 cm = 180, 3-6 cm = 63, 6-9 cm = 11; 63 with cortex 2 polished; Pieces 46.8% Grams 53.9% | 241.2 gr 12.4% 452 Pieces 46.5%; 0-1 cm = 337, 1-3 cm = 105, 3-6 cm = 9, 6-9 cm = 1; 13 with cortex; Pieces 46.6% Grams 15.3% | 365.7 gr 18.8% 1 Piece 0.2%; 1 Piece 7.2 x 5.3 x 5.1, 322 gr; 1 Piece 5.2 x 3.7 x 1.7 | 973 | 0-1 cm = 537, 1-3 cm = 307, 3-6 cm = 115, 6-9 cm = 12 | 85; Polished 4 |
| Without Core | 1574.7 gr | | | | | | | | |
| TR 1E | 656.4 gr | 47.1 gr 7.2% 7 Pieces 1%; 1-3 cm = 4, 3-6 cm = 2, 6-9 cm = 1; 2 with cortex 2 polished; Platform Thckn 0.4-0.7 cm | | 499.6 gr 76.1% 439 Pieces 59%; 0-1 cm = 233, 1-3 cm = 172, 3-6 cm = 32, 6-9 cm = 2; 28 with cortex 21 polished 3 modified | 109.7 gr 16.7% 298 Pieces 40%; 0-1 cm = 183, 1-3 cm = 111, 3-6 cm = 4; 22 with cortex | | 744 | 0-1 cm = 416, 1-3 cm = 287, 3-6 cm = 38, 6-9 cm = 3 | 52; Polished 23 |

Table A: Continued

( Page 17 )

| Provenience | Weight | Complete Flake | Broken Flake | Flake Fragment | Debris | Core | Total No. | Size Class | Cortex |
|---|---|---|---|---|---|---|---|---|---|
| TP 13 - 4 | 1709.2 gr | 105.3 gr 6.2% 6 Pieces 0.3% | 230.8 gr 13.5% 43 Pieces 2% | 1017.9 gr 59.5% 1345 Pieces 62.3% | 356.1 gr 20.8% 763 Pieces 35.4% | | 2157 | 0 - 1 cm = 1153 1 - 3 cm = 940 3 - 6 cm = 63 6 - 9 cm = 1 | 64 |
| | | 1 - 3 cm = 2 3 - 6 cm = 3 6 - 9 cm = 1 | 1 - 3 cm = 21 3 - 6 cm = 22 | 0 - 1 cm = 648 1 - 3 cm = 674 3 - 6 cm = 23 | 0 - 1 cm = 505 1 - 3 cm = 243 3 - 6 cm = 15 | | | | |
| | | Platform Thckn 0.5 - 1.3 cm | 1 with cortex Platform Thckn 0.3 - 0.7 cm | 34 with cortex 21 polished | 29 with cortex | | | | Polished 21 |
| TP 13 - 4 | 798.1 gr | 85.5 gr 10.7% 5 Pieces 0.6% | 77.6 gr 9.7% 18 Pieces 2% | 458.3 gr 57.4% 651 Pieces 71.5% | 177.2 gr 22.2% 236 Pieces 25.9% | | 910 | 0 - 1 cm = 431 1 - 3 cm = 442 3 - 6 cm = 37 | 31 |
| | | 1 - 3 cm = 1 3 - 6 cm = 4 | 1 - 3 cm = 10 3 - 6 cm = 8 | 0 - 1 cm = 311 1 - 3 cm = 319 3 - 6 cm = 21 | 0 - 1 cm = 120 1 - 3 cm = 112 3 - 6 cm = 4 | | | | |
| | | 1 with cortex Platform Thckn 0.4 - 1.6 cm | 1 with cortex 1 polished Platform Thckn 0.3 - 0.7 cm | 17 with cortex 13 polished | 12 with cortex | | | | Polished 14 |

Table A: Continued

( Page 18 )

## III. TOOL MANUFACTURING EXPERIMENTS AND THEIR EVALUATION

### 3.1 Pedrological reality

Basalt is principally comprised of pyroxene and plagioclase with lesser amounts of some combination of olivine, Fe-Ti oxides, apatite, and glass. Basalt does not contain quartz. When the volcanically originated basalt emerges to the surface and atmosphere, it cools down fastly. When it cools down slowly it forms gabbroic rocks. Even when basalt consists of a wide spectrum of chemical composition it shows a continuum that splits into two basalt types - alkali olivine basalt and tholeiitic basalt. The wide ranging appearance of basalt is explainable through depositional and post-depositional alterations. Oxidation is the main factor of basalt alteration, resulting from the great concentration of iron in basaltic rock. When water supports the cooling phase, it becomes purose and oxidates faster because the smaller hydrogen molecules diffuse out of the hot body, and less mobile oxygen molecules participate in oxidative reactions. The degree of oxidation determines the varicolored appearance of basaltic rocks. Black, blue-green-yellow, red-brown, and gray are the most common colors. Basalt has a mat sheen and a fine grained structure that breaks rough and uneven after cracking. ( Text free after M.G. Best " Out of igneous and metamorphic petrology " NY 1985:62-196 )

The specific gravity of basalt is 2,6-3,11. The hardness according the Moh's scale is 6-6,5 ( Semenov 1964:34-5 ). The author's experiments showed a wider hardness range of 5-7.

Thin sectioning both of the Waikalua and experimentally used material was not made. The following analysis are presented done by Mac Coy and Cleghorn for the Mauna Kea Adz Quarry (Cleghorn, Weisler, Dye, and Sinton 1983 ) and by Clark and Riford for the Waikalua material which they could trace back to four different sources:
1. Ko'olau Caldera, 2. Waiahole Quarry, 3. Kailua Adz Quarry, and 3. Kane'ohe region. ( Clark/Riford 1986:75 )

In general the Mauna Kea basalt consists of fine to very fine grained ( 158 grains/mm ) adesite composed primarily of plagioclase, and olivine with or without alteration products occurring in minor amounts; plagioclase feldspars are the dominant phenocrysts, with either augite, pyroxene, or olivine with or without alteration products being subdominant. The occurrence of minor minerals is restricted to biotite and calcite. ( Cleghorn et al. 1983:245-6 ) Clark and Riford examined seven thin sections of the Waikalua material. They could divide the basaltic material into four clearly distinguishable groups:

" **Group 1**. Samples Sa15, Sa461, Sa566, and "road fill" are all intersertal amygdaloidal basalt with relatively coarse textures ( 50-60 grains/mm ). The ground mass is predominantly plagioclase feldspar laths with approximately equal amounts of clinpyroxene and an opaque mineral. The opaque minerals are commonly needlelike, and often from lattice structure. Opaque and secondary mineral phencrysts are present in small numbers. Quartz in veinlets and amygdules typically shows undulatory extinction.

**Group 2**. Sample Sa567 is a relatively coarse-grained ( 72 grains/mm ) intersertal basalt. The ground mass is predominantly plagioclase feldspar laths with approximately equal amounts of clinoproxene and an opaque mineral. Some of the opaques are elongated. Phenocrysts are relatively common and are mostly secondary minerals. Unaltered phenocrysts are an orthopyroxene, probably hypersthene.

**Group 3**. Sample Sa365 is a relatively coarse-grained ( 85 grains/mm ) intersertal basalt. The ground mass is predominantly plagioclase feldspar laths with smaller amounts of clinopyroxene and an opaque mineral. The only phenocrysts are euhedral plagioclase feldspar up to 1.25 mm long.

**Group 4**. Sample Sa926 is an exceedingly fine-grained ( 450 grains/mm ) basalt composed of glass that is clouded with extremely small opaque mineral crystals. Within this matrix are numerous euhedral plagioclase feldspar crystals up to 0.25 mm long and a few subhedral clinopyroxene crystals about 0.05 mm long. "
( Clark/Riford 1986:73 )

The prehistorically used basalt could not be employed for the experiments as the quarries are now on private property and not accessible. So it was decided to use the Mauna Kea material that was at hand. The measurements taken after Mohs show a hardness of 7 for both basaltic materials, even though the pedrographic analysis displays different grain sizes.

### 3.2 Adze manufacturing

After a fugitive presorting of the Waikalua flakes it was decided to restrict the tool manufacturing to the traditional Hawaiian adze manufacture. The main decision criteria were the characteristic features of the flakes. Several complete flakes definitely pointed to a refinement of the adze preforms, as they were rectangular in shape ( displays the thickness of the adze preforms ) and showed crushings at the striking platform as well as at the distal ends, where they laid on the anvil. ( See photo No.26) Most of the flakes were small with a thin striking platform, showing cortex, which points to refinement or secondary reduction. ( Williams 1989:55-59 ) Many, however, were so small, that they could not be clearly assigned to a phase in Williams proposed reduction model, but if polish was present the rejuvenation and reworking stage ( Williams 1989:60-1 ) seemed to be appropriate. In this experiment, primary as well as secondary reduction involved percussion flaking using the technique of freehand percussion and on-anvil bipolar flaking, as described by Cleghorn ( 1982 ).

## A. Primary reduction

### a) Pre-manufacturing

Eight basalt blocks were found to be suitable and selected for the adze manufacturing ( Photo No. 27 ). Flakes with special edge angles were stricken from block 1 and block 4 exclusively ( See section C ). Each block was previously weight,

Block 1 = 6190 gr
Block 2 = 2450 gr
Block 3 = 3640 gr
Block 4 = 2820 gr
Block 5 = 1250 gr
Block 6 = 1420 gr
Block 7 = 1790 gr
Block 8 = 940 gr

to examine the weight loss towards
a) the blanks
b) the preforms and
c) to see how much flaked material fell out of the grid and/or through the screen.

Twenty-two hammerstones were collected either from the Moleka stream, Makiki valley or the Kalei and Manoa stream, both in Manoa valley. ( Photo No.28) The main criteria for the selection were not only dimensions, weight and hardness, but also the outline ( Table B ). Round water-worn stones that are said to be the typical strikers for adze manufacture, as well as pointed, waterworn intenders were gathered. Each hammerstone was photographed in the typical way that it was held in the manufacturing process (Photo Series). An appropriate chipping floor was selected and demarcated with string in the previously 2x2 m unit then extended to a 3x2 m unit. The chipping floor was overgrown with some kind of plant tendril and very little grass. However, most of the floor was not overgrown at all showing reddish-brown soil with few pebbles in the matrix. As this location was used for several stone tool manufacturing experiments before, it had to be brushed carefully and even stepped in flakes had to be removed. An anvil was selected and placed in that way that it was closer to one side of the unit, opposite to the direction of the blows. ( Photos No. 29,30 )

### b) Manufacturing

The respective raw material block was held in an angle of 35 degrees to 50 degrees towards the working edge of the anvil, so that one side of the block became fully supported by the anvil edge. The angle of the blows ( blow angle ) employed to the block edge, opposite to the one sitting on the anvil, varied from 50 degrees to 70 degrees. The first timid blows did not even chip small pieces from the extremely hard material. While increasing the blow intensity, it became obvious that most of the selected hammerstones would not suit their purpose. They broke in pieces. The hammerstone fragments were immediately collected so that they would not influence the flake scatter pattern and the weight measurements. Hammerstones 1, 4, 5, and 6 were found to be most suitable for

the primary reduction, whereat the pointed intenders did more accurate work than the simply rounded ones. When the striker did not exactly hit the margin region of the block and at the same time the blow was executed in a 90 degree angle towards the block, two flakes were then often chipped off. ( "Secondary-multiple-flakes" according to Jelinek et al.1971:198-200 )

A primary flake with negative and positive percussion bulb as well as a secondary flake with only a positive percussion bulb, was recognizable. The chipped off flakes showed, in general, feather termination at the lateral ends, while the distal end, caused by the anvil, was flat and/or crushed. The proximal end was normally formed. If a tip of the anvil was used to support the block, it could happen that either the intender or the tip of the anvil chipped a flake off. In the case that the percussion was not intense enough to divide the block in the full length, smaller flakes were chipped off that showed feather termination at the distal ends. This usually happened when the block was very thick.

The flakes fell freely on the ground, they were not held. Only few flakes broke while hitting other flakes or block fragments on the chipping floor. The frequent cleaning of the anvil surface resulted to an accumulation of tiny flakes at that side of the anvil they were wiped. The only possibility to control the chipping of the basaltic material was on the edge of the anvil. When the block was laid flat on the anvil it could happen, that a blow applied to a lateral end of the block caused the breakage of it in the middle. It also was found that it is easier to work along a flat side of the block, mostly were cortex was present. This flat side was used as a basis for the establishment of a regular, rectangular shape.

The material of the six blocks yielded six more or less recognizable blanks with regular shape. ( Photo No. 31 ) The weight of the blanks was measured to 3917 gr. ( see sizes out of table C )

### c) Post manufacturing

The flake scatter pattern was photographed and drawn, ( Fig 3 ) and the flakes were counted by 5x5 cm units to develop a density variation. Definite chips from the anvil were collected out of the other flakes. Flakes that would be suitable for cutting, scraping, etc. experiments were selected and singly bagged, while the few flakes that had fallen outside of the 3x2 m unit were not considered. The unit and the anvil were brushed again and the heaped up soil with the flakes was bagged to be sift with the same sized sieve used at the Waikalua excavation.

## B. Secondary reduction

### a) Pre-manufacturing

The blanks were examined for their suitability to be further worked either as quadrangular or triangular preforms. The intended outline of the working preform was sketched with chalk on the blanks. The flat, cortex side of the blanks was always used as the top of the working preform.

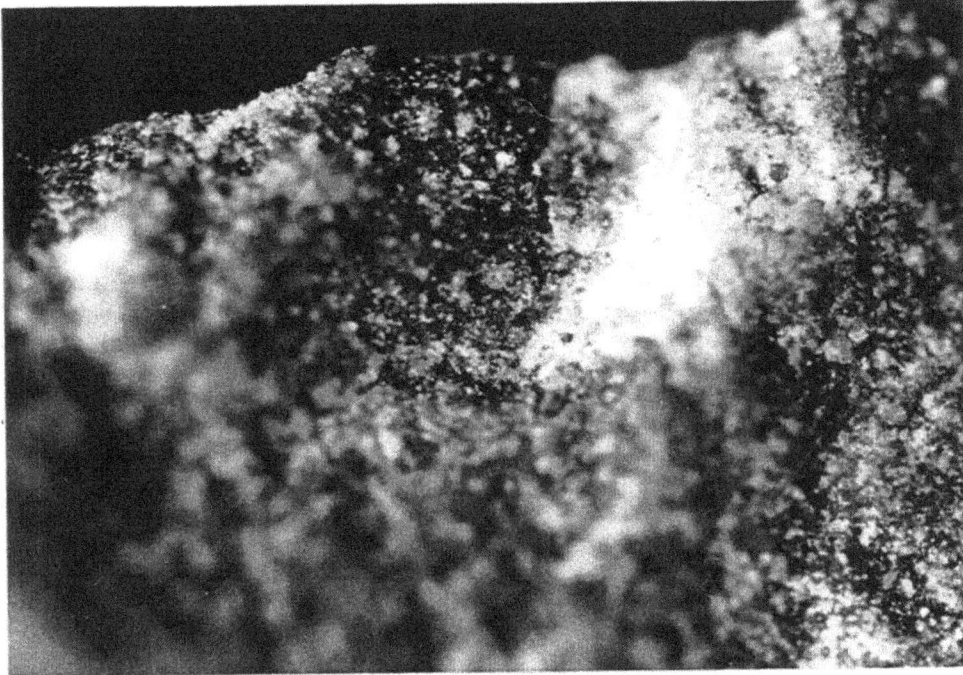

( Photo 26: Crushing caused through the anvil )

( Photo 27: Basalt blocks )

( Photo 28: Hammerstones )

22

| Object | Location | Hardness acc. Mohs' | Length in cm | Width in cm | Thickness in cm | Weight in gr |
|---|---|---|---|---|---|---|
| 1 | Moleka Stream Makiki Valley | 6 + 0. 5*= 6. 5 | 16. 4 | 10. 5 | 6. 6 | 1343. 0 |
| 2 | Kalei Stream Manoa Valley | 4 + 0. 5 = 4. 5 | 15. 8 | 10. 4 | 6. 8 | 1033. 6 |
| 3 | Moleka Stream Makiki Valley | 6 + 0. 5 = 6. 5 | 14. 5 | 9. 1 | 5. 9 | 958. 8 |
| 4 | Moleka Stream Makiki Valley | 6 + 0. 5 = 6. 5 | 13. 6 | 8. 1 | 5. 2 | 749. 3 |
| 5 | Manoa Stream Manoa Valley | 6. 5 + 0. 5 = 7 | 13. 2 | 6. 7 | 6. 0 | 692. 0 |
| 6 | Manoa Stream Manoa Valley | 6. 5 + 0. 5 = 7 | 12. 9 | 6. 5 | 4. 8 | 525. 9 |
| 7 | Kalei Stream Manoa Valley | 5. 5 + 0. 5 = 6 | 12. 3 | 7. 8 | 7. 1 | 913. 4 |
| 8 | Kalei Stream Manoa Valley | 4. 5 + 0. 5 = 5 | 12. 0 | 9. 3 | 5. 8 | 735. 2 |
| 9 | Moleka Stream Makiki Valley | 6 + 0. 5 = 6. 5 | 11. 3 | 7. 2 | 5. 6 | 535. 2 |
| 10 | Manoa Stream Manoa Valley | 5 + 0. 5 = 5. 5 | 11. 2 | 9. 2 | 6. 1 | 685. 7 |
| 11 | Manoa Stream Manoa Valley | 4. 5 + 0. 5 = 5 | 11. 1 | 8. 6 | 6. 4 | 597. 7 |
| 12 | Manoa Stream Manoa Valley | 5 + 0. 5 = 5. 5 | 9. 7 | 9. 2 | 6. 4 | 649. 0 |
| 13 | Moleka Stream Makiki Valley | 5. 5 + 0. 5 = 6 | 9. 2 | 8. 1 | 7. 0 | 672. 0 |
| 14 | Manoa Stream Manoa Valley | 5. 5 + 0. 5 = 6 | 9. 2 | 6. 1 | 4. 2 | 274. 5 |
| 15 | Manoa Stream Manoa Valley | 4. 5 + 0. 5 = 5 | 8. 8 | 8. 1 | 5. 8 | 478. 5 |
| 16 | Manoa Stream Manoa Valley | 5 + 0. 5 = 5. 5 | 8. 4 | 7. 8 | 4. 0 | 365. 6 |
| 17 | Moleka Stream Makiki Valley | 5. 5 + 0. 5 = 6 | 8. 3 | 5. 1 | 3. 8 | 212. 1 |
| 18 | Manoa Stream Manoa Valley | 5 + 0. 5 = 5. 5 | 8. 1 | 6. 0 | 2. 4 | 142. 1 |
| 19 | Manoa Stream Manoa Valley | 4. 5 + 0. 5 = 5 | 7. 3 | 6. 5 | 5. 9 | 347. 2 |
| 20 | Kalei Stream Manoa Valley | 4. 5 + 0. 5 = 5 | 6. 6 | 4. 8 | 4. 1 | 122. 0 |
| 21 | Moleka Stream Makiki Valley | 5 + 0. 5 = 5. 5 | 5. 8 | 4. 8 | 2. 1 | 68. 0 |
| 22 | Kalei Stream Manoa Valley | 4. 5 + 0. 5 = 5 | 5. 2 | 4. 5 | 3. 7 | 85. 3 |

*The surface of the stones is strongly eroded and rolled in the river so that it became softer. After cracking some stones and conducting measurements acc. Mohs' a mean value of 0. 5 was considered to be accurate to add to the surface measurements

( Page 23 )          Table B: Measurements of the hammerstones

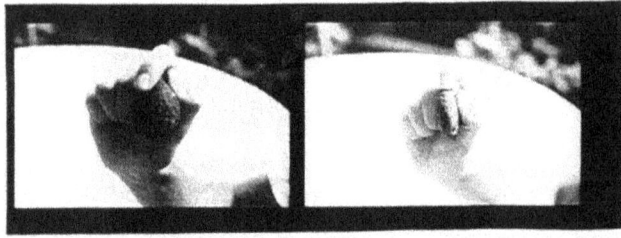

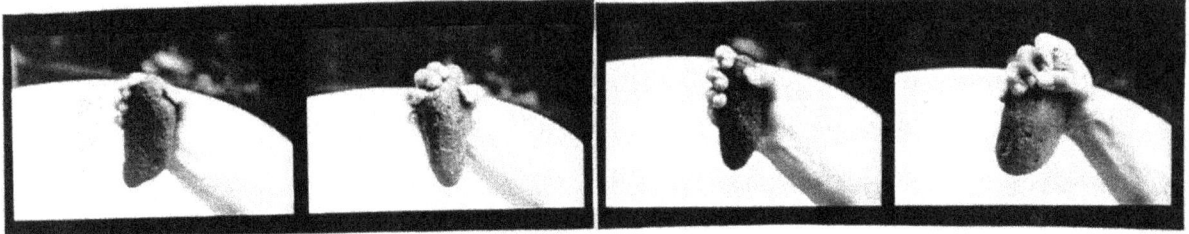

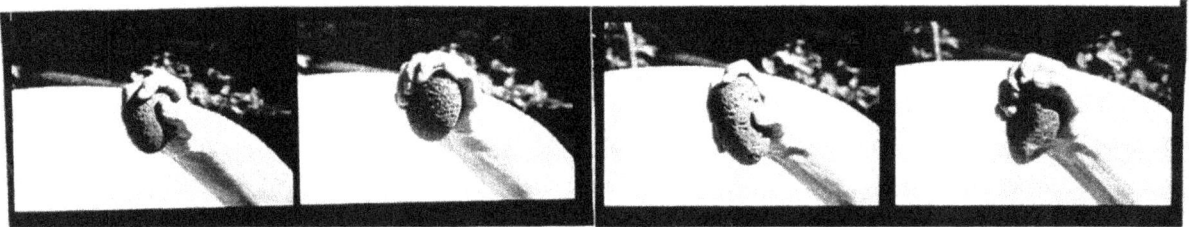

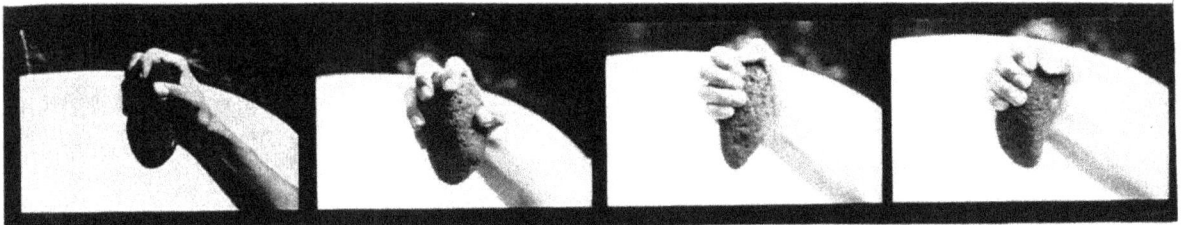

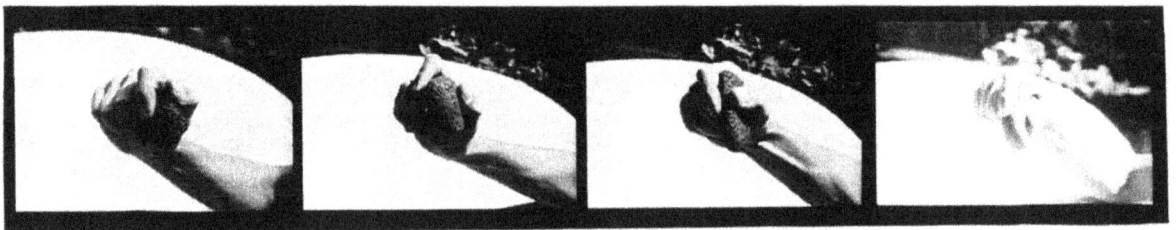

( Photo Series: Handling of hammerstones )

( Photo 29: Chipping floor before extension )

( Photo 30: Anvil )

## b) Manufacturing

It was tried to produce reverse trapezoidal, tanged and un-tanged adze preforms with quadrangular as well as one adze with triangular cross section. In this reduction stage, hammerstones 6, 9, 14, 17, 18, and 21 were found to be most suitable for this task. Hammerstones 14 and 18 broke in the advanced manufacturing process. To obtain more accurate chipping results, the extreme edge of the anvil was used. While this technique was applied, the breakage of the basaltic material could be controlled. The over the anvil edge protruding part of the blank chipped almost always in the desired way. In this phase, also the angle of the producing flakes could be determined through the blow angle. This newly obtained knowledge was used to produce flakes with special angles ( see below ). The drawback was that this method could only be used to reduce the thickness of the blanks or to smooth the preform sides. In the moment, when the preform could not be fully supported by the anvil edge due to an uneven broken surface, the breakage was beyond the control of the stone worker. Problems with endshock and perverse fracture caused most commonly the breakage of the almost finished preforms, and this led to their discard. Experiments, were it a chisel or a pointed anvil, that would solve this problem were not undertaken; but it seems to be most likely, that the point of the applied force could be controlled and as such the breakage. Four of the six blanks broke while trying to work the cutting edge of the intended adze. Two were discarded immediately, as they broke in the middle, the two others were tried to work to smaller adzes, with more or less success. All together two usable adze preforms, one with quadrangular and one with triangular cross section, and two quasi preforms were worked with a weight of 1855 gr. ( see sizes out of table C, also photo no. 32 )

The produced waste flakes were in general smaller in number and shape, and less of them showed a feather termination on the distal end, as they were chipped of a quadrangular blank. Several showed definite crushing on the proximal end caused by the hammerstone as well as on the distal end caused by the anvil. Because of the more deliberate work and the steeper angle, the blank was held towards the anvil, what caused the flakes to fall on the ground next to the anvil. The flake scatter pattern was limited to a small area ( Figure 4 ). Cortex chips were small but common because of the applied method described above.

## c) Post manufacturing

Again the flake scatter pattern was photographed and drawn, and the flakes were counted by 5x5 cm units to develop a density variation. Chips from the anvil or hammerstones were collected as well as suitable flakes for the cutting, scraping, etc. experiments selected and singly bagged. The unit and the anvil were carefully brushed, and the heaped up soil with the flakes was bagged to be screened afterwards. No flakes had fallen outside the unit.

## C. Production of flakes with special edge angles

The remaining blocks 1 and 4 were used to strike flakes with relative edge angles ranging from 5 degrees to 90 degrees. In general, intervals of 10 degrees were chosen to be accurate enough to suit the task properly. The exact number of the flakes and their distribution towards the edge angle intervals, can be seen in the following table:

| | |
|---|---|
| 5 - 15 = 3 | 55 - 65 = 13 |
| 15 - 25 = 6 | 65 - 75 = 10 |
| 25 - 35 = 18 | 75 - 85 = 5 |
| 35 - 45 = 25 | 90 = 1 |
| 45 - 55 = 22 | |

Total: 103

The first step was to produce a relatively thin, rectangular block form with flat sides that could be fully supported by the anvil edge. As earlier stated, this is one of the preconditions in controlling the breakage of the basaltic material. Because of its previously proved suitability, hammerstone 4 was used exclusively to strike the flakes from the block. By varying the blow angle or the angle of impact it was relatively easy to control the angle of incidence and to produce the intended flakes.

( Photo 31: Produced blanks )

( Photo 32: Produced preforms )

( Photo 35: Extended chipping floor )

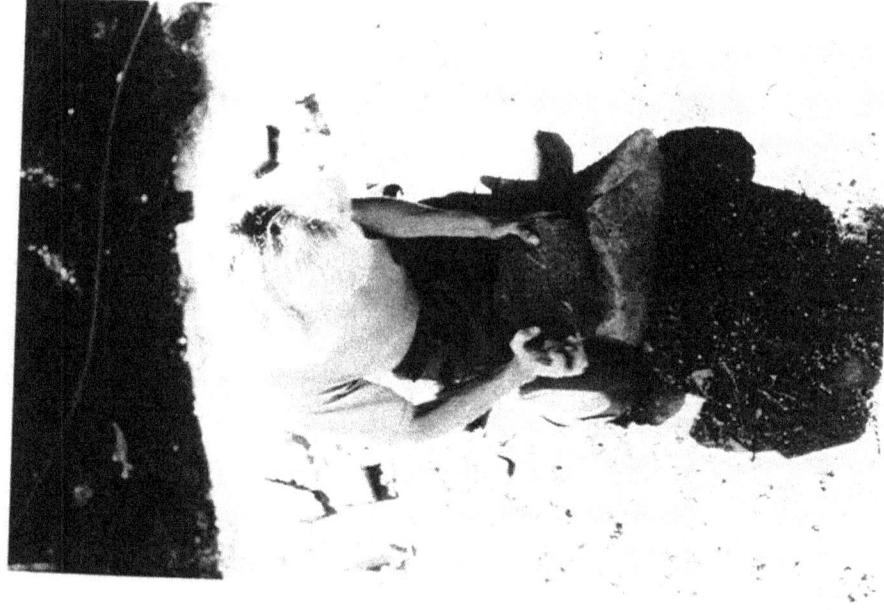

( Photos 33 and 34: Author striking flakes from block 1 )

( Page 28 )

| Reduction | Weight | Complete Flake | Broken Flake | Flake Fragment | Debris | Core | Total No. | Size Class | Cortex |
|---|---|---|---|---|---|---|---|---|---|
| Primary Reduction | 7502.5 gr | 663.9 gr 8.8% — 19 Pieces 0.5% — 1-3 cm = 1, 3-6 cm = 11, 6-9 cm = 7 — 8 with cortex — Platform Thckn 0.4 - 2.0 cm | 509.3 gr 6.8% — 37 Pieces 1% — 1-3 cm = 1, 3-6 cm = 29, 6-9 cm = 7 — 8 with cortex — Platform Thckn 0.4 - 1.7 cm | 2976.2 gr 39.7% — 1556 Pieces 42.1% — 0-1 cm = 921, 1-3 cm = 460, 3-6 cm = 160, 6-9 cm = 14, 9-12 cm = 1 — 68 with cortex | 715.3 gr 9.5% — 2073 Pieces 56.2% — 0-1 cm = 1775, 1-3 cm = 229, 3-6 cm = 68, 6-9 cm = 1 — 74 with cortex | 2637.8 gr (35.2%) — 6 Pieces (0.2%) — 853.1 gr — 1 Piece 12 x 11.8 x 6.7; 1 Piece 8.7 x 6.9 x 5.7 = 522.5 gr; 1 Piece 8.6 x 6.4 x 5.5 = 301.1 gr; 1 Piece 8.6 x 6.9 x 6.6 = 364.2 gr; 1 Piece 7.7 x 5.3 x 5.2 = 294.1 gr; 1 Piece 6.7 x 4.8 x 4.8 = 302.8 gr | 3691 | 0 - 1 cm = 2696, 79.2%; 1 - 3 cm = 696, 18.9%; 3 - 6 cm = 268, 7.3%; 6 - 9 cm = 24, 0.6%; 9 - 12 cm = 1, 0.03% | 158 |
| Without Core | 4864.7 gr | Pieces 0.5%, Grams 13.6% | Pieces 1%, Grams 10.4% | Pieces 42.2%, Grams 61.2% | Pieces 56.3%, Grams 14.8% | | | | |
| Blanks | 3917 gr | Lost Material | | 71 gr | | Blank Fragments | | | |
| Secondary Reduction | 2024 gr | 17.8 gr 0.9% — 5 Pieces 0.6% — 1-3 cm = 3, 3-6 cm = 2 — Platform Thckn 0.2 - 0.7 cm | 122.4 gr 6.0% — 28 Pieces 3.1% — 0-1 cm = 1, 1-3 cm = 10, 3-6 cm = 17 — 10 with cortex — Platform Thckn 0.2 - 0.5 cm | 731.7 gr 36.2% — 453 Pieces 50.8% — 0-1 cm = 259, 1-3 cm = 172, 3-6 cm = 18, 6-9 cm = 6 — 29 with cortex | 258.1 gr 12.8% — 403 Pieces 45.1% — 0-1 cm = 349, 1-3 cm = 48, 3-6 cm = 6 — 21 with cortex | 894 gr (44.1%) — 3 Pieces (0.4%) — 428.6 gr — 1 Piece 8.5 x 5.6 x 4.8; 1 Piece 7.8 x 5.2 x 4.7 = 276.4 gr; 1 Piece 5.5 x 4.7 x 4.2 = 189 gr | 892 | 0 - 1 cm = 609, 68.5%; 1 - 3 cm = 233, 26.2%; 3 - 6 cm = 43, 4.8%; 6 - 9 cm = 4, 0.5% | 60 |
| Without Blank Fragm | 1130 gr | Pieces 0.6%, Grams 1.6% | Pieces 3.1%, Grams 10.8% | Pieces 51%, Grams 64.8% | Pieces 45.3%, Grams 22.8% | | | | |
| Preforms | 1855 gr | Lost Material | | 38 gr | | | | | |

Outcome: One quadrangular adze 14.2 x 5.3 x 3.8 cm by 534.2 gr
One triangular adze 12.7 x 6.2 x 4.8 cm by 538.2 gr
One quadrangular adze 10.7 x 5.4 x 4.2 cm by 420.6 gr
One quadrangular adze 12 x 5.4 x 3.7 cm by 362.0 gr

(Page 29)

Table C: Primary and secondary reduction of the adze manufacturing process

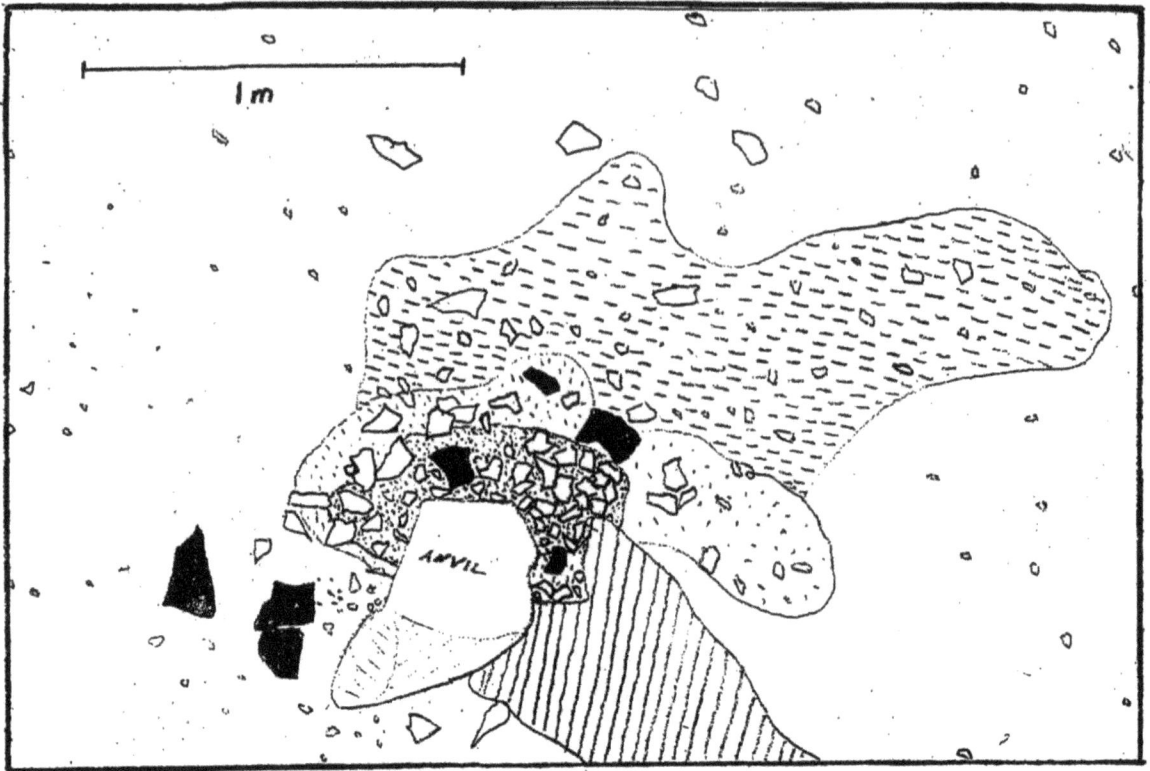

( Figure 3: Flake scatter pattern of primary reduction )

Legend:  Over 30 flakes per 5x5 cm unit
Disturbed area ( Working area of stone worker )
Up to 15 flakes per 5x5 cm unit
Up to 5 flakes per 5x5 cm unit
0 - 2 flakes per 5x5 cm unit
Core ( Fig 3 ), Broken adze fragments ( Fig 4 )

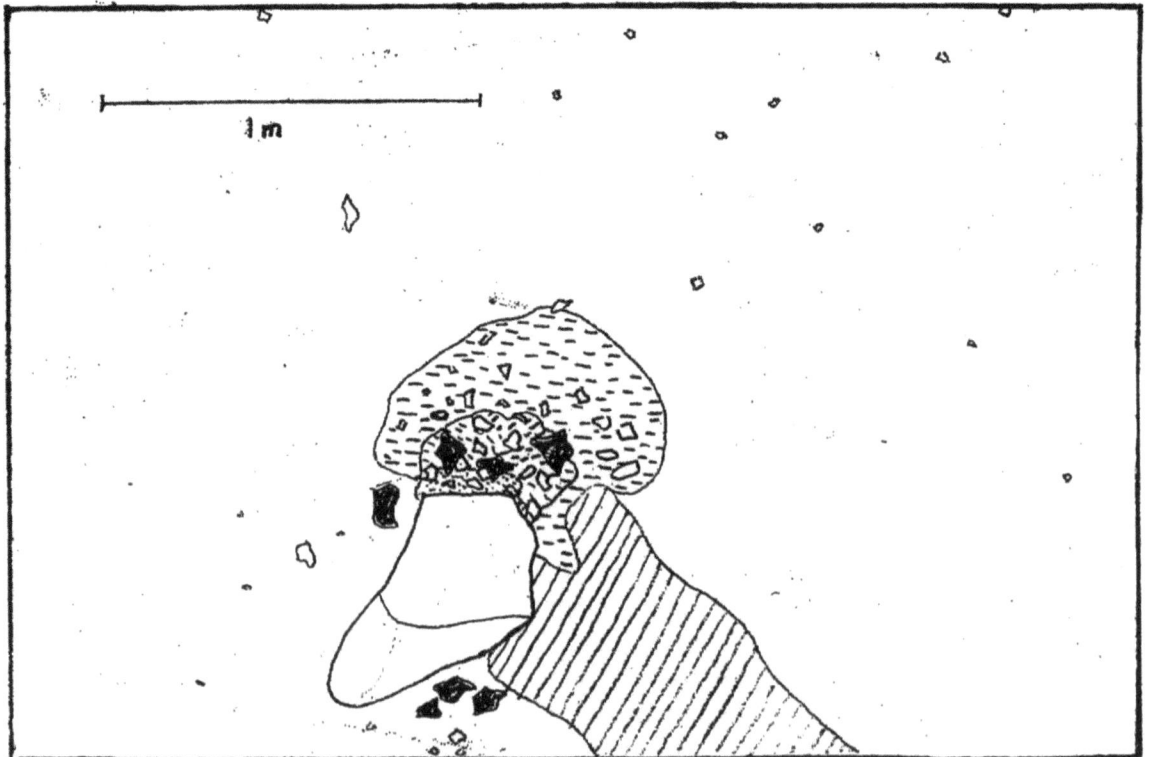

( Figure 4: Flake scatter pattern of secondary reduction )

## 3.3 Flaking attributes of basalt

Even though basaltic material shows a rough and uneven fracture, it displays every single criteria, observable in several of the flakes, we would expect by flaking flint. Both types, as far as it concerns the Waikalua and Mauna Kea basalt, have a hardness of 7 on the Mohs' scale. Nevertheless, flint breaks easier, conchoidal, and its breakage is controllable. It is most likely that this fact results from the different molecular structure of both materials. While flint tends to chip naturally, basalt does not. It also seems that in the basaltic material, if loaded dynamically at some point, the force of impact will not be transmitted throughout the whole material, especially in longitudinal direction. While increasing either the blow velocity or the force, the brittle material reaches its critical point and breaks. Exactly this critical point beyond the elasticity ( elastic property ) of the material, that tended to absorb the shock waves produced by the dynamic load, is reached easier with flint than with basalt. This implies that the stone worker has to hit the material harder, faster or with a heavier intender. All these factors result in a less controllable manufacturing procedure, as the material will be hit less accurately. This is especially true when working with an anvil, which requires to strike the margin region where the flake was situated. If the block is not worked on the edge of the anvil, and instead laid flat on it, the anvil will reflect the applied force and may break the block or even worse the preform in an unintended way, so that it will be rendered useless and discarded. The chipped basaltic flakes appear to be similar to the flint flakes as long as their production could be controlled over the edge of the anvil and the intender hit the margin region of the block accurately. As described above, the striking platform is intact and the bulb of percussion intersects the striking platform. The lateral ends or margins exhibit feather termination, only the distal end is disturbed through the supporting anvil. If a flake shows these attributes it is defined as a complete or if slightly damaged as a broken flake. As can be seen in table A, the number of the complete respectively broken flakes is small within the Waikalua material, what will support the above mentioned theory. The huge number of other diagnostic flakes indicates positive percussion features, such as force lines or parts of the percussion bulb, but the point of the applied force is absent. Presuming the stone workers at the Waikalua site were at the height of their skill, it becomes obvious that they could not have solved this breakage problem sufficiently. Other Hawaiian debitage studies will probably support this statement. The amazingly high amount of broken preforms, found at nearly every extensive manufacturing site, becomes explainable when one tries to work the cutting edge of the intended adzes without the full support of the anvil edge. (See secondary reduction )

## 3.4 Quantity and quality of the flakes produced in com - parison to the Waikalua material

To conduct a comparable, quantitative analysis of the flakes produced in the first and second reduction phase, similar finding realities had to be established. As mentioned earlier, the brushing of the chipping floor led to a soil-flake mixture, probably similar to every excavated unit, that had to be screened. The same sized screen that was employed at the Waikalua excavation, was applied to the soil-flake mixture. Used was an 1/8 inch screen, which means that only particles smaller than 32 mm fall through. The screen was only shaken, no trowel or bare hands were used to force the material through it in order to avoid the crushing and breakage of the flakes. The remains in the screen were put on window glass and the flakes were separated from the larger soil particles, pebbles, and organic material. The flakes were sorted according to size. Flakes under 1 cm were put in one bag, flakes over 1 cm in another one, and finally, flakes that could be applied to further experimentation were singly bagged. The same sorting and measuring procedure that was employed to the Waikalua material, was also applied to the experimentally produced flakes. ( See section II )

Restricting factors in the expressiveness of the experimental flakes in regards to the Waikalua flakes,were the damage of the latter material through trampling, the smallness of the excavation units, no complete chipping floor was laid open, and the fact that most of the flakes were recovered from posthole fillings. Even though detailed, comparative analysis will be exaggerated, general traits in size, number, and quality are recognizable. Over 50% of the Waikalua and nearly 70% of the experimentally produced flakes are under 1 cm in size and 40% respectively 20% range in size from 1 - 3 cm. These small flakes are splinter products and show only a few characteristic flaking features. Most of them are either flake fragments or debris. It also becomes obvious that there are only a few high quality flakes, ( broken or complete ) present. As earlier mentioned, these flakes only occured when the intender hit the margin region of the block accurately, which implies a controlled blow.

Cortex is not limited to a specific size or quality of the flakes, it appears equally throughout the categories. The lack of core or blank fragments at the Waikalua site points to a preform refinement, or if polished flakes occur, to rejuvenation and resharpening of finished adzes.

## 3.5 Comparison of waste flakes with especially produced cutting, scraping, etc. flakes.

As the circumstances and purposes of the flake production were different, the obtained material displayed disparate attributes. The relatively high amount of complete and broken flakes, up to 30% of the target population, is striking. The complete flakes show feather termination not only on the lateral ends, but also on the distal ends. They are longer and generally sharper than the " accidentally " produced flakes, so that they would suit their cutting, scraping, etc. purposes more efficiently. The reason for the occurrence of those flakes is two-fold. On the one hand the most suitable, pointed intender, already proven of its accuracy, was used and on the other hand every single flake was carefully worked on the anvil edge. The striking block part from which the flake should occur, hung over the anvil edge, so that the distal end of the future flake could show only minor or no crushing caused by the anvil. Also, because of the controlled flaking, there were only few splinter products, which makes a chipping floor of this kind clearly distinguishable to the adze

31

reduction floor. These reflections lead to the certain conclusion that flakes at the Waikalua site, if used in any way, produced from adze reduction rather than separate production.

## IV. APPLICATION OF EXPERIMENTALLY PRODUCED FLAKES

### 4.1 Selection of contact material

The fundamental question for the selection of the material to be worked with the flakes was: " What types of plants or animals were at the disposal of the Hawaiians in the time period from AD 1070 - 1405 ? " Beggerlys investigation of " edge damage on experimentally used scrapers of Hawaiian basalt " ( Beggerly 1976 ) was finished after scraping various native Polynesian woods. The same four Hawaiian wood species she used were also selected for this experiment. They were not taken over uncritically. After consultation of several biologists and botanists, who all confirmed the correctness of Beggerly's selection, the decision was made to use these wood species. These were Hibiscus Tilliaceus ( oheohe hau ), Aleurites moluccana ( kukui ), Acacia koa ( koa ), and Metrosoderos Collina ( 'ohia'a-lehua ). These wood species have been mentioned as having been used by ancient Hawaiians. 'Ohia'a-lehua was supposedly used for weapons, tools, and images, while kukui found its use for containers, house timbers, and occasionally canoes. Hau was exclusively used for canoe out-riggers and fishnet floats (Handy/Handy 1972). Koa, on the other hand, was needed for the construction of canoes, house posts, and calabashes ( Kraus 1972 ). Kukui and hau were classified as medium-soft, koa and 'ohia'a-lehua as medium-hard contact material. The wood was a gift from the Foster Botanical Gardens. Except for the koa, what was cut one week before the experiments, the wood was freshly cut and worked within the next three days. ( Photos No. 36 - 39 )

Other contact materials were fish, pig, and bird. The fish was purchased from the Tamashiro fishmarket. Acanthurus Triostegus or Convict Tang ( Manini ), Adioryx Xantherythrus or Hawaiian Sqirrelfish ( Alaihi ), and Priacanthus Meeki or Hawaiian Bigeye ( Aweoweo ) were selected to be used in the experiments. The hardness of fish flesh was classified as soft, the hardness of the fish bone as medium-hard. As the author did not want to contribute to the drastic extinction of the endemic Hawaiian birds, frozen chicken was chosen instead, as an example of the wide range of Hawaiian birds. Bird flesh was classified as soft, bird bone as hard contact material. Mike, a butcher apprentice, allowed the cutting up of a 1/2 a year old pig, that was killed two hours before the experiment. ( His boss still does not know that we cut up one of his pigs with basalt flakes ) The pig flesh was classified as soft material, the bone as hard.

A last contact material were leaves and small branches of the above mentioned wood. This material was classified as soft.

### 4.2 Investigation of edge damage prior to the use of the tools for experiments

Every usable edge of the experimentally produced flakes was examined under 20x, 50x, 100x, and/or 200x magnification. A NIKON polarizing OPTIPHOT-POL microscope with reflected light was used for the examination. This microscope was equipped with a rotating stage, so that the object did not have to be touched, if needed to turn to better light conditions. This was especially helpful when observing under high magnification, as the point of investigation could be held fixed. A variety of filters were at the authors disposal, mostly employed to screen the brightness of fields of crushing towards those with less light reflective attributes. Only with this little trick,was it possible to examine the latter fields closely. The power source was a 12 V - 50 W halogen lamp attached to the microscope ( Photo No. 40/41). The applied bulb had 120 V - 40 W intensity. The photos were taken with a NIKON FX 35 WA camera. The time of exposure was controlled automatically by a NIKON UFX II exposure meter. The additional light source shortened the shutter time for about 6 - 12 seconds depending on the brightness of the object and the magnification employed. Even the slightest previous edge damage was noted ( Table D ). The damaged part of the tool was photographed, ( Photo Series ) and its position on the flake was circled on a sketch of the respective flake ( Figure 5 - 7 ). Twenty-two of the hundred and three flakes were previously damaged, three of them so heavy that they had to be sorted out. These were flakes 4, 11, and 76. They showed either step terminated microflake scars, heavy crushing, and/or several cracks or notches. ( Photos No. 42 - 43 ) In the following table are the tools mentioned that displayed slight to heavy edge damage.

( Photo 37: Ohia-a'lehua )

( Photo 38: Oheohe Hau )

( Photo 39: Kukui )

( Page 33 )

( Photos 40/41: Photographic appliances )

| Tool | Damage | Photo No. | Drawing No. |
|---|---|---|---|
| 2 | Slight crushing | 11 | 1 |
| 3 | Small edge fracture | 18 | 2 |
| 4 | Heavy edge damage;several overlapping;step terminated microflake scars;cracks | 17 | 3 |
| 8 | Small grooves and cracks | 20 | 4 |
| 11 | Heavy edge damage - crushing | 1 | 5 |
| 21 | Slight damage - small notches | 3 | 6 |
| 25 | Heavy edge damage;several natural retouches; but a second undisturbed edge | 5 | 7 |
| 26 | Slight damage - notch | 14 | 8 |
| 32 | Slight damage - notch | 9 | 9 |
| 40 | Medium damage - notch and natural retouch | 10 | 10 |
| 52 | Slight damage - notch | 16 | 11 |
| 53 | Medium damage - two notches | 4 | 12 |
| 62 | Slight damage - retouch | 22 | 13 |
| 71 | Medium damage - little notch in two larger notches | 15 | 14 |
| 73 | Slight damage - retouch | 7 | 15 |
| 76 | Heavy edge damage;several overlapping;step terminated microflake scars | 19 | 16 |
| 78 | Slight edge damage - retouch | 2 | 17 |
| 85 | Slight edge damage - notch | 13 | 18 |
| 90 | Medium edge damage - notch and groove | 6 | 19 |
| 92 | Slight edge damage - notch | 21 | 20 |
| 95 | Slight edge damage - notch | 8 | 21 |
| 97 | Slight edge damage - notch | 12 | 22 |

Table D: Edge damage on experimentally produced flakes prior to use

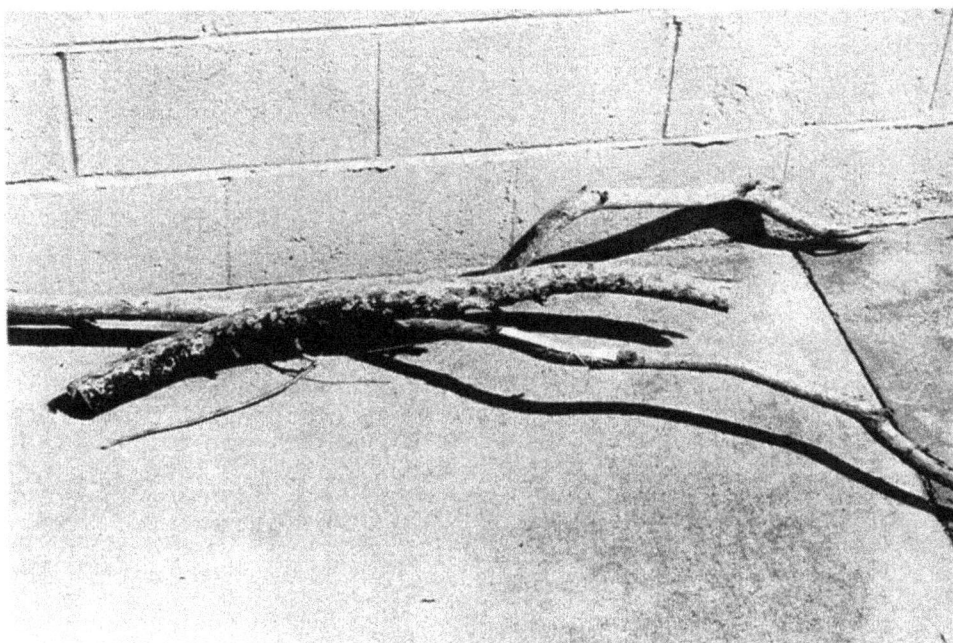

( Photo 36: Contact material koa )

( Photo 42: Heavy previous edge damage )

( Photo 43: Heavy previous edge damage )

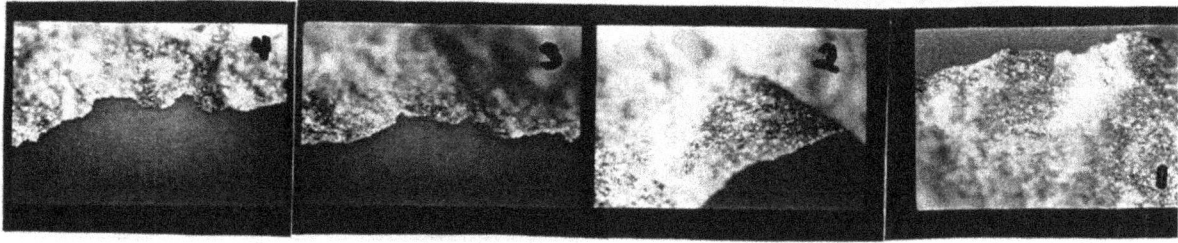

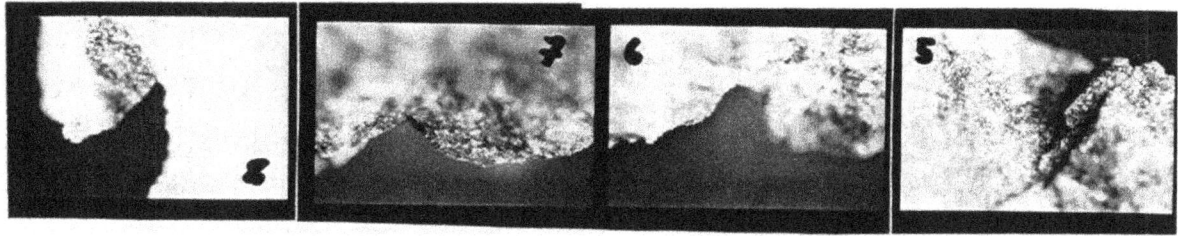

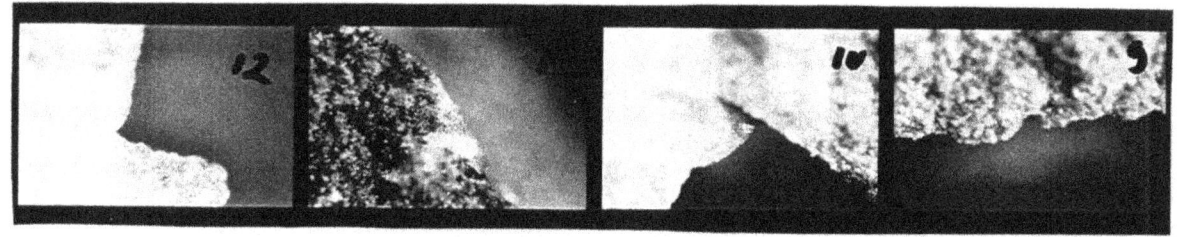

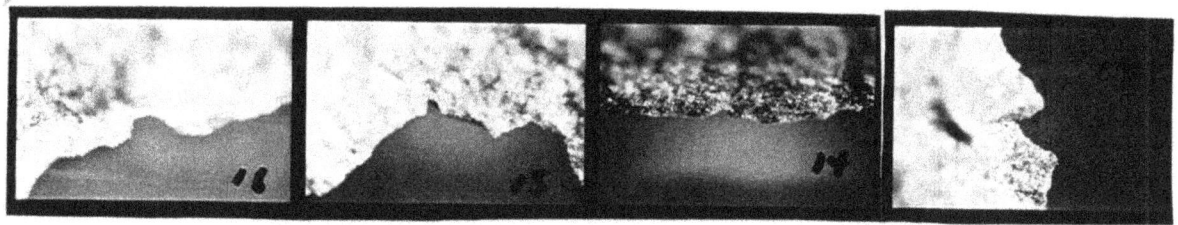

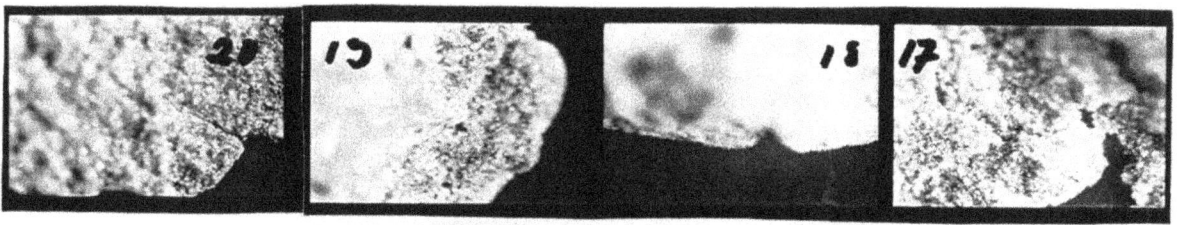

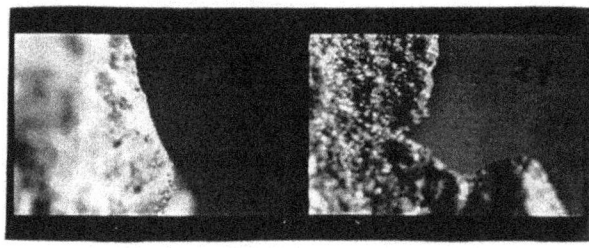

( Photo Series: Previous edge damage of experimentally used flakes )

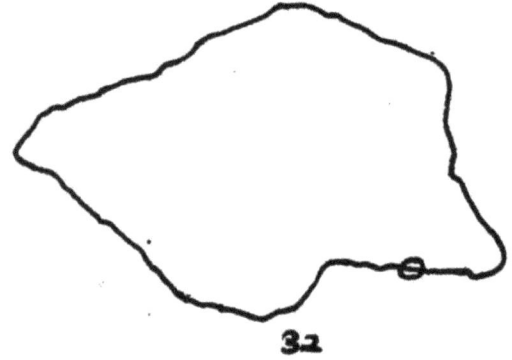

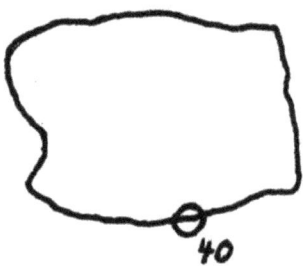

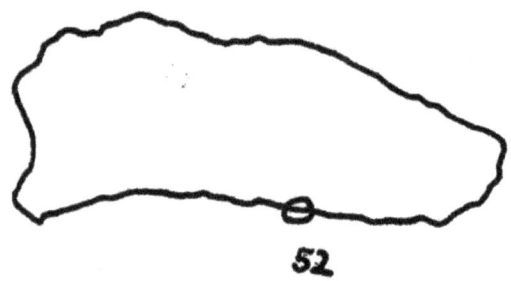

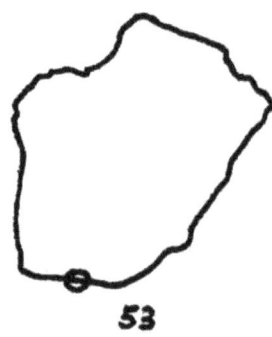

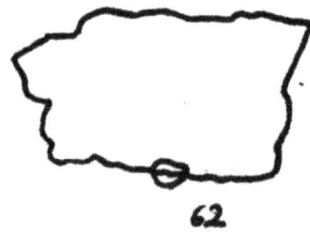

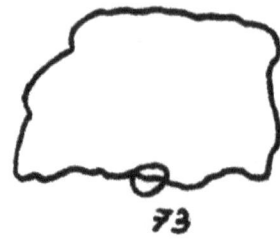

( Fig. 5: Flake outlines with location of edge damage )

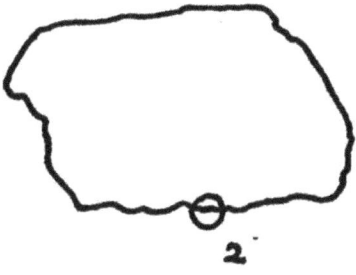

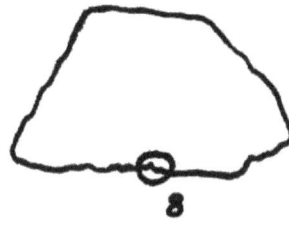

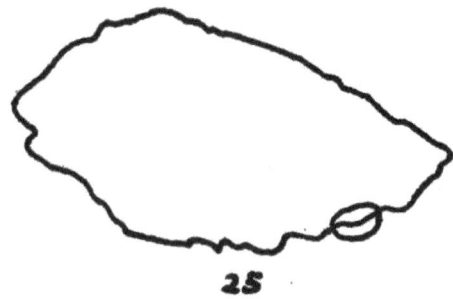

( Fig. 6: Flake outlines with location of edge damage )

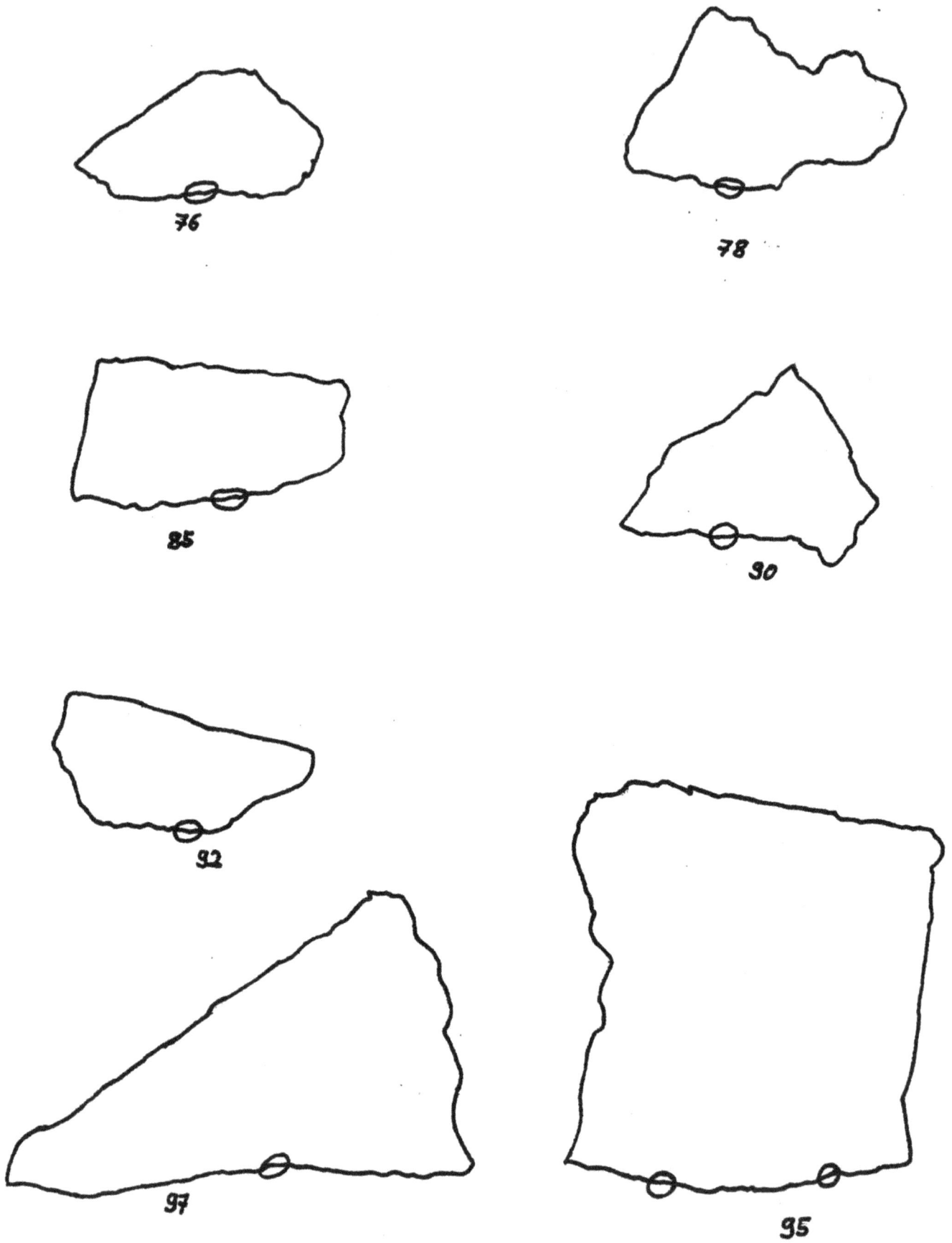

( Fig. 7: Flake outlines with location of edge damage )

## 4.3 Evaluation of the quality and suitability of the flakes in terms of sawing and scraping etc.

### a) Sawing and cutting of bone

As a rule, flakes with smaller edge angles cut and saw better than those with larger angles. Restricting factors to the rule are the thickness, weight and dimensions of the respective tool. If the tools were thin, they broke often, especially under strong pressure. The breakage did not seem to effect the cutting or sawing attributes of the tools as long as they were large enough to be held comfortably. The major advantage of the equal thinness of the blade, was the ability to make even deep cuts into the bone, which was impossible, when the cross section of the tool enlarged. The heavier a tool was, the less pressure had to be applied, which led to less breakage and as such to a longer use-life of the tool. Flakes with edge angles ranging from 40 degrees to 90 degrees were absolutely unsuitable for the cutting and sawing purpose. They either scratched the bone material or cut/saw only a small groove. When strong pressure was applied, it often led to the crushing of the bone material. Exception to the rule was tool FF COa 1, with an edge angle ranging from 45 degrees to 55 degrees. This tool had the advantage that the thickness of the cutting edge was constant, but the grip was thickened. These features made it almost to the ultimate cutting and sawing tool, as it could be applied with strong pressure without breaking and because of the constant thickness it was able to cut/saw deeply.

On the average, medium pressure seemed to be appropriate to obtain a careful cut. Strong pressure tended to crush the contact material, what often rendered the bone useless for subsequent working processes. Three minutes pig/chicken bone and five minutes fish bone cutting were the maximum time spans that the tools could be employed before being absolutely blunted, when using the most suitable tools. In this space of time, the tools could be applied to the working material with 180 - 240 strokes depending on the contact material. The pressure, rather than the velocity, made a measurable difference in the degree of bluntness.

### b) Cutting of flesh

Cutting flesh actually requires a fairly sharp tool edge. If this is not given, the flesh was rather ripped off against the flake edge then cut. Using tool FF SP 57, for example, the general shape of the producing flesh part was not predictable, as the cutting was not controllable. Especially small but sharp flakes were highly suitable to cut up flesh easily. Larger tools were usable to cut sheer flesh, but useless to deflesh bone carefully. If the only intention was to separate flesh parts rapidly, neglecting the outcome, larger tools like FF SP 95 were most suitable. The triangular shape and the weight of this tool made it possible to cut through flesh or bone in seconds. In general, tools with edge angles up to 50 degrees worked best, restricted only through inadequate size. Flakes with angles larger than 50 degrees did not work at all. The just ripped the flesh in little pieces.

Often observable was a denticulation of the tool edge after use. This was particularly visible on tools used for pig skin and pig flesh or sinuous flesh cutting. Possible explanation for this, could be the different hardness of the contact materials that led to partial breakage or the disparate pressure distribution while ripping flesh against the tool edge.

Soft to medium pressure seemed to be appropriate to obtain a careful cut. Strong pressure tended to rip and flatten the contact material, so that we can not speak of a cutting process. Fish flesh divided easily, almost without pressure. Pig flesh and chicken flesh are of a tougher consistency and need stronger pressure as well as a sharper tool edge to be divided. The softness of fish flesh versus pig or chicken flesh is reflected by the degree of dullness of the employed tools applied to chicken or pig flesh definitely cuts worse caused by attrition, the tools used to cut up fish flesh seem not to be effected from the contact material at all. After 300-350 strokes or about 4-5 minutes of cutting pig or chicken flesh most tools were blunted.

### c) Whittling of wood

To whittle wood effectively, the wood worker has to select a flake that displays the following attributes: The flake has to be extremely sharp and thin, to intrude the wooden material easily and to whittle with little pressure. It has to be hard enough, so that it does not break if stuck and the when wood worker has to wiggle the flake in order to free it. On one hand the tool has to be large enough, to be handled comfortably and leave sufficient space for the chips to glide along the tool surface. On the other hand, the largesse of the tool should not effect the thinness especially the extreme forward edge. If the forward edge is sharp then it does not matter if the tool cross section is triangle or constant in shape. Edge angles of 30-55 degrees seem to be most suitable for whittling purposes, while smaller angles, mostly related to tool thinness are unsuitable as the tool breaks. (Exp. CF COa 16 ) Wider angles are improper for whittling, as the tool takes of the bark rather than getting into the wood.( Exp. FF COa 5 ) In order to whittle with tools with wider angles, stronger pressure has to be applied which leads to early blunting. An exception to the rule is tool FF SP 99 with an edge angle of 65-75. Extreme sharpness is the only plausible explanation for it. To whittle branches it was found to be adequate to use those flakes that showed a notch in the same size than the diameter of the whittled branch. Using such a tool, the first wood layer of the branch was taken off quickly. It seems appropriate to clean the tool edge often, as wood mush adversely affects the cutting properties of the tool. It was also found, that even slightly seasoned wood was impossible to whittle with the flakes. On the average, medium pressure was sufficient to whittle non-seasoned wood easily. Strong pressure leads to rapid bluntness and unclean whittling. The tools were blunted relatively early in the whittling process. A medium of 170 strokes by two minutes of whittling was measured. This relatively low average stroke number resulted from the fact that hard wood was almost impossible to whittle, so that the tools blunted early. When whittling soft wood like kukui, the tools were blunted after 250-300 strokes. ( Exp. FF SP 42 )

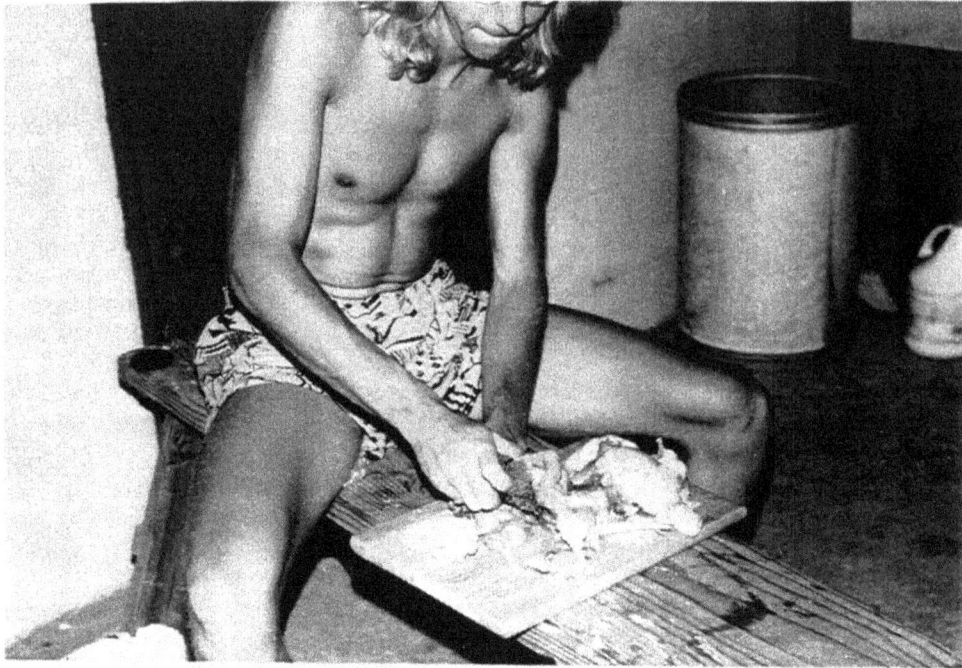

( Photo 44: Author defleshing a chicken )

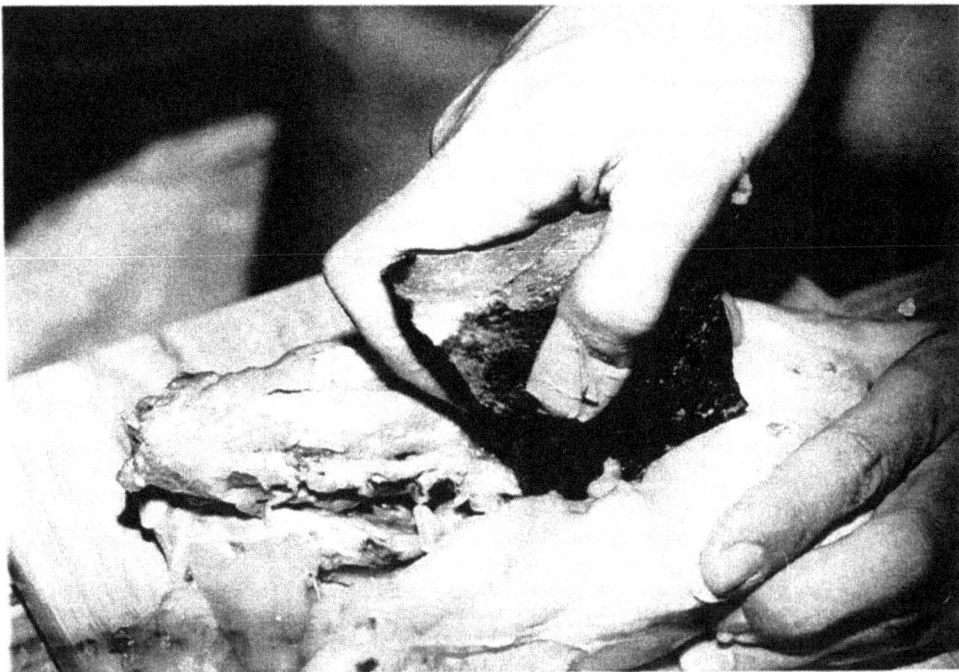

( Photo 45: Close-up view )

( Photo 46: Author sawing kukui )

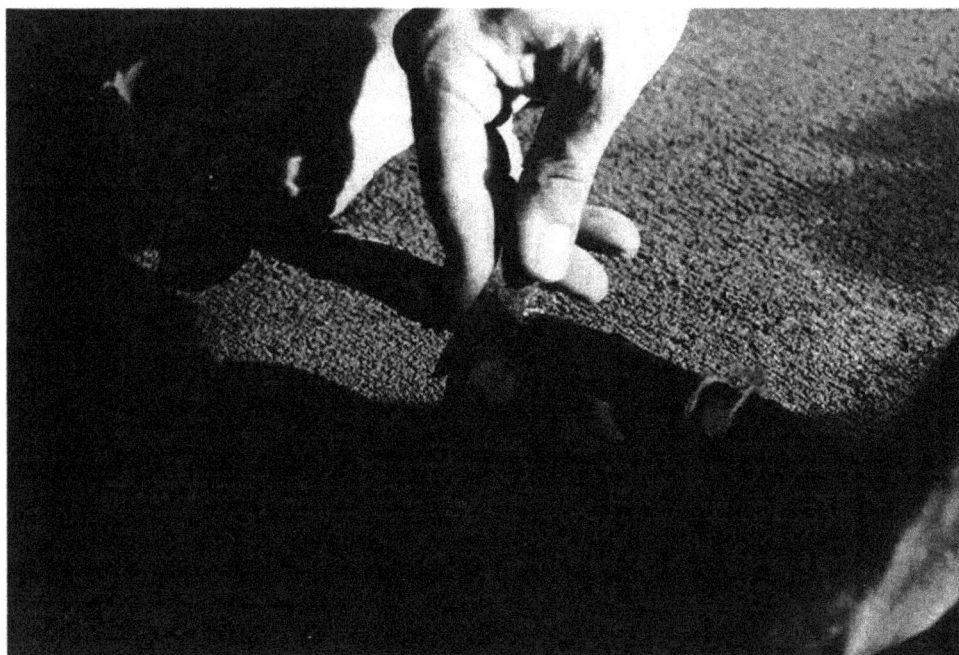

( Photo 47: Close-up view )

## d) Sawing of wood

Larger tools were needed to fulfill a sawing motion on wood. The first reason for this is the frequent breakage of parts of the tool edge, which let the flake shrink rapidly. The second reason for this is the increasing risk of injury, especially to the fingertips, that the wood worker has to face when the tool becomes too small. Another necessary attribute is that the tool used for sawing purposes should display a flat, dull side, opposite to the cutting edge. This is extremely important if the wood worker wants to avoid serious wounds of the forefinger, which has to be used to apply pressure on the tool. On one hand, the tool should be thin and sharp to bite in the wood and cut deeply, on the other hand, it should be hard enough to resist even impetuous attempts to free a stuck tool. Flakes with a constant cross section should be preferred to those with a triangular one, even if the latter are sharper. It seems to be reasonable that a tool with constant cross section is able to cut deeply in the contact material and may divide it, as one with a triangular shape will saw a notch and get stuck, where the cross section of the tool enlarges. There is no special edge angle that would be more suitable than another one. If a flake showed the attributes mentioned above, it was acceptable to be used as a sawing tool. It was found that flakes are only useable to divide branches up to three centimeters in diameter. Thicker branches were only divisible with the " sawing around " technique, as the cutting edge thickened so that a new notch next or opposite to the old one had to be sawed. Special prominence has to be given to tool CF COa 14. This tool was applied to the extremely hard wood ohia`a-lehua with slight pressure. In contrast to most of the other tools that were applied to hard contact materials with soft or medium pressure, tool CF COa 14 sawed well and deep. The reasons could be explained in the thinness and sharpness of the tool. Total bluntness was reached on medium-soft material after 215 strokes by 1 1/2 minutes. Medium to strong pressure was most practical to saw quick and deeply. The tool itself had to be cleaned often from the wood mush and the sawing incision had to be cleaned out with a flicking motion.

## b) Scraping of wood

Scraping as well as planing requires special preparation of the working wood. As the intention of scraping and planing wooden material was probably to smooth, respectively plane, the surface the arts and crafts and the wood had to be pre-worked. First the bark was taken off with a knife and branches then were removed. Secondly the wood was divided into three centimeter thick strips with an iron saw. The so prepared wood, was considered to have the same properties of a raw worked canoe or sculpture. The scraping tool itself should not be too sharp, as for example tool FF SP 89, so that it does not cut into the wooden material. Tools with edge angles under 35 degrees were unsuitable for the scraping as they broke through the transverse motion due to their thinness. The most appropriate shape of a scraping tool could be described as slightly triangular in the cross-section with two dull sides. One dull part should be at the opposite side of the cutting edge to be enclosed with four fingers and another

one at a lateral end of the tool, depending on right or left handed use, to be held with the thumb. The tool should not be so small that it hurts the user when the finger knuckles hit the contact material. Characteristically for the tools used for scraping is the breakage phase of the first two or three strokes. Eventual unevenness of the extreme forward edge are smoothed so that the solid tool edge has contact with the wooden surface. The same phenomenon is observable if the tool is slightly convex or concave.

Seasoned wood is less promising to work with, as the attempt to scrape the slightly seasoned wood specimen hau shows. ( Tool FF SP 96 ) As long as the pressure was increased, the hardness of the wood itself seemed not to effect the scraping abilities of the flakes. Tool BR SP 32 was applied to 'ohia'a-lehua with strong pressure and worked beautifully until it was dull after 412 strokes. The applied pressure should be adjusted to the hardness of the contact material. The harder the wood the stronger should be the applied pressure. Slight pressure is definitely unsuitable. The tools are blunted at about 350 - 400 strokes by 3 - 4 minutes.

## f) Planing of wood

The working wood was prepared in the same way as it was done for the scraping process. The flake was employed to the wood comparable to the function of a modern plane. As such, the flake should display the following features. It should be large enough to be held comfortably with the whole hand or the fingertips of both hands. It should be dull at the side where it is held and should guarantee an injury free use. An extreme triangular cross-section and a fairly sharp working edge are guarantors for successful working.

The planed chips should be able to glide freely along the upper tool edge so that long and regular chips can be taken off. Tools with edge angles under 35 degrees were absolutely unsuitable for planing purpose as they broke through the transverse motion, because of their thinness. Straight or slightly convex working edges work best while concave ones tend to cut too deep in the contact material, so that the tool get stuck. The heavier a tool is, the better it works, and the less pressure has to be applied, as the tool FF SP 93 shows.

The slightly seasoned hau wood was almost impossible to plane, only a few splinter were taken off ( Exp. FF COa 22 ), while the other wood specimen were easily planable. The purpose of planing is to get an even surface either to be further worked with the scraping tool or to be used in this stage. Most tools fulfill this purpose, but were blunted after 500 - 600 strokes by 5 - 7 minutes of working time.

## 4.4 Determination of the most convenient angle of use for scraping, cutting, etc. in order to ascertain the probable tool use or to exclude tools from special functions.

As mentioned earlier, this part shall establish a theoretical framework for the classification of flakes to special functions because of their attributes considering also clearly recognizable use-wear patterns. This framework shall enable to ascertain the possible use of flakes for definable purposes and under special consideration of use-wear their actual use.

## a) Sawing and cutting of bone, fish or wood

The significance of this work is that the establishing angle of the worked material, rather then the flake angle, determines the angle of skew or use. If the only intention is to cut a material, the tool will be held perpendicular to the working object. This is especially true when cutting bone or wood. Flesh, as a rule, will also be cut with a tool held in a 90 degrees angle towards the cutting object. An exception is the attempt to deflesh a bone. In this case the tool will be held in such a way that it gets most access to the cutting part and, as flesh will not hurt the tool users fingers, when applying the tool with various angles. Common attributes of such tools are the extreme sharpness, a small edge angle, and, except for flesh, the large size. These vague attributes allow not even a guess of tool use without a cautious examination of the use-wear. If the use-wear analysis shows rounding of the extreme forward edge and smoothing or polish of the dorsal and ventral aspects of the tool, then it was probably used for sawing or cutting. Flesh cutting can be supposed through a denticulation typical for tools used to cut flesh with a ripping motion against the tool edge.

## b) Whittling of wood

Not only for cutting and sawing the angle of use is of great importance, but also for the whittling abilities of a tool. A mean angle of 50 - 60 degrees was established to be most suitable for the whittling purpose. This angle of skew allows the worker to whittle the contact material easily, which implies a not to deep cut in order to take off long chips without hurting his/her fingers. As suggested in section 1.2, hafting of the tools may have been a possible way to use tools with smaller use angles or even tools with normally inappropriate edge angles. The typical outcome of the use of flakes with smaller edge angles and an unfitting small angle of skew is immediate breakage and injuries of the thumb. When the angle of skew is too large, a deep cut with breakage is the consequence. The common result of the use of flakes with wider edge angles and an inappropriate small angle of skew

is a more scraping then whittling motion. A wider angle of skew can only scratch the material and maybe take off the soft bark. Exceptionally useful for the whittling, are those tools with a notch or concave curvature that suits the whittling branch. Such a tool is applicable with even a steeper angle of skew and, if the tool is large enough with a correspondingly smaller angle In general, tools with an edge angle of 30 - 55 degrees, held towards the object in an angle of 50 - 60 degrees, are appropriate for the whittling purpose. Use-wear characteristics of a tool used for whittling are the rounded forward edge, and the extensive field of smoothing or polish along the dorsal side of the tool that had permanent contact to the contact material, and the striation or interrupted fields of polish on the ventral side.

## c) Scraping ,and planing wood

Although wood scraping and planing shall fulfill the same purpose, that is to smooth the contact material, tools used for this are held in different angles towards the wooden surface. While scraping is possible with an angle of skew of 40 - 50 degrees, planing should be done with a use angle of 0 - 20 degrees in order to obtain the best results. While the planing tool will be pushed, the scraping tool will be drawn over the contact material. As such, also the observable use-wear characteristics are different. The flake employed for a planing motion shows, similar to the whittling tool, an extended field of smoothing or polish on the dorsal side and striation or interrupted fields of polish on the ventral side caused by the planed chips. The forward edge is rounded. A distinction between a whittling and a planing tool is doable through extension measurements of the polished field on the dorsal side ( the bigger, the more probable a planing tool ), the general shape of the tool ( triangular cross-section for planing tools ), and the edge angle of the tool ( over 50 degrees definitely a planing tool ). The scraping tool, on the other hand, shows polish only on the ventral side accompanied by a rounded forward edge. In general tools with edge angles of 35 - 70 degrees for scraping and 40 - 90 degrees for planing, held in an angle of 40 - 50 degrees respectively 0 - 20 degrees towards the object, are appropriate for the scraping respectively planing purpose.

| Tool | Angle Edge / To. Obj. | Contact Material | Direction | Elapsed Time in min | Strokes No | Pressure | Remarks |
|---|---|---|---|---|---|---|---|
| FF SP100 | 45 - 55 / 60 - 90 | Leaves;Ohia-a'lehua | MainlyUni | 1.5 | 132 | Medium | Fits well in hand;Suitable;Except leaves also 13 little branches removed; Branches are a little dry;Tool is still usable ( Drawing ) |
| FF SP 45 | 55 - 65 / 60 - 90 | Leaves ; Hau | MainlyUni | 1 | 79 | Medium | Branches thicker so it takes longer than before;Have to saw when material is resistant;Still usable;Does not fit well in hand |
| FFCOa 1 | 45 - 55 / | Pig Bone | Bi | 2 | 198 | Strong | Almost perfect for this special task;Saws fastly deep; 2 bones;2cm in diameter sawed; Tool is still sharp |
| CFCOa15 | 25 - 35 / | Pig Bone | Bi | 4.5 | 315 | Strong | Tool looses edge material fastly;1 thick (3cm) bone was sawed Tool is blunted after 254 strokes; Tool was suitable |
| FFCOa18 | 35 - 45 / | Pig Bone | Bi | 2 | 153 | Strong | Parts of the tool edge break;however other parts are still functional; Tool was suitable |
| FFCOa 8 | 25 - 35 / | Manini Bone | Bi | 3 | 191 | Medium | Bone breaks more than being sawn;Edge parts break; Tool seems blunted after 187 strokes |
| FF SP 73 | 25 - 35 / | Alaihi Bone | Bi | 2 | 134 | Medium | Cuts bone easily;Tool hits wooden board often;Tool is still usable |
| CFCOb 2 | 25 - 35 / 90 | Alaihi Bone | Bi | 2 | 158 | Medium | Sawing is almost impossible;Bone breaks;Fish bone was probably only cut or ripped with the hands |
| FF SP102 | 45 - 55 / 90 | Manini Bone | Bi | 2 | 127 | Medium | Does not work;Crushes the bone under pressure;but does not saw;Tool is unsuitable |
| FF SP 46 | 55 - 65 / ? | Manini Bone | Bi | 1 | 123 | Medium | Does not work;Edge angle too wide;Will not saw |
| FF SP 78 | 35 - 45 / ? | Chicken;Flesh/Bone | Bi | 1 | 82 | Medium | Does a really good job;Blunted at 0.5 min by 21 strokes; Will not cut the bone any more |
| CF SP 58 | 45 - 55 / ? | Chicken;Flesh/Bone | Bi | 1 | 92 | Medium | Works well;Absolutely suitable;Still usable afterwards |
| FF SP 57 | 55 - 65 / ? | Chicken;Flesh/Bone | Bi | 1 | 71 | Strong | Works well like the previous one;Tool is heavy and thick that probably helps. Motion was more cutting and ripping it off against the flake edge |
| FF SP 98 | 65 - 75 / ? | Chicken;Flesh/Bone | Bi | 1 | 85 | Strong | Does not work too well although it does cut a bit;Not blunted yet |
| FF SP 90 | 35 - 45 / ? | Aweoweo;Flesh/Bn. | Bi | 2 | 164 | Medium | Fish falls apart easily;Also fish bone is cut fastly;Needs almost no pressure; Tool is not blunted at all |
| BF SP101 | 55 - 65 / 90 | Pig Bone | Bi | 2 | 179 | Strong | Tool does not fit well in hand;Poor cutting abilities; Saws only bones up to 2 cm in diameter |
| FF SP 49 | 35 - 45 / ? | Aweoweo;Flesh/Bn. | Bi | 2 | 132 | Medium | Hard to cut especially skin;Needs more pressure than the tool applied to cooked fish; Tool is still usable |
| CFCOa19 | 45 - 55 / ? | Manini;Flesh/Bone | Bi | 1 | 94 | Strong | Unsuitable flake;Rips the flesh;Pressure too strong;Tool too thick |
| BFCOa23 | 45 - 55 / ? | Manini Flesh | Uni | 2 | 145 | Medium | Does not cut well; Cutting with extreme forward edge works a little better;Still usable;Hardly affected |
| FF SP 43 | 45 - 55 / ? | Manini Flesh | Bi | 2.5 | 201 | Soft | Once through skin it cuts even with soft pressure;but the thickness of the tool causes the ripping of the flesh when cutting deeper |

Table E: First observations of the experimentally produced flakes while use

( Page 46 )

| Tool | Angle Edge / To. Obj. | Contact Material | Direction | Elapsed Time in min | Strokes No | Pressure | Remarks |
|---|---|---|---|---|---|---|---|
| BF SP 77 | 55 - 65 / | ? | Manini Flesh | Bi | 2 | 211 | Medium | Unsuitable for fish cutting purpose;Rips fish flesh;No damage on tool |
| FF SP 52 | 65 - 75 / | ? | Manini Flesh | Bi | 1 | 117 | Medium | Same as above ( BR SP 77) |
| CFCOa 6 | 15 - 25 / | ? | Manini;Flesh/Bone | Bi | 5 | 251 | Soft | Cuts well; 1 1/2 fish were defleshed;Tool is still usable |
| CFCOa 3 | 25 - 35 / | ? | Alaihi Flesh | Uni | 1.5 | 79 | Medium | Tool is very sharp;Work proceeds fastly;Edge splittering was the consequence when the bone was hit;Tool is still usable |
| BF SP 66 | 35 - 45 / | ? | Aweoweo Flesh | Bi | 3 | 187 | Medium | Unsuitable for cutting;but divides cooked flesh easily |
| CF SP 41 | 5 - 15 / | ? | Chicken Flesh | Bi | 0.5 | 41 | Medium | Does not cut through tough skin - or takes a long time;Breaks |
| CF SP 81 | 25 - 35 / | ? | Chicken Flesh | Bi | 1 | 95 | Medium | Definitely cuts better than previous tool |
| FF SP 33 | 25 - 35 / 90 - | ? | Pig Flesh | Bi | 5 | 325 | Medium | Tool fits purpose well;Cuts easily;Tool is still usable |
| FF SP 55 | 65 - 75 / | ? | Pig Flesh | Uni | 3 | 294 | Medium | Cuts well;Four pig ribs were defleshed;Not blunted |
| FF SP 79 | 65 - 75 / | ? | Pig Flesh | Bi | 3 | 313 | Medium | Would need more pressure in order to obtain better cutting results;The uni-directional motion causes the ripping of the flesh from the bone;Three ribs were defleshed |
| FFCOa17 | 45 - 55 / | ? | Pig Flesh | Uni | 3 | 301 | Strong | Flesh is cut fastly but uncontrolled because of the strong pressure;Tool seems to be blunted afterwards |
| FFCOa10 | 45 - 55 / | ? | Pig Flesh | Bi | 2.5 | 254 | Medium | Cuts well;Still usable afterwards;Cuts even thick sinews |
| FF SP 92 | 15 - 25 / | ? | Chicken;Fl./Sinews | Bi | 1 | 94 | Medium | Works well;Does a good job ( once through skin ) |
| FF SP 27 | 35 - 45 / | ? | Chicken;Flesh/Bone | Bi | 1 | 128 | Medium | Does a really good job but a bigger tool would be more effective |
| BF SP 36 | 25 - 35 / | ? | Chicken;Fl./Sinews | Bi | 4 | 301 | Medium | Cutting slowly;Defleshing a leg;Tool works very well;The small tool can get close to the bone and control what is cut;Problems with the sinews which are thick;Tool hit wooden board several times; Blunted after 285 strokes |
| FF SP 67 | 25 - 35 / | ? | Pig;Flesh/Sinews | Bi | 3 | 202 | Medium | Tool edge brittles;Fastly blunted; Unsuitable tool |
| BFCOa25 | 25 - 35 / | ? | Pig;Flesh/Sinews | Bi | 3 | 189 | Medium | Tool does a good job;Still usable afterwards; The tool is too small ( not enough weight ) to cut thick sinews |
| FF SP 72 | 25 - 35 / | ? | Pig;Flesh/Bone | Bi | 3 | 174 | Strong | Tool looses lots of edge material;Almost blunted at the end;One pig shank was cut |
| FF COa 7 | 35 - 45 / | ? | Pig;Flesh/Sinews | Uni | 2.5 | 201 | Soft | Cuts flesh well but only small sinews because of the soft pressure applied;Tool looses few edge material |
| FF SP 95 | 45 - 55 / | ? | Chicken;Fl./Sinews | Bi | 3 | 304 | Medium | Absolutely suitable;Cuts through everything in seconds;Blunted after 292 strokes |
| FF SP 62 | 35 - 45 / | ? | Pig;Fl./Sinews/Bone | Bi | 3 | 211 | Medium | Looses edge material when hitting the bone;Cuts flesh and sinews well; Still usable |
| FFCOa21 | 25 - 35 / | ? | Chicken;Fl./Sinews | Bi | 1 | 68 | Medium | Cuts well;Defleshes bone maybe scrape a little;Not blunted |
| FF SP 74 | 35 - 45 / | ? | Pig;Fl./Sinews/Bone | Uni | 5 | 473 | Medium | Tool works very well;Still usable at the end of experiment |
| FF SP 83 | 55 - 65 / | ? | Pig;Flesh/Sinews | Bi | 2 | 199 | Medium | Cuts well and fastly;Highly suitable;Not blunted afterwards |

Table E: Continued

( Page 47 )

| Tool | Angle Edge / To. Obj. | Contact Material | Direction | Elapsed Time in min | Strokes No | Pressure | Remarks |
|---|---|---|---|---|---|---|---|
| CFCOa26 | 35 - 45 / 30 - 40 | Koa | Uni | 9 | 1243 | Strong | Even though handled with strong pressure tool seems to be still usable; But recognizably worse cutting after 351 strokes |
| FF SP 63 | 65 - 75 / 40 - 50 | Koa | Uni | 3 | 298 | Strong | Absolutely unsuitable for this purpose;Rips surface;Blunted after 168 strokes |
| BF SP 32 | 35 - 45 / 40 - 50 | Ohia-a'lehua | Uni | 6 | 611 | Strong | Absolutely blunted after 412 strokes;Edge rounging visible |
| FF SP 96 | 45 - 55 / 40 - 50 | Hau | Uni | 2 | 213 | Medium | Tool is very suitable as long as scraped with the wood graining Tool is still usable at the end of the experiment |
| FF SP 68 | 45 - 55 / 50 - 60 | Kukui | Uni | 1 | 105 | Medium | Angle towards object is too steep;Tool edge breaks and is unserviceable after 64 strokes |
| BF SP 64 | 55 - 65 / 40 - 50 | Kukui | Uni | 2.5 | 284 | Medium | The forward edge aspect breaks because of the rough surface of the tool;Now the tool fits its purpose;Does a good job |
| FF SP 89 | 55 - 65 / 40 - 50 | Ohia-a'lehua | Uni | 1 | 92 | Medium | This tool would be more suitable for whittling or carving however it is successful; Blunted after 89 strokes |
| FF SP 56 | 65 - 75 / 40 - 50 | Hau | Uni | 1 | 107 | Slight | Smoothes the surface nicely but would need more pressure because of its littleness;Still usable |
| FF SP 94 | 75 - 85 / 40 - 50 | Kukui | Uni | 2 | 317 | Medium | Tool was not always controllable because of the high velocity applied;Some edge aspects break; however tool is still usable |
| FF SP 80 | 75 - 85 / 40 - 50 | Ohia-a'lehua | Uni | 1 | 189 | Slight | Tool would need more pressure in order to work successfully; Only slight smoothing of wooden surface;On roots and knots still rough surface;Tool is still usable |
| CFCOa13 | 35 - 45 / 30 - 40 | Kukui | Uni | 4 | 451 | Medium | Tool scrapes small parts of the material off and smooths the surface;Only the dorsal side is used;At 243 it's blunted and parts of the edge broke at 245. Nice surface;really smooth by 3 min. |
| FF SP 86 | 35 - 45 / 40 - 50 | Hau | Uni | 2.5 | 273 | Medium | Works well even on hau;Tool still usable;it hardly affected it |
| FF SP 48 | 45 - 55 / 20 - 30 | Koa | Uni | 1.5 | 95 | Medium | Tool is too small;Thumb rasps over contact material;Unsuitable |
| FF SP 39 | 65 - 75 / 15 - 25 | Koa | Uni | 1 | 83 | Medium | Tool is too small;Hurts the fingers;Scratches material |
| FF SP 38 | 75 - 85 / 15 - 25 | Koa | Uni | 4 | 399 | Medium | Works well but tends to whittle because of the angle towards the contact material; Should contact the material directly |
| BFCOa24 | 35 - 45 / 15 - 25 | Ohia-a'lehua | Uni | 8 | 997 | Medium | Absolutely suitable;Takes of the last unevennesses of the wood; Dorsal aspect of the tool has visible polish |
| FFCOa22 | 35 - 45 / 20 - 30 | Hau | Uni | 3 | 401 | Medium | Less prosperous for planing;Still rough parts;Tool is still usable |
| FF SP 75 | 45 - 55 / 30 - 40 | Kukui | Uni | 1 | 71 | Medium | Angle towards material too steep;Edge parts break;Unsuitable |
| FF SP 97 | 55 - 65 / | Kukui | Uni | 10 | 1254 | Strong | Works perfectly;Absolute suitable;Still usable;Best tool so far |
| FFCOa12 | 65 - 75 / | Ohia-a'lehua | Uni | 5 | 492 | Strong | Works as good as previous tool;Smooths surface after a short time; Still usable afterwards |
| FF SP 93 | 90 / | Hau | Uni | 7 | 647 | Medium | Tool lies well on the contact material because of it's heaviness; Does a good job; Still usable at the end |

Table E: Continued

| Tool | Angle Edge / To. Obj. | Contact Material | Direction | Elapsed Time in min | Strokes No | Pressure | Remarks |
|---|---|---|---|---|---|---|---|
| CFCOa14 | 35 - 45 / 90 | Ohia-a'lehua | Bi | 0.5 | 79 | Slight | Even with slight pressure it saws well;Tool still usable;Suitable |
| FF SP 29 | 35 - 45 / 90 | Kukui | Bi | 5 | 1107 | Medium | Highly suitable;Cut around branch and cut different notches because too thick to cut way in. Getting blunted (slightly) at 395; Finally blunted at 522 strokes |
| FFCOa20 | 35 - 45 / 90 | Hau | Bi | 1.5 | 217 | Medium | Cuts fastly and pretty deep;Suitable;Still usable at 217 strokes |
| FFCOa 9 | 45 - 55 / 90 | Hau | Bi | 1 | 155 | Strong | Two edge parts broke after 3 strokes;After 92 strokes a 1.5 cm branch was cut in half and almost cut through a second;2 flakes chipped off |
| CF SP 87 | 45 - 55 / 60 - 90 | Kukui | MainlyUni | 1.5 | 127 | Strong | 11 1/2 branches cut off;Most suitable for cutting in;breaking small branch;then cutting the remaining portion |
| FF SP 54 | 75 - 85 / 90 | Kukui | Bi | 0.5 | 107 | Slight | Scratched the material |
| CFCOa16 | 15 - 20 / 90 | Ohia-a'lehua | Bi | 1 | 245 | Medium | Two edge parts broke after 15 seconds;Blunted after195 strokes |
| BF SP 59 | 15 - 20 / 90 | Kukui | Bi | 0.5 | 134 | Medium | Fairly sharp-works beautifully;Tool is still usable;Width of tool too thick to get deeper in wood but sharpness is perfect |
| FF SP 61 | 25 - 35 / 90 | Kukui | Bi | 1.5 | 293 | Medium | Tool too thick but highly suitable otherwise-still sharp until about 215 strokes;Sawed all around branch because too thick to go into it far |
| CF SP 84 | 25 - 35 / 90 | Kukui | Uni | 2 | 99 | Medium | Cut with extreme forward edge(because uni);Makes deep cuts; Still sharp at end;Cut 6-7 different notches because couldn't get deep;Highly suitable |
| CF SP 65 | 35 - 45 / 90 | Koa | Bi | 1 | 167 | Slight | Scratches rather than biting in;Slightly blunted at 132 strokes but still usable;Does cut it but takes a long time |
| FF SP 35 | 65 - 75 / 90 | Koa | Bi | 1 | 211 | Strong | Cuts deeply pretty fast but limited in deepness by thickness of the tool;Blunted after 184 strokes |
| CF SP 34 | 10 - 15 / 90 | Koa | Bi | 2 | 352 | Medium | Tool edge brittled;was blunted after 250 strokes;Unsuitable tool |
| FF SP 88 | 25 - 35 / 90 | Koa | Bi | 0.5 | 124 | Strong | Blunt after 88 strokes |
| BF SP 30 | 10 - 15 / 45 - 50 | Kukui | Uni | 3.5 | 150 | Medium | Flake broke after 120 strokes;but the working edge was not affected;Tool is still suitable/sharp;Tool is too thin for whittling |
| BF SP 28 | 15 - 25 / 50 - 60 | Kukui | Uni | 2 | 157 | Medium | Works very well;Mainly using notch that fits branch;At 64 strokes much of edge broke on hard part of the wood;Starts to get blunted at 92;Have to stop and clean off fibers (10-15 sec) Still usable at the end of the experiment |
| FF SP 85 | 25 - 35 / 40 - 50 | Ohia-a'lehua | Uni | 1 | 91 | Medium | Suitable;Whittles easily;Angle absolutely unsuitable;Hand goes over the wood;Absolutely usable at 91 |
| FF SP 71 | 25 - 35 / 70 - 80 | Hau | Uni | 1.5 | 148 | Medium | Angle too steep - a lot of fibers on tool;Only bark comes off; Microscar;tiny break; Stopped to clean off the tool surface as it would slow down the experiment;Tool seems to be blunted |

Table E: Continued

( Page 49 )

| Tool | Angle Edge / To. Obj. | Contact Material | Direction | Elapsed Time in min | Strokes No | Pressure | Remarks |
|---|---|---|---|---|---|---|---|
| FF SP 42 | 25 - 35 / 50 - 60 | Kukui | Uni | 4 | 333 | Slight | Part of edge broke with the first stroke;This part of wood may be a bit seasoned;hard;Have to clean tool off;Works pretty well; Blunted after 272 strokes |
| FFCOb 5 | 35 - 45 / 50 - 60 | Hau | MainlyUni | 2.5 | 187 | Medium | Works very well;Difficult to get into the wood;Have to clean fibers off;Takes bark off very well |
| BF SP 53 | 35 - 45 / 50 - 60 | Hau | Uni | 1 | 38 | Strong | Not very suitable;Blunted after 17 because tool broke over whole length of egde |
| BF SP 37 | 35 - 45 / 50 - 60 | Ohia-a'lehua | Uni | 1 | 73 | Medium | Not very suitable;Blunted but not sure when |
| FF SP 44 | 45 - 55 / 50 - 60 | Kukui | Uni | 1 | 172 | Medium | Works well;Occasionally stop to clean the tool;Not blunted |
| CF SP 82 | 45 - 55 / 50 - 60 | Kukui | Uni | 1 | 158 | Medium | Clean tool occasionally;Works pretty well;Not blunted |
| FF SP 47 | 45 - 55 / 50 - 60 | Ohia-a'lehua | Uni | 1 | 86 | Strong | Tool worked well but slowed down by roots of tiny branches; Not blunted afterwards |
| FF SP 69 | 45 - 55 / 50 - 60 | Ohia-a'lehua | Uni | 3.5 | 391 | Medium | Works well; Blunted at 141 strokes |
| FF SP 31 | 55 - 65 / 50 - 60 | Kukui | Uni | 1 | 58 | Strong | Whittles very well;Gets deep in the material;Can do only short strokes because it goes so deep |
| FF SP 51 | 55 - 65 / 50 - 60 | Ohia-a'lehua | Uni | 1 | 91 | Medium | Works well;Cuts deep;Parts of the edge brake;however still usable |
| FF SP 99 | 65 - 75 / 50 - 60 | Kukui | Uni | 1 | 64 | Medium | Cuts really deep;Very successful |
| FF SP103 | 75 - 85 / 50 - 60 | Kukui | Uni | 1 | 63 | Medium | Definitely not suitable;No whittling is possible;Only scraping |
| CF SP 60 | 15 - 25 / 50 - 60 | Koa | Uni | 1 | 68 | Medium | Unsuitable;Broke after 5 strokes;Blunted after 21 strokes;Wood is too hard for this small flake |
| BF SP 50 | 35 - 45 / 50 - 60 | Koa | Uni | 1 | 52 | Slight | Wood is just too hard;it's seasoned;can't do anything-so it's more scraping |

Key: To. Obj. = Towards object
Uni = Unidirectional
Bi = Bidirectional

Table E: Continued

(Page 50)

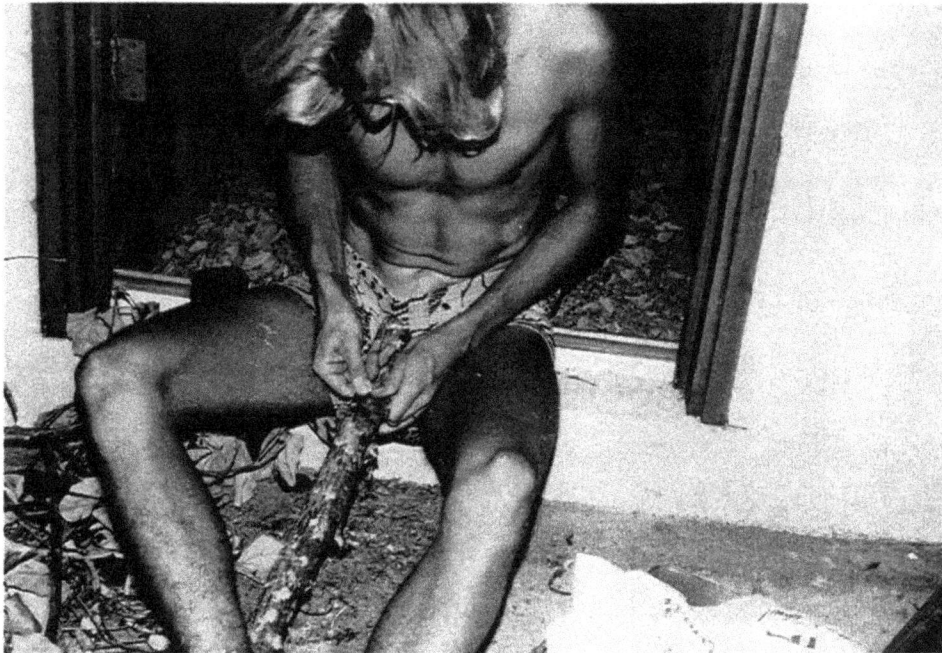

( Photo 48: Author planing koa )

## V. HIGH AND LOW POWER USE-WEAR ANALYSIS OF EXPERIMENTAL BASALT TOOLS

### 5.1 Introductory remarks

Even though the analysis of observed microwear on experimental basalt tools, established by Richards in 1989, is far more extended than the present examination, it seems to be appropriate to use at least the same or a similar recording method. An assimilation in the recording method would have the advantage of easy comparison and quick detection of absurdities. In the following, the reader will find a descriptive enumeration of microflake scars ( defined by Richards 1989:61 ), edge rounding, polish, striation, and denticulation of the 103 used tools. At the end of every use-wear examination there will be a comparative analysis with previously done research.

The reader is strongly advised to consult the appendixes A+B where the described microwear is completely tabulated and some illustrations of the experimental tools are provided.

### 5.2 Green plants ( small branches )

Two tools were used on small branches and leaves of 'ohia'a-lehua, hau, and kukui. ( Tools FF SP 100, FF SP 45 ) The leaves and small branches were taken off of the wood that was acquired from the Foster Botanical Gardens. The flakes were employed with the right hand, while the left one held the cutting branches respectively leaves so that the contact

material was under tension and a pure cutting/slicing motion was possible. Medium pressure was sufficient to secure good to excellent cutting results. The duration of the cutting experiments ranged from 1 to 1 1/2 minutes by 79 - 132 strokes. The tools were still usable afterwards.

Microflake scars: Only few microflake scars were observable and the majority of them were small in size ( 75 % ). Snap (50 % ) and feather ( 50 % ) scars are the two most common microflake termination types. The dorsal, as well as the ventral side, displayed microflake scars in almost equal numbers. The scar configuration is always scattered independent on the hardness of the contact material.

Edge rounding: The edges are either unmodified or slightly rounded.

Polish/Smoothing: Dorsal and ventral edge smoothing are always detectable. Depending on the curvature and the surface of the tool the polish is either continuous or scattered along the edge, but always pitted. Tool FF SP 100 displays an area of heavily developed polish on parts of the ventral side of the tool. The polished areas are usually along the cutting edge.

Striation: Only tool FF SP 100 shows striation on some of the areas of heavy polish. These striations were only visible under a magnification of at least x 250. The orientation of the striae is principally parallel to the edge. The striations are short, narrow, and not very deep.

Denticulation: The denticulation of the forward edge is in-

51

termitted and shallow as the tools seldomly hit contact material parts of different hardness, as for example knot-holes.

Comparison: The highly reflective polish observed from Odell and Odell-Verecken ( 1980:114-115 ) and Richards (1989:70 ) was not recorded in the present study. This may be caused by the extreme different time of tool employment. In the present study, the tool use was probably to short to develop such a reflective polish and also the contact material is not absolutely comparable. Overall, the obtained results confirm Richards investigation.

### 5.3.1 Unsoaked bone sawing

Twelve basalt tools ( Tools FF COa 1, CF COa 15, FF COa 18, FF COa 8, FF SP 73, CF COb 2, FF SP 78, CF SP 58, FF SP 98, FF SP 57, FF SP 102, and FF SP 46 ) were used to saw fresh, unsoaked pig, fish, and chicken bone for 1 to 4 1/2 minutes by 71 to 315 strokes. The bones were previously defleshed from all flesh, sinews, and smaller bones. They were placed on a cutting board and held with the left hand. The tool was vigorously drawn back and forth with medium to strong pressure.

Microflake scars: Although small in size, several hinge ( 40,2 % ) and step ( 42,4 % ) scars were detectable, while snap-terminated scars were seldom ( 9,2 % ), but large in size. Feather scars are uncommon ( 8,1 % ). The dorsal side shows slightly more microflake scars then the ventral one, and the scar configuration is always scattered due to the small numbers of scars on each tool, on the average about 7 per tool.

Edge rounding: The edges are mostly worn out to absolute bluntness. Only the medium hard contact material fish bone leads to medium and slight rounding.

Polish/Smoothing: The dorsal, as well as the ventral edge aspect, is strongly polished over the whole length of the cutting edge. Especially when cutting/sawing the hardest of the bones, pig bone, polish is heavily developed. The polish is bright, extreme smooth-textured and seldomly pitted. Only on some tools used on fish bone, pitted polish is observable. Grainy-textured dull polish was only twice detectable, both times on tools used for chicken bone sawing/cutting.

Striation : Definite striations situated parallel to the cutting edge of the tools were always observed on tools employed to pig bone. It extended along the dorsal and ventral side of the entire cutting edge. It was seldomly intermitted. The sawing/cutting of fish bone developed almost no striation. An exception is tool CF COb 2 that shows striation on the dorsal side of the tool probably caused while hitting the cutting board. The development of striation on the tools applied to chicken bone is dependent on the size of the bone. Smaller bones tend to leave few and scattered striation while larger bones develop extended and clearly visible use-wear. All the striation was visible under a magnification of x150 - 200.

Denticulation: Because of the extreme strain of the basaltic material and the early developed bluntness, no denticulation was recorded.

Comparison: Contrary to Kamminga's ( 1978:151-156, 544-545 ) detected predominant large snap scars, with smaller scars within them, the present study confirms Richards (1989:76 ) observations of common hinge and step microflake scarring. A contradiction, on the other hand, is the prominent bright smooth-textured, but seldomly pitted polish that is rare and mostly pitted in Richards investigation. Grainy- textured dull polish is almost absent in the present study, but common in Richards. Neither Montgomery (1979) nor Kamminga ( 1978 ) detected striation. Richards (1989:76) found possible striation, while the author sees striation as characterization of bone cutting and sawing.

### 5.3.2 Cooked bone sawing

Two tools ( FF SP 90 and BF SP 101 ) were used to saw cooked fish and pig bones for 2 minutes by 164 to 179 strokes. The pig bone was previously defleshed, while the fish was cut/sawed through flesh and bone. Both contact materials were placed on a cutting board and held like the previously described unsoaked bones. Medium pressure was sufficient for fish, while strong pressure was a necessity for the pig bone.

Microflake scars: The tool employed to fish flesh and bone displayed mainly hinge ( 60 % ) and snap ( 40 % ) scars in the absence of feather and step scars, while the tool used for pig bone cutting showed mainly snap ( 30 % ) and step ( 40 % ) scars, while hinge scars ( 20 % ) were seldom and feather ones ( 10 % ) rare. The present scars were small in size. The ventral side of the tool shows slightly more microflake scarring then the dorsal, and the configuration of the scars is always scattered probably due to the small number of scars on each tool.

Edge rounding: Tool FF SP 90 shows slight edge rounding while tool BF SP 101 is strongly rounded doe to the extreme use conditions.

Polish/Smoothing: Polish is nearly continuous along the dorsal as well as the ventral edge aspects of tool BF SP 101 and intermitted by tool FF SP 90. The polish is bright and extreme smooth-textured, shiny, and seldomly pitted. Pitted, grainy-textured, and dull polished tool parts are present on the tool used for fish flesh and bone cutting.

Striation: Even under high magnification ( x250 - 300 ), striation was only detectable on tool BF SP 101. The striation is situated parallel and unintermittedly extended along the cutting edge.

Denticulation: The extreme tool abrasive contact material blunted the flakes rapidly so that no denticulation could be developed.

Comparison: No comparative experiment with basaltic material is known.

### 5.4.1 Slicing whole fish

Two basalt tools ( FF SP 49, CF COa 19 ) were used to cut up fresh fish. In a cutting/slicing motion, flesh, bones, scales and skin were cut through. The elapsed time of the experiments was 1 respectively 2 minutes by 94 and 132 strokes. The applied pressure varied from medium to strong. The fish was placed on a cutting board, secured with the left hand and cut in the previously described way.

Microflake scars: Snap ( 55,6 % ) and hinge ( 33,3 % ) scars were the main observable use-wear characteristics on both tools. Feather terminated scars ( 11,1 % ) were rare, and step terminated scars were not present. The scars were small in size and scattered, due to their small number. Only one microflake scar overlapped another one on tool CF COa 19. There are slightly more scars on the ventral side of the tools then on the dorsal ones.

Edge rounding: Slight rounding of the extreme forward edge is discernible.

Polish/Smoothing: As could be seen in section 5.3.2 fish bone and flesh leaves grainy-textured, pitted, and dull polish. The polish is exclusively located on the tool edge

Striation: Absent

Denticulation: Tool FF SP 49 displays intermitted and shallow denticulation of the extreme forward edge, while tool CF COa 19 shows none.

Comparison: Contrary to Odell and Odell-Vereecken (1980) and Richards ( 1989:85 ) the present study shows snap and hinge terminated scars, as by far the most common type with lesser amounts of feather terminated scars. While Odell and Odell-Vereecken saw overlapping feather and hinge terminated microflake scars,as main characteristic, Richards experiments emphasize feather terminated scars with common step and few hinge scars.

### 5.4.2 Slicing fish flesh

Four basalt tools ( Tools BF COa 23, FF SP 43, BR SP 77, and FF SP 52 ) were used to slice fresh flesh into fillets. Contact with bone, skin, or the cutting board was strictly avoided. Soft to medium pressure was applied. The cutting time was 1 - 2 1/2 minutes by 117 to 211 strokes.

Microflake scars: Except for tool BR SP 77, where one feather terminated scar was found, no microflake scars were discernible.

Edge rounding: Absent

Polish/Smoothing: Absent

Striation: Absent

Denticulation: Absent

Comparison: The author is of the opinion that Richards ( 1989:85-86 ) only found use-wear on his tools because of the usage of vitreous basalt and the occasional contact of the tool with bone and skin parts. In the present study the difference between an unused and an actually applied tool was not discernible.

### 5.4.3 Defleshing fish bone

Two tools ( CF COa 6, CF COa 3 ) were used to deflesh fish bone carefully whereby occasional contact occurred. Tool and fish were always held in that way that the bone was easily accessible. The cutting board was never hit. The elapsed time ranged from 1 1/2 to 5 minutes by 79 - 251 strokes.

Microflake scars: The relatively " high " amount of microflake scars is explainable only through the contacting of the fish bone. Although small in size, step ( 50 % ) and feather (41,7 % ) terminated scars are dominant on the tools, while hinge ( 8,3 % ) scars are uncommon and snap scars are absolutely absent. The scar configuration is always scattered.

Edge rounding: The extreme forward edge and parts of the dorsal, respectively ventral side are slightly rounded.

Polish/Smoothing: Dorsal and ventral edge smoothing is not always detectable and if so then it is intermitted and hardly perceptible. The polish is grainy-textured, mostly pitted and of dull appearance. The polished areas are exclusively located near the forward edge of the tool.

Striation: Absent

Denticulation: Surprisingly, tool CF COa 3 shows on parts of the edge deep denticulation even though the cutting board was never hit. This is only explainable through the relative edge thinness of the tool, that caused edge breakage even though the contact material was soft. Tool CF COa 6 displays intermitted and shallow denticulation.

Comparison: No comparative analysis are known.

### 5.4.4 Slicing cooked fish flesh

One basalt tool ( BR SP 66 ) was employed to cooked fish flesh with a cutting/slicing motion. The fish bone was previously removed and the cutting board was only nicked a few times by the tool. The duration of the experiment did not exceed 3 minutes by 187 strokes. Medium pressure was applied.

Microflake scars: Absent

Edge rounding: Absent

Polish/Smoothing: Absent

Striation: Absent

Denticulation: Absent

Comparison: No comparative analysis is known

### 5.5.1 Slicing flesh

Six basalt tools were used to cut/slice fresh chicken and pig flesh. The tools ( CF SP 41, CF SP 81, FF SP 33, FF SP 55 and FF COa 17 ) were applied with medium to strong pressure. The contact material was mostly placed on a wooden cutting board or held freely with the left hand. The board itself was seldomly hit, so were bone or skin parts. The elapsed time of every experiment varied from 1/2 to 5 minutes, sufficient time to stroke 41 to 325 times.

Microflake scars: Surprisingly high amounts of microflake scars were detected, in the course of which the dorsal side showed slightly more of them. Feather ( 40,9 % ) and step (38,65 % ) terminated scars were dominant, while snap (13,65 % ) and hinge ( 6,8 % ) terminated scars were seldom to uncommon. All of the scars are small in size and shallow. The scar configuration is always scattered along both edge aspects.

Edge rounding: In general, the edges display slight edge rounding. Only tool FF SP 79, employed with a half scraping motion, shows slight to strong edge rounding.

Polish/Smoothing: Nearly all of the tools show at least slight edge smoothing, but often also areas of heavily developed polish. These polished areas are uniformly extended along the tool edge of the most vigorously used tools. Dull, grainy polish is predominant, bright, grainy polish is present only on tool FF SP 79. Tools CF SP 41 and CF SP 81, applied to chicken flesh present only traces of polish.

Striation: Only tool FF Sp 79 shows short striation, parallel to the cutting edge. The striation is located on areas of heavily developed polish and only detectable under a magnification of x 300.

Denticulation: By cutting and ripping flesh against the tool edge, typical denticulation is observable. The denticulation is mostly unintermitted and shallow to deep along the extreme forward edge. The cause of the denticulation is the breakage of the tool's edge through the ripping motion of the tool.

Comparison: The present study confirms Richards (1989:88-89 ) observed use-wear characteristics. Feather and step terminated scars are by far the predominant microflake scars. Odell ( 1980 ) observed only bifacial, feather terminated scarring and Montgomery ( 1978 ) no use-wear at all. Richards interprets this through the relatively low magnification employed. In general, microflake scars were visible not under a magnification of x 150.

### 5.5.2 Slicing cooked flesh

Tool FF COa 10 was employed to previously cooked pig flesh. This flesh was obtained from the supermarket in a non-frozen state. The flesh was cooked for about 30 minutes. The flesh parts as well as sinewy parts had to be divided in a slicing motion. As usual the contact material was placed on a cutting board and held with the left hand. It was carefully avoided to contact the board in order to attain correct results. The duration of the experiment was 3 minutes by 254 strokes. Medium pressure was applied.

Microflake scars: Step terminated ( 50 % ) are most frequent, and feather ( 25 % ) and snap ( 25 % ) terminated scars, also show equal numbers. Hinge scars are absent. Due to the small amount of detectable scars, this result should be seen critically, as one other microflake scar could alter the outcome immensely. The observed scars are small in size and shallow in appearance. The scar configuration is always scattered, due to the small number of scars.

Edge rounding: Slight rounding of the edges was recorded.

Polish/Smoothing: On the dorsal side of the tool there were traces of dull, grainy polish and some spots of brighter, but also grainy polish. The ventral side of the tool showed no traces of smoothing or polish. This one-sided polish is miraculous, as both sides of the tool were equally stressed. The polish of the dorsal side is scattered and intermitted along the tool edge.

Striation: Absent

Denticulation: The tool FF COa 10 displayed intermitted and shallow denticulation, as the flesh was softer in the cooked state and was not ripped against the tool edge.

Comparison : The author acquired no knowledge of experiments with cooked flesh, executed with non-vitreous basalt tools.

### 5.5.3 Dismembering ( Cutting/Slicing )

Seven basalt tools ( FF SP 92, FF SP 27, BF SP 36, FF SP 67, BF COa 25, FF SP 72, and FF COa 7 ) were used to dismember a chicken and several pig parts in a cutting/slicing motion. The chicken was first cut in half and then carved into platable pieces. The dismembering of the pig mainly involved cutting off the legs, cutting through skin , flesh, and ribs. Although it seems that primarily hard contact material was cut, cartilage and bone was seldomly touched. The individual tool was varied from 1-4 minutes by 94 -301 strokes. Soft to medium as well as strong pressure was applied, depending on the expected hardness of the contact material. The chicken was placed on a cutting board, the pig on the ground.

Microflake scars: Step terminated ( 48,2 % ) as well as feather terminated ( 42,9 % ) microflake scars are by far the most common type present on the tools. Snap scars ( 3,6 % ) are uncommon and hinge scars are rare ( 5,3 % ). It is curious that the amount of microflake scars rises proportionally to the strain of the tool, a phenomenon also observed in Richards investigation. The ventral side of the tool shows more microflake scars than the dorsal one, which might be caused through slight scraping of the contact material. The scar configuration reflects the high amount of microflake scars. The distribution varies from scattered to continuous, and in one case overlapping scars.

Edge rounding: Tools that cut mainly flesh and sinews display slight to strong edge rounding, while the tools, used to cut flesh and bone show strong edge rounding.

Polish / Smoothing: Some tools like FF SP 92 that were used to cut through flesh and sinews, only sometimes display traces of dull, grainy polish. The polish is mostly pitted. The more vigorously used tools, like FF SO 72, show nearly continuous bright, grainy polish along the forward edge.

Striation: As a rule, striation can be found on those tools that contacted bone parts often. The striation is intermitted and shallow, and on tool FF SP 27 almost unitermitted but still shallow. The striae observed on the tools BF SP 36 and FF COa 7 was restricted to the ventral respectively dorsal side, short in extension and only visible by x 300 magnification.

Denticulation: Due to the extreme strain of some tools and the subsequent bluntness, no denticulation was observable, while tools used less vigorously show intermitted and shallow denticulation.

Comparison: Richards distinguished in his investigation between "dismembering ( slicing )" and "dismembering (sawing/slicing )" probably because of uni- or bi-directional motion. ( 1989:89-91 ) Although the working process is similar, ( he found different polish structures, and in one case striation ), Odell ( 1980b ) described, similar to this study, a denticulated edge and bifacially distributed microflake scars. Kamminga ( 1978:476-478 ) noticed edge dulling, blunting and microflake scars. The present experiments confirm the dominance of small step and feather scars.

### 5.5.4 Dismembering grilled flesh ( Cutting/Slicing )

Two basalt tools ( FF SP 95, FF SP 62 ) were used to dismember a previously grilled chicken and parts of a pig in a cutting/slicing motion. The chicken was roasted on a stick over an open fire to insure the authenticity, but the pig was roasted in the oven. The chicken was cut up in the previously described way, and the pig parts, mainly consisting of the forelegs and rib parts, were cut while nicking bone parts temporarily. The elapsed time of each experiment was 3 minutes by 211 to 304 executed strokes. The applied pressure was medium.

Microflake scars: Thirteen microflake scars were observable

and the majority of them were small in size. Feather terminated ( 53,8 % ) and step terminated ( 38,5 % ) scars were dominant with on hinge terminated ( 7,7 % ) scar and no snap terminated scars. The dorsal as well as the ventral side displayed microflake scars in almost equal numbers. The scar configuration is always scattered, due to the small amount of scars.

Edge rounding: Due to the unequal strain of the tools, slight edge rounding is perceptible on tool FF SP 95, used only to cut flesh and sinews, and slight to strong edge rounding is observable on tool FF SP 62, used to cut, not only flesh and sinews, but also bone.

Polish/Smoothing: Totally absent is polish or smoothing on tool FF SP 95, while the other tool displays dull, grainy, and pitted polish on both edge aspects to equal amounts. The polish is intermittedly arranged along the ventral and dorsal tool side.

Striation: Absent

Comparison: No comparative study is known.

### 5.5.5 Defleshing bone ( Cutting/Slicing )

Three basalt tools were used to deflesh either chicken or pig bones. ( Tools FF COa 21, FF SP 83, and FF SP 74 ) The cutting/slicing motion mainly involved defleshing of chicken legs and parts of the breast as well as pig shanks and the upper part of the pigs hind leg. Both the chicken and the pig were placed on a cutting board that was occasionally nicked. The individual tool use varied from 1 to 5 minutes by 68 to 473 strokes. Medium pressure was sufficient to insure good cutting results.

Microflake scars: A relatively high number of microflake scars was found on tool FF SP 74, probably due to its vigorous use. All the tools showed mainly feather ( 44,1 % ) and step ( 44,1 % ) terminated microflake scars. These scars were small in size and scattered along the tool edges. Tool FF SP 74 displayed a continuous and sometimes overlapping scar configuration. The dorsal and the ventral side were stressed equally as the ventral and dorsal scar ratio shows.

Edge rounding: The tools that were used to cut flesh and sinew parts show slight edge rounding; the tool that hit bone parts occasionally displays strong edge rounding.

Striation: Tool FF SP 74 appeared to have possible striation on both edge aspects. The striation is short, narrow, and shallow. It is situated parallel to the tool edge.

Denticulation: Tool FF COa 21 and FF SP 83 display intermitted and shallow denticulation, while tool FF SP 74 shows none.

Comparison: Richards defleshed bone with a scraping as well as slicing motion ( Richards 1989:91,92 ). The comparable slicing motion resulted in almost the same use-wear pattern as in the present study. Astonishing was only the high amount of microflake scars on tool FF SP 74 and its possible striation.

### 5.6.1 Scraping dry bark and wood

Two tools ( Tools CF COa 26 and FF SP 63 ) were used to scrape dry koa bark and wood. The koa was cut about one week before the actual use in the experiments. The scraped wood had always intact bark on the parts that were employed for scraping employed. The main used branch of the wooden material was 4 - 5 cm in diameter. The branches that disturbed the scraping motion were removed. The contact material was worked in a sitting position, in which one side of the branch was grasp and secured with the feet, and the other one held with the left hand. The tool was scraped with the right hand over the contact material. Strong pressure was a necessity to scrape off wooden material. The individual tool use varied from 3 to 9 minutes by 298 to 1243 strokes.

Microflake scars: The presence of microflake scars is restricted to the dorsal side of the tools. This involves mainly feather ( 33,3 % ) and step ( 55,6 % ) terminated scars. An exception is a single hinge ( 11,1 % ) terminated scar on the ventral side of tool FF SP 63. All scars were small in size and scattered along the dorsal tool edge.

Edge rounding: The edges, especially the dorsal edge aspects, are slightly rounded.

Polish/Smoothing: The dorsal edge aspect shows heavy, very smooth, and seldomly pitted polish, while the ventral edge aspect displays no smoothing at all. The polish is almost continuously extended along the mainly used tool edge.

Striation: Absent

Denticulation: Absent

Comparison: The predominant step and feather terminated scars confirm Richards ( 1989:93 ) investigation about microflake scars. The absence of striation and the heavy polish contradict his observations, especially when considering the fact that the author worked with non-vitreous basalt tools. Schutt ( 1982:Appendix 2 ) also used glassy basalt tools, but could not detect striation at all. Instead she found feather and step terminated scars, and on more than half of the investigated tools, definite polish.

### 5.6.2 Scraping fresh bark and wood

Ten basalt flakes ( Tools BR SP 32, FF SP 96, FF SP 68, BR SP 64, FF SP 89, FF SP 56, FF SP 94, FF SP 80, CF COa 13, and FF SP 86 ) were used to scrape fresh wood of different hardness. Ohia'a-lehua was the hardest employed wood, hau medium, and kukui the softest. The bark was previously taken off of most of the wood, whereby bark regions were touched. In some cases the wooden material was already preworked and flattened so that a pure scraping motion on even material was possible. The contact material,

as well as the tool, were held in the previously described way. The author experimented with various pressure applications to reinforce the effectiveness of the scraping tools. The elapsed time per experiment varied from 1 to 6 minutes by 92 to 611 strokes.

Microflake scars: Few microflake scars were detectable on the tools. The more vigorously used tools, like tool BR SP 32, display a higher amount of mainly step ( 48,5 % ) and feather ( 51,5 % ) terminated scars. The scars are small in size and normally scattered along the dorsal tool edge. An exception is tool BR SP 32 that shows a continuous and in two cases overlapping scar configuration on the dorsal side and a scattered one on the ventral side.

Edge rounding: The edges are unmodified on the ventral edge aspect and slightly rounded on the dorsal one.

Polish/Smoothing: Neither polish nor traces of smoothing are self-evident for scraping tools. Three of the ten employed tools show no polish at all. Most of the other tools show only traces of polish or smoothing scattered along the dorsal side of the tools. Solely tools BR SP 32, BR SP 64, and FF SP 94 display sometimes extended and heavily polished areas. This polish is bright, grainy, very smooth and seldomly pitted.

Striation: Absent

Denticulation: Absent

Comparison: Even on the most vigorously used tool was no striation detectable. Neither Kamminga ( 1978:651 ) nor Montgomery ( 1978:273-274 ) or Schutt ( 1982:Appendix 2 ) were able to identify striation on for scraping of fresh wood employed tools. Although this study confirms Richards ( 1989:94 ) observed feather and step scars, other researchers ( see above ) obtained other results.

### 5.6.3 Planing dry wood

Three basalt tools ( Tools FF SP 48, FF SP 39, and FF SP 38) were used to plane koa in a seasoned state. The scraped wood had only few intact bark parts that were fastly and easily planed off. In the planing process, different to the scraping motion, the tool is pushed over the contact material. The working branch was held and secured with the feet on one end, while the other side of the branch was pressed in the belly. Medium pressure was always sufficient to insure good planing results. The individual tool use varied from 1 to 4 minutes by 83 to 399 strokes.

Microflake scars: The most common microflake scar type is feather terminated ( 63,2 % ), followed by step ( 26,3 % ) and few hinge terminated ( 10,5 % ) scars. Differently to the scraping motion also the ventral side is involved in the development of use-wear. The ventral side shows only feather terminated scars. The scar configuration is scattered on the dorsal side, and, if scars are present also on the ventral side.

Edge rounding: The edge aspects are unmodified to slightly

rounded on the ventral side of the tool and slightly rounded on the dorsal side.

Polish/Smoothing: At least on the dorsal side of the tools, polish is always present in sufficiently observable amounts. The polish is bright, very smooth and never pitted. The ventral side displays only traces of polish at those areas where chips glided along the ventral edge aspect. Tool FF SP 38 has areas of heavy polish and overlapping areas of less heavy polish.

Striation: Short, narrow and not very deep striation is observable on the areas of heavy polish of tool FF SP 38. The other tools show no polish.
Denticulation: Absent

Comparison: No comparative study is known.

### 5.6.4 Planing fresh wood

Seven tools ( BR COa 24, FF COa 22, BR SP 91, FF SP 75, FF SP 97, FF COa 12, and FF SP 93 ) were used to plane fresh wood with different hardness. These woods include 'ohia'a-lehua, hau, and kukui. The wood branches were cut longitudinally so that the inner, even part of the wood could be planed. In order to secure the contact material, the wood-worker used a gap of two wooden planks that were part of a bench as a vice. The applied pressure varied from medium to strong, depending on the planing abilities of the respective tool. 1 to 10 minutes was the time variation of every experiment. This time was sufficient to stroke 71 to 1254 times.

Microflake scars: Mainly feather ( 55,8 % ) and step ( 32,6 % ) terminated scars, with smaller amounts of hinge ( 7 % ), and few snap ( 4,6 % ) terminated scars were present on the basalt tools. The scars were generally small but, in one case (Tool BR COa 24 ) large in size. The vigorously used tool FF SP 97 counted by far the highest amount of microflake scars observed. The scar configuration of the dorsal side was usually scattered, on one tool continuous and on another one continuous and often overlapping. The ventral side showed none or a scattered scar configuration due to the small number of observed scars.

Edge rounding: The dorsal edge aspect was slightly, but often also strongly rounded, while the ventral edge aspect was unmodified or slightly rounded.

Polish/Smoothing: The dorsal side of the tools was always polished or at least smoothed. The more vigorously used tools had areas of bright, extreme smooth polish; less strained tools showed dull to bright, grainy polish. Some tools showed polish also on the ventral side. The polish was dull, grainy and pitted.

Striation: The three most vigorously used tools sometimes showed extended but narrow striations along the dorsal edge aspect of the tool. The striation was perpendicular to the tool edge.

Denticulation: Absent

Comparison: No comparative analysis is known.

### 5.6.5 Sawing fresh wood and bark

Several branches of ohia-a'lehua, hau, and kukui were sawed with 10 basalt tools ( Tools CF COa 14, FF SP 29, FF COa 20, FF COa 9, CF SP 87, FF SP 54, CF COa 16, BF SP 59, FF SP 61, and CF SP 84) The branches were not debarked or pretreated in any other way. The diameter of the branches ranged from 1cm - 6cm. The sawing motion took place perpendicular to the longitudinal axis of the contact material. The tools were vigorously drawn back and forth. Slight, medium and strong pressure was applied to test the sawing abilities of the tools. The tools were used between 0.5 and 5 minutes, sufficient time to stroke 79 to 1107 times.

Microflake scars: The predominant microflake scar type was feather terminated ( 43,6 % ) followed by step ( 37,2 % ) and snap terminated ( 16,7 % ) scars, and lesser amounts of hinge terminated ( 2,5 % ) scars. Most scars were small in size and almost equally distributed over the dorsal and ventral edge aspects. Tool FF SP 29 that was employed for 5 minutes by 1107 executed strokes counts 16 microflake scars in total. Due to the high amount of microflake scars, the scar configuration of tool FF SP 29 was continuous and often overlapping, while the other tools displayed only a scattered scar configuration.

Edge rounding: Tool BF SP 59 represented an exception to the rule in that the edges were strongly rounded. This tool showed only slight edge rounding, probably due to the short time of use.

Polish/Smoothing: Polish or even smoothing were only seldomly present. The most heavily used tools presented a dull, but partially bright grainy polish with fields of extremely smooth and non-pitted surface structure. This kind of polish was continuously extended only on tool CF SP 87 and partially on tool CF SP 84. Solely the dorsal side was polished on tool FF COa 9.

Striation: Striation was generally absent, but present on tool CF SP 87. The striation was short, narrow, and not very deep. It was located parallel to the edge.

Denticulation: Absent.

Comparison: Contrary to Kamminga's ( 1978:590 ) mainly detected snap terminated microflake scars, the present study confirms Richard's ( 1989:96 ) ascertation of predominate feather, common step, and some snap terminated scars. Also Schutt ( 1982: Appendix 2 ) confirms the previously described microflake scar presence and distribution. Montgomery ( 1978:274 ) does not even mention the kind of microflake scars she found. The present study contradicts Richard's investigation concerning the amount of polish found on the tools. The number of tools with polish was smaller than Richard's.

## 5.6.6 Sawing dry wood and bark

Four basalt tools were used to saw koa in a dry stage. These tools were CF SP 65, FF SP 35, CF SP 34, and FF SP 88. The wood was not previously prepared in any way. The contact material was held with a vice on one end while the other end was held with the left hand. The diameter of the branch used was 3cm. Also here, the sawing motion was perpendicular to the longitudinal axis of the contact material. Slight, medium, and strong pressure was applied even though slight pressure was absolutely unsuitable for koa sawing purposes. The individual tool use varied from 0.5 - 2 minutes, which led to 124 to 352 strokes.

Microflake scars: Feather ( 52,2 % ) and step terminated (30,4 % ) microflake scars were the most common types. Snap ( 13 % ) and hinge terminated ( 4,4 % ) scares were seldom. Most scars were small in size and scattered along the tool edge. The dorsal and the ventral tool side showed an equal amount of microflake scars.

Edge rounding: In two cases the author recorded strong edge rounding, in two others slight edge rounding of the dorsal as well as the ventral edge aspects.

Polish/Smoothing: Polish was definitely present on tool CF SP 34. The polish was bright and smooth, but occurred only in spots. Slight smoothing and traces of polish were also visible on tool FF SP 35, but restricted to the dorsal side.

Striation: Possible striation was observed on tool FF SP 34. The dorsal and ventral side showed short intermitted and shallow striae.

Denticulation: Absent.

Comparison: Schutt ( 1982: Appendix 2 ), as well as Richards, ( 1989:97 ) detected similar use-wear to those described in the present study. Contrary to their investigations, the author found possible striation on one of the used tools.

## 5.6.7 Whittling fresh wood and bark.

16 basalt tools were used to whittle ohia-a'lehua, hau and kukui along the longitudinal axis of the contact material. Tools BF SP 30, BF SP 28, FF SP 85, FF SP 71, FF SP 42, FF COb 5, BF SP 53, BF SP 37, FF SP 44, CF SP 82, FF SP 47, FF SP 69, FF SP 31, FF SP 51, FF SP 99 and FF SP 103 were applied with slight, medium, and strong pressure. The contact material was held in the same way as the wood used for planning. The diameter of the employed branches ranged from 1 cm to 5,5 cm. The individual tool use varied from 1 to 4 minutes employment, in the course of which 38 to 451 strokes could be done.

Microflake scars: Feather terminated scars ( 49,5 % ) were dominant, but also common were step terminated scars

( 38,2 % ). Snap ( 11,2 % ) scars are seldom. Although the scars were small in size, so they appeared larger than the scars on the tools employed for planning and scraping. The scar configuration was only in one case continuous, but in general scattered along the tool edge. The dorsal and the ventral side of the tools showed an equal amount of microflake scars.

Edge rounding: The edge aspects were slightly to stongly rounded, depending on the strain of the tool.

Polish/Smoothing: Polish was seldom, but when present, often only in traces. Tool BF SP 30, as well as Tool FF SP 69, displayed bright, smooth-pitted, grainy polish, while other tools showed dull to bright, smooth, and grainy polished spots.

Striation: Except for tool FF SP 69, that showed narrow and short striae on the dorsal side of the tool, striation was absent.

Denticulation: Absent

Comparison: The presently observed use-wear was similar to Schutts ( 1982:Appendix 2 ) results. Richards ( 1989:99 ) found more polish, and also the observed striation seemed to be clearer.

## 5.6.8 Whittling dry wood and bark

Two basalt tools ( Tools CF SP 60 and BF SP 50 ) were used to whittle dry wood with slight to medium pressure. The contact material was not pretreated in any form, and held in the previously described way. The used branch had a diameter of 3 cm. The tools were used 3 minutes by 52 respectively 63 executed strokes.

Microflake scars: Mainly feather and step terminated scars were observed ( 53,8 % respectively 46,2 % ). The scar configuration was always scattered due to the small number of scars.

Edge rounding: The edges are strongly rounded.

Polish/Smoothing: The polish of the edges was uniform, bifacial and extensive. Bright, very smooth, and non-pitted polish was prevailing, while patches of dull to bright, smooth-pitted polish was also present.

Striation: Absent

Denticulation: Absent

Comparison: While Schutt ( 1982:Appendix 2 ) did not observe polish at all, the present study confirms Richards (1989:99-100 ) investigated polish structure. Striation could not be found on the employed tools.

# VI. HIGH AND LOW POWER EXAMINATION OF THE WAIKALUA MATERIAL

## 6.1 Introductory remarks

The applied observing and recording methods were the same as those used to examine the experimentally produced flakes. Two factors that rendered the investigation more difficult were the determination of action and contact material. This determination, already done and proven to be possible in the blind tests, turned out to be even harder, as the historical tools were sometimes strongly patinated or recently scratched or broken through improper handling and storage. Nevertheless, the reader will find a descriptive enumeration of the 34 investigated basalt tools and their observable use-wear. At the end of the listing a short summary shall show absurdities and eventual discoveries.

Also here, the careful reader will consult the appendixes C and D, where the following microwear is completely tabulated and several pictures of the Waikalua tools are provided.

## 6.2 Tool interpretation

FF W 1: This tool was characterized through the absence of

microflake scars of any kind, but showed slight edge rounding of the dorsal as well as the ventral edge aspect. The sides were smoothed along the cutting edge, but the smoothed surface was always pitted. Striation was absent, so was denticulation. The bifacial edge rounding and smoothing points to cutting or sawing. Sawing usually develops strong edge rounding and obvious polish, so that a cutting motion seemed to be more appropriate. Soft contact material, fish or flesh, that does not always develop denticulation was implied due to the few impacts it left on the tool.
Evaluation: Unreliable conclusion

CF W 2: Six dorsal microflake scars were observed, all small in size. Feather ( 66,7 % ) and step terminated ( 33,3 % ) scars were the mainly observed microflake scars. The scar configuration was scattered. Slight dorsal edge rounding and dull, grainy, but very smooth polish was recorded. Striation and denticulation were absent. The exclusive strain of the dorsal side of the tool with absolutely no traces of use-wear on the other side pointed to a scraping motion. Whittling, as well as planing, would leave at least recognizable traces of use-wear on the ventral side or edge aspects trough chips that glid along the tool's surface. The intensity and extension of the use-wear indicated medium-hard contact material.
Evaluation: Reliable conclusion

CF W 3: No use-wear

CF W 4: Four microflake scars were detected, three on the ventral and one on the dorsal side of the tool. This involved mainly feather ( 50 % ), but also step ( 25 % ) and hinge terminated ( 25 % ) scars. The scars were scattered along the tool edge. All scars were small in size. Both edge aspects were slightly rounded, and the spotted polish was dull to bright, grainy, and not very smooth. The appearance of the microflake scars pointed to bi-directional motion, probably cutting, and the intermitted and shallow denticulation will be explainable through the tool employment on the soft contact material flesh.
Ealuation: Reliable conclusion

FF W 5: Like the previous tool, this one was used to cut or slice the soft contact material flesh. The common microflake scars, mainly feather ( 44,5 % ) and step terminated ( 33,3 % ) scars with lesser amounts of snap ( 11,1 % ) and hinge terminated ( 11,1 % ) scars pointed through their arrangement to a bi-directional motion. Due to their small number and size the microflake scar configuration was scattered. The dorsal and ventral edge aspect rounding was slight. The almost continuously extended areas of polish were dull to bright and grainy. The typical denticulation in unintermitted and deep.
Evaluation: Reliable conclusion

FF W 6: This tool showed one feather terminated ( 100% ) microflake scar on the dorsal side of the. There were no other hints of usage. Knowing that cutting up fish flesh leaves almost no discernible use-wear, this tool could have either been used to fulfill the fish cutting purpose or was not used at all.
Evaluation: Unreliable conclusion

FF W 7: No use-wear

FF W 8: No use-wear

CF W 9: Only two microflake scars of the dorsal side were explored. Feather ( 50% ) and step terminated (50% ) scars seem to be characteristic for the special tool use. A scattered scar configuration is self-evident, and the slight edge rounding supports the idea of timid tool use. Only scraping, planing, and whittling are possible tool uses, but the latter ones develop more definite use-wear even by timid use. ( See experimental tools ) Scraping of soft material seems to be most probable.
Evaluation: Unreliable conclusion

FF W 10: No use-wear

CF W 11: The highest amount of microflake scars was found on this tool, while dorsal and ventral scars are represented in equal numbers. Feather ( 40 % ) and step terminated ( 50 % ) scars were domi-

nant, while hinge terminated ( 10 % ) scars were rare. Due to the smallness of the scars, their configuration is scattered along the tool's edges. Parts of the edge aspects of the tool were slightly, others strongly rounded. The polish was dull, grainy and mostly pitted. The observed striation of the dorsal tool side is intermitted and shallow. The microflake scars, as well as the intermitted and shallow denticulation, point to a bi-directional cutting or slicing motion with ripping against the tool edge. Soft to medium-soft material was worked.
Evaluation: Reliable conclusion

CF W 12: No use-wear

BF W 13: No use-wear

CF W 14: Similar use-wear characteristics as those of tool CF W 9 were found. Two dorsal feather terminated ( 100% ) microflake scars were observed that were scattered along the tool edge. The edges were slightly rounded, while polish, striation and denticulation were absent. The same evaluation criteria, as used for tool CF W 9, led to the opinion that soft material was scraped.
Evaluation: Unreliable conclusion

BF W 15: No use-wear

FF W 16: The seven microflakes found were composed mainly of feather ( 42,85 % ) and step terminated ( 42,85 % ) scars. Hinge terminated ( 14,3 % ) scars are uncommon. The scar configuration was scattered and the edge rounding is slight to strong. Dull, grainy, and mostly pitted polish were predominant, but some spots also show bright, very smooth and non-pitted polish. The intermitted and shallow denticulation supports the general traits of flesh cutting/slicing. All in all the tool shows a great similarity to the previously investigated tool CF W 11. Both tools were probably used to dismember flesh.
Evaluation: Reliable conclusion

FF W 17: No use-wear

FF W 18: No use-wear

CF W 19: NO use-wear

CF W 20: No use-wear

FF W 21: NO use-wear

BF W 22: Tool BF W 22 showed all characteristics a flake used for whittling should display. Mainly feather ( 37,5 % ) and step terminated ( 50 % ) scars contribute to the relatively high amount of microflake scars. Snap terminated ( 12,5 % )

scars were uncommon and the scar configuration was scattered. The dorsal tool edge aspect was strongly rounded, while the ventral one showed intermitted and slight rounding. The polish of the dorsal side was almost continuously extended along the tool edge and appears bright and very smooth. The ventral polish on the other hand was seldom and only present in spots of dull, grainy polish traces. Striation and denticulation were absolutely absent. The observable strain of the tool, evidently caused through a whittling motion, pointed to the working of medium-hard material.
Evaluation: Reliable conclusion

BF W 23: Even though similar work might have been executed, the use-wear characteristics were not as clear as on the previous tool. This has been explained through the working of softer, exactly medium-soft material. The four microflake scars were composed of three feather ( 75 % ) and one hinge terminated ( 25 % ) microflake scars. The few scars are scattered along both edge aspects. Slight edge rounding was visible, but no polish could be detected. Striation and denticulation were also present.
Evaluation: Unreliable conclusion

FF W 24: No use-wear

CF W 25: No use-wear

CF W 26: No use-wear

FF W 27: This strongly stressed tool displays dorsal and ventral microflake scars almost in equal numbers. Feather terminated ( 71,4 % ) microflake scars are the predominant type, but also step (28,6 % ) terminated scars are common. The scars were small in size and scattered along the tool edges. The observed polish on both edge aspects was dull and grainy with some spots of bright and extreme smooth, non-pitted occurrence. The polish is almost uniformly distributed along the supposedly used edge aspects. Striation, located parallel to the tool edge, is observable on the ventral side of the tool. The striation was short, narrow, and shallow. Denticulation is absent. Although the polish does not fit the proposed use-wear characteristics at every point, the author reserves himself the right to interpret the tool as having been used to saw medium-hard material. The main points that led to this interpretation were the distribution of the feather and step terminated scars to almost equal amounts on both tool edges, parallel to the tool edge oriented striation, and the main traits the tool displays in terms of polish/smoothing.
Evaluation: Unreliable conclusion

BF W 28: Six observed microflake scars were exclusively found on the dorsal side of the tool, an unmistakable indicator of an executed scraping or planing motion. The scars were composed of mainly step ( 50 % ) and feather terminated (33,3 % ) but also lesser amounts of snap terminated ( 16,7 % ) microflake scars. All scars were small in size and scattered along the dorsal tool edge. Consequently, the dorsal edge of the tool shows stronger edge rounding than the slightly rounded ventral one. Polish was also observable at the dorsal side of the tool and occurs bright, extremely smooth and non-pitted. The polish is almost uniformly distributed along the mainly used tool edge. Striation and denticulation were absent. As the characteristics for scraping and planing actions were similar, a distinction would only be possible through extension measurements of the polish or striation, which proved to be unreliable and often misleading in the interpretation. Other tools ( CF W 2 and CF W 8 ) could be recognized as pure scraping tools as the ventral side was unmodified, and planing as well as whittling would leave at least recognizable traces of use-wear. The use of medium-soft contact material seemed to be suitable in view of the number and appearance of the microflake scars.
Evaluation: Reliable conclusion

FF W 29: No use-wear

CF W 30: No use-wear

CF W 31: The few ( two ) observable microflake scars were found on the dorsal as well as the ventral side of the tool, and consisted of a ventral step ( 50% ) and a dorsal hinge terminated ( 50% ) microflake scars. Accordingly, the scar configuration was scattered and also the edge rounding was only slight on both sides. Polish, striation and denticulation were absolutely absent. The conclusion of whittling of soft material derived from the outer appearance of the tool as it was extremely thin and displayed a small edge angle. The lacking denticulation excluded the cutting/slicing of flesh.
Evaluation: Unreliable conclusion

CF W 32: No use-wear

FF W 33: The four microflake scars appearing only on the dorsal tool side pointed to a scraping/planing motion. The scars were composed mainly of feather ( 50 % ), but also of snap ( 25 % ) and step terminated ( 25 % ) microflake scars. The scar configuration was scattered. Slight dorsal edge rounding and dull, grainy, but very smooth dorsal polish were recorded. Striation and denticulation were absent. The interpretation of a sole scraping tool is founded on the same argumentative points used to characterize tool CF W 2 as a scraping tool.
Evaluation: Reliable conclusion

FF W 34: No use-wear

### 6.3 Summary

The high and low power examination of the selected Waikalua flakes established 14 out of 34 tools as being used. One tool ( FF W 6 ) displayed use-wear, but could not be assigned to a special activity or the used contact material. Eight times the author could definitely determine the tool use and/or the contact material the tool was employed to. The remaining six times only an unreliable conclusion was possible. Striking, is the correspondence of the previously established use-wear characteristics for various tool uses. ( Section 4.3 and V. ) One notices that the Waikalua flakes display generally less use-wear than comparatively used experimental flakes. The use-wear is less obvious and needs higher magnification to be detected. As a rule it can be stated, that the higher the employed magnification, the smaller is the accuracy to relate use-wear to definite tool use. This implies that the interpretation of the use of the Waikalua flakes is less accurate than the use stated for the experimental flakes. ( Compare blind tests )

An contradiction that should be mentioned here is the discrepancy between the previously established optimal edge angle for whittling tools and the edge angle of the Waikalua flakes determined as whittling tools. Mostly the edge angle of the tools is too small to be used for whittling, even though the use-wear characteristics point toward that.

## VII. EXAMINATION OF PLANT RESIDUES

### 7.1 Phytolith analysis

Corn gloss or sickle sheen, a phenomenon that has been proven to be caused by phytolith adhering to the tool surface, it is still not fully explained. In spite of some disagreement, most experts state that phytolith is a sediment build-up through plant residues, mainly silica. The production of phytolith starts in the ground water were hydrated silica creates phytolith supporting milieu, that will be absorbed through the plants roots and carried through the vascular system. The most proliferous phytolith production and

monly used explanation model, would be the thermal melting of plant material through friction between tool and the respective plant. This would cause the spreading of siliceous material across the tool surface, while the morphology of the individual particle would be destroyed. Kamminga ( 1979 ) and Anderson ( 1980 ), who are vehement representatives of the chemical bounding theory emphasize the importance of water to generate phytolith on the tool surface. Anderson states that next to the water and heat production of the tool work, the tool surface alteration is highly depended upon the texture of the tool. The finer the grain structure of the tool, the less siliceous material may adhere to the tool surface.

Considering that phytolith is subject to chemical corrosion

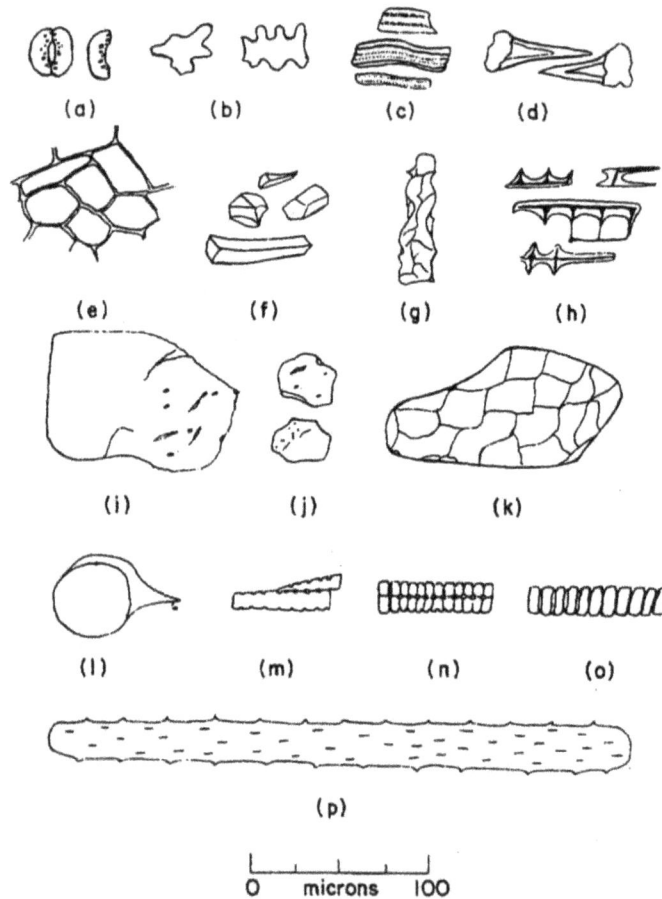

Distinctive non-grass opal phytoliths: (a-e) deciduous tree type; (f-h) coniferous tree types; (i-k) dicotyledonous herb types; (l-p) monocotyledonous herb types. (From Rovner 1971, *Quaternary Research* 1(3):350.)

( Figure 8: Distinctive phytolith key )

accumulation seems to be in the stems and leaves of the plant. Newcomber ( in Hayden 1979:190 ) found evidence that phytolith might actually penetrate the tool surface, and Anderson ( 1980:188 ) localized apparent dissolution of flint tool surfaces that were affected by phytolith. Del Bene contradicts the occurrence of chemical bounding between the phytolith and the tool surface as he observed indubitable exfoliation of a phytolith layer on the surface of a Near East sickle blade ( Del Bene 1979:171, Figure 5 ) Another com-

and mechanical abrasion or simply breakage in soil deposits, the question of the durability of phytolith arises. Several factors may influence the preservation of a phytolith layer on stone tools. Post depositional alteration through highly alkaline soils, post depositional displacement ( landslide, river ), the respective phytolith form and its thickness on the tool surface may adversely affect the resistance of the phytolith layer. The age of the phytolith layer is a factor that should not be overlooked. Generally, when mechanical breakage and corrosion increases with the age of the deposit, the chances of preservation become smaller.

The usefulness of phytolith analysis is seen in its ability to identify either the original flora or the material that was contacted by the tool. Since there are many different, but specific phytolith specimens, a recognition and a distinction between them might only be possible if previously investigated in experiments and written down in distinctive phytolith keys. ( Brown 1984, Piperno 1984, Rovner 1983, compare also fig. 8 ) This has not been done for Hawaii yet, but still could be encouraged for the future. Nevertheless, the author decided to carry out a phytolith analysis, as the earlier mentioned phytolith keys also show phytolith specimen of tropical wood comparable to the wood stock in Hawaii.

Hurcombe ( 1985:83 ) showed that careful studies are not limited to the use of a Scanning Electron Microscope ( SEM ), often it is sufficient to conduct residue observation and photography with a light microscope. For the present phytolith as well as the following botanical-chemical analysis

the reliable OPTIPHOT-POL, polarizing microscope was used. Every edge that was established to have been used ( see section VI ) was examined under 150 x and 250 x magnification. Unfortunately, no sickle sheen or corn gloss that could point to phytolith and as such to the use of the tool as a cutting/scraping utensil could be observed. An examination of the experimentally used flakes delivered a similar desolate picture. Assuming the presence of phytolith does not imply visible sickle sheen or corn gloss, the plant residues that have been exfoliated from the cutting edge of the tools had to be investigated. In order to accomplish this, the residues had to be mounted on slides. ( Procedure see section 7.2 ) Also here, no known or comparable phytolith structures were observed.

There are three possible explanation models that could explain his phenomenon. The first is that there is/was no phytolith at all. A second possibility could be the use of an alkaline solution to exfoliate the plant residues of the tool surface. ( see section 7.2 ) An alkaline solution could have damaged or destroyed the phytolith layer, while it was useful

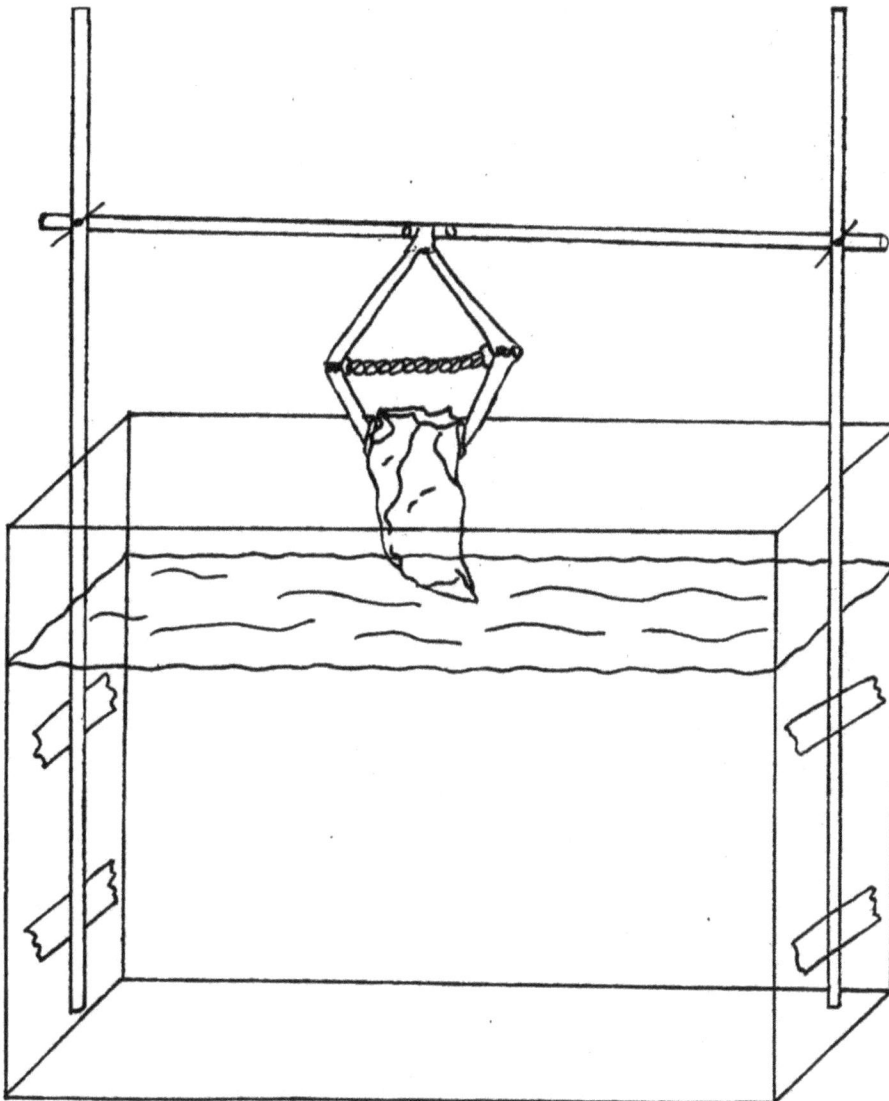

( Figure 9: Apparatus to retain height in relation to solvent )

to recover other plant residues. Another explanation would be that the extremely fine texture of the basaltic material did not allow the build-up of phytolith material.

## 7.2 Botanical-Chemical experiments in order to exfoliate and investigate plant and/or animal residues.

Since the high power examination of the Waikalua material examined several spots of definite organic residues that could not have been further investigated as long as adherent to the tool edge, methods had to be worked out to exfoliate the residues from the tool. The basic problem was to employ solvents that would be able to fulfill this purpose, but would not damage or destroy the residues. Scraping the plant material from the surface was impossible, as no sufficient amounts were present. An acidic solvent on the one hand would have destroyed valuable information while desolving residue parts, an alkaline solvent on the other hand might have caused the vanishing of the phytolith layer. Considering the fact that phytolith analysis in Hawaii is still at the beginning and potential information that could have been gained would be little. the latter possibility was chosen. After the consultation of experts in the crime laboratory of the Honolulu Police Department, it was decided to use saline and/or extra strength CSP ( Compact Sodium Phosphate ) cleanser, commonly used to clean the cozy bathroom. Due to the meticulous work involved, the treatment of the tools was troublesome and time consuming. Experience showed that just dipping the tool in the solution was insufficient to dissolve the residues on the tool's surface. Even an electrolytic bath left plant parts on the tool and delivered insufficient plant material for the analysis. The best method, which can be demonstrated was the brushing off of the residues with a little toothbrush. Therefore the working surface of the tool had to be constantly immersed in the solvent. In order to soak and brush only those parts of the flakes that had contact with the supposedly cut material, a little apparatus was built. ( See fig. 9 )

The main function of this outfit was the steady retention of the height of the flake in relation to the solvent's surface. This was necessary in order to state that only plant material adherent to the tool's working surface that actually came in contact with the worked material was collected. The obtained solution was poured into test tubes and centrifuged. Then the surplus water was poured out, and the rest that contained mainly plant material was distributed on dishes. The dishes were put into a drying chamber for 45 minutes at a low temperature. In a last step, the residues were mounted on slides in order to examine them under the light microscope.

In the following there will be a verbal description of the residues found on four tools. These tools were CF W 2, described as a scraping flake, employed to medium-hard wood, BF W 22, seen as whittling tool on medium-hard material, FF W 27 used to saw medium-hard wood, and FF W 33 established as a flake used for scraping medium-soft contact material. Again an OPTIPHOT-POL polarizing microscope was used, but this time with transmitted light. The magnification varied from 50x to 200x, depending on the translucence of the material.

Residue A: Various rod shaped and apparently broken structures were observed. At some places the rods joined each other and formed crosses. The main bar widened to one side and appeared to be less fragile than the crossing ones. Some parts were extremely translucent, others appeared to be almost black. The color of the substance ranged from yellow to brown. ( Tool CF W 2 )

Residue B: Definite cell structures were observed. The single cells joined each other by their smaller sides and formed slightly irregular rows. Each row was connected to another row of equal or unequal shape and extension so that an irregular honey comb like formation was the outcome. Several rods that were as fine as hair were crossing the structure. The color ranged from yellow to reddish-brown. (Tool BF W 22 )

Residue C: A c-shaped particle with varying width. It seemed to be broken on the lateral ends, while it shows longitudinally no interruptions except for a deep incision towards the middle of the object. Several parallel dotted lines structured the surface, while three indefinable spots disturbed the equal appearance. The object was highly translucent and of light brown color. ( Tool FF W 27 )

Residue D: This irregularly shaped substance showed no clearly discernible plant like characteristics. Some parts in the middle of the object seemed to be thicker and less fragile than the outer ones. No regular lines or patterns could be observed. A light brown color was predominant. ( Tool FF W 33 )

After these preliminary observations the slides were sent to the Department of Botany at the University of Hawaii at Manoa for further investigation. The objects were examined microscopically ( Zeiss Photomicroscope II ) and tested for the presence of lignin. Next to cellulose, lignin is one of the most important wooden components that lead to the lignification of the plant cell if accumulated in it. The presence of lignin can be proven through histochemical tests with Ploroglucinol-HCL that leads to a stain reaction. If the color changes to red, lignified cells are present. The previously described occurrence of the residues found on the tool BF W 22 pointed to sclerenchyma through the longish, rod-shaped strings that were criss-crossing each other. The positive stain reaction ( red ) supported the explanation of a stabilizing tissue. Residue B showed no stain reaction with Phloroglucinol-HCL, therefore so it could not contain lignin. The general appearance and some unique features pointed to plant fiber. Residues C and D were found to be Xylem elements that once transported the nutrients though the plant. ( See results and photographs in appendix E )

The botanical-chemical experiments seem to support the previously stated tool use ( See section VI. ). Even though the flakes that have been assigned to the cutting or slicing of flesh showed no positive blood reaction, so they also displayed no plant residues. This could lead to the hypotheses that no detectable residues will remain on the tool's surface if flesh or other animal parts were worked. The same can be stated for timid or short tool use on soft plant material that will leave no discernible residues on the cutting edge of the tools. It also seems that residues tend to be more numerous on tool areas with surface irregularities. The roughness of the tool supports the residue adherence and conservation, as the indentions take up the residues and hinder use as well as post depositional factors to destroy or alterate them. Finally, it can be said that plant residues may be present on tools that have been used on medium to hard contact material for a time of at least one minute. These residues may further support the microwear traces so that a definite determination about tool use seems possible.

### 7.3 Botanical-chemical experiments of randomly chosen samples ofrocks and macrofloral remains

The originally planned approach to go to the former excavation site and collect samples from various layers was not practicable. There was absolutely no possibility to get access to this now privately used area. The information obtained suggested the area had been developed. Future scientists who may work on a fundamental basalt, volcanic glass, or flint flake analysis should be advised to avoid working with material of a site that they will not have access to for further research.

The only half way legitimate possibility to obtain at least some results, was the investigation of already collected hammerstones and other rock material from the same layer/filling. This rock material was also previously washed by the employees of the Bishop Museum. The same procedures already applied to the prehistoric basalt flakes were also employed to the rock material. In spite of most careful work, almost no plant material could be recovered. In one case, several tiny roots were observed. These roots were not worked as they displayed no incisions or other hints of breakage or damage commonly found on plant material that was contacted by the working edge of the stone tool.

It can be stated that plant material that overgrew the artifacts after their discard, may not be preserved on the stone tools if previously washed. This plant material is only loosely adherent to the tool surface and not pressed into indentions like the worked plant material. Even though a sufficient amount of unworked plant material may be preserved, it can easily be distinguished from worked plant material as it shows the undisturbed outer epidermis, no single fibers, and no uncovered Xylem elements.

### 7.4 Comparison of the botanical-chemical results with the faunal and floral analysis of the Waikalua site

Even though Clark and Riford ( 1986:87-95 ) presented an exemplary faunal analysis, it was of no use for the present work as no faunal residues were found on the stone tools. Unfortunately, the floral analysis was not as good as the faunal analysis so that only the use of kukui can be reliably concluded ( 1986:95 ). Since the author of the present study was already in Germany when he wrote this section there was no possibility to get access to possible existing regional investigations of this area. Future works should consider those comparisons as valuable to prove hypotheses developed in the use-wear and botanical-chemical experiment part.

## VIII. BLIND TESTS

Blind tests, compulsory for every use-wear study, since they were proved to be useful and accurate ( Keeley and Newcomber 1977, Odell and Odell-Verecken 1980, Gendel and Pirnay 1982, Unrath et al. 1984/6 ), were also conducted in the present study. The tests should objectively evaluate the effectiveness of the applied method to determine use-wear and the accuracy and skillfulness of the investigator.

One set of five basalt tools were used from each of the three subjects to perform cutting, scraping, whittling, sawing, and planing actions on different material. These fifteen tools resulted from the manufacturing process of flakes with special angles ( See III c ). The flakes were randomly selected from the bystanding three subjects, to see if they suit their intended purpose. Each of the three subjects bagged the flakes singly and handled them cautiously before and after their usage. The tools were carefully washed, so that they would not give any hint of their usage through residues on the tool's surface. The investigator did not see those flakes again, until he examined them under the microscope. ( low and high power )

A few restrictions were placed on the subjects use of the blind test tools. As contact material they had to use fish, bird, or pig flesh, small plants, bone, or one of the four kinds of wood. A contact material key as well as abbreviation usage were provided before ( Table F ). The contact material itself was contributed by the author. The subjects could choose between uni- or bi-directional movement of the tool. They could vary in the actual time of use, the number of strokes, and the applied pressure. The tools had to be used unhafted. Another possibility was either not to use the tool or to use it for, at most, two different materials or actions.

Subject:
Sex:        Age:

| Tool: | Length: |
|---|---|
|  | Width: |
|  | Thickness: |

Edge Angle:        Action: Longitudinal = L
Used area(s)                  Transverse = T
Action:           Contact material:
Contact material:  Flesh (Fish,Bird,Pig)
Pressure:         Small plants = Soft (S)
Strokes:           Soft Woods Kukui,Hau
Elapsed time:      Sinew = Medium-Soft (MS)
Direction: Uni-    Hard Woods 'ohia'a-lehua,koa
Comments:         Fish bone = Medium-hard (MH)
                  Bird/Pig bone = Hard (H)
                  Pressure: Soft = SO
                  Medium = ME
                  Strong = ST

Table F: Tool information, required in the blind test and abbreviation key.

All the information had to be written down on a previously prepared sheet, any special occurrences or changes had to be mentioned with comments. Also on this sheet the four possible areas of use were shown schematically, so that they could be used in abbreviations ( Table F ).

The blind tests discussed here were two-fold. Five tools from test (A) were examined prior to the observation of microwear traces on the experimental basalt tools, the other ten tools were examined after an interpretive framework had been devised for the interpretation of wear traces observed on the tools.

Prof.Dr. Helmut Ziegert in Hamburg functioned as a middleman. The subjects as well as the author independently submitted him their filled out sheets respectively the examined microwear traces and their interpretation. After the experiments were completed and the author returned to Germany, the results were put together.

Results:

### Prior to any microwear examination

Test: A
Subject: A     ( male,24 )
Tool: 1
Function: This tool was used longitudinally to cut up a pig shank with medium pressure. Flesh as well as bone was cut. Only area 2 of the tool was affected. ( 5 min, 155 strokes ) The tool was used bidirectionally.
Evaluation: The longitudinal direction was recognized. Area 2 was definitely assigned to cut hard material and was used more often  than area 3, however, area 3 appeared to have been used to cut soft plants because of several microflake scars. A uni- or bi-directional use of the tool could not be identified.
Points: Action: 1 Contact material: 1/2 Direction: 0 Area: 1/2

Tool 2
Function: This tool was used transversely to whittle kukui with soft pressure. Initially used area 3 broke so that area 1 was used. ( 7 min, 230 strokes ) Unidirectional use.
Evaluation: The transverse direction was recognized. Area 3 as well as area 1 were assigned to breakage as well as use while working on medium-soft material. The uni-directional use could be identified.
Points: Action: 1 Contact material: 1 Direction: 1 Area: 1

Tool: 3
Function: The flake was not used.
Evaluation: The tool was either assigned to cutting of soft material with soft pressure because of slight rounding of the edge of area 2 or no use. If used no direction could be identified.
Points: Action: 1/2 Contact material: 1/2 Direction: 1 Area: 1/2

Tool: 4
Function: This tool was used at first longitudinally to saw 'ohia'a-lehua with strong pressure and in a second step transversely to whittle hau with medium pressure. The tool was bidirectionally used. ( 12 min, 370 strokes ) Area 2 was used in both cases.

66

Evaluation: Only the use of the tool on hard material was identified. Longitudinal as well as transverse direction was observed. Area 2 was recognized to be the used edge. Bi-directional movement was noted.
Points: Action: 1 Contact material: 1/2 Direction: 1 Area: 1

Tool: 5
Function: This tool was longitudinally and transversely used to deflesh fish with soft pressure. Uni- and bi-directional application of the tool. Area 3 was employed. ( 10 min, 220 strokes )
Evaluation: Area 3 as well as area 2 appeared to have been used for longitudinal cutting of soft material. Bi-directional use was more guessed than seen.
Points: Action: 1/2 Contact material: 1 Direction: 1/2 Area: 1/2

Total accumulated points: 14 1/2
Action: 4 Contact material: 3 1/2 Direction: 3 1/2 Area: 3 1/2
Total possible points: 20
  Action: 5 Contact material: 5 Direction: 5 Area: 5

Even though the author had previous knowledge only with flint artifacts and their examination under low power magnification, great accuracy was achieved. 72.5 % of the total possible point amount was concluded ( in one case guessed ) correctly. This test already shows that it is possible to assign use-wear characteristics to performed tool uses.

**Examination at the end of any microwear investigation**

Test: B
Subject: B   ( female, 27 )
Tool: 1
Function: This tool was used longitudinally for cutting and sawing of chicken bone. Strong pressure was applied. Area 1 was employed exclusively ( 5 min, 325 strokes ). The motion was bi-directional.
Evaluation: Bi-directional motion was concluded because of the arrangement of five microflake scars ( negative percussion bulb shows the point of incidentally applied force ). Area 1 was recognized to have been used for cutting or sawing of hard material. The dorsal, ventral, as well as the extreme forward edge of this area were strongly rounded. Also area A1/A2 was mentioned to be crushed, probably through hitting the ground when the tool slipped off the contact material. When the author questioned the subject B about that afterwards, she confirmed the theory.
Points: Action: 1 Contact material: 1 Direction: 1 Area: 1

Tool: 2
Function: This tool was used transversely on two areas, area 2 and area 3. With the first area kukui was scraped with medium pressure. 'Ohia'a-lehua was planed with strong pressure with the second area. Both motions were uni-directional.
Evaluation: The use of the two areas was seen. The rounding of both edges displayed definitely transverse action as only the forward edge and the ventral side of the respective areas were rounded. The hardly recognizable use-wear of area 2 would actually point to soft material, but medium-soft material was concluded, as scraping of the provided soft material seems to be impossible. No points will be given for this, as it

could not be determined through observation. Area 3 displayed more obvious wear patterns. The contact material was described as hard. Uni- or bi-directional motion was not seen because of the lack of microflake scars. Uni-directional motion was concluded.
Points: Action: 1 Contact material: 1/2 Direction: 1/2 Area: 1

Tool 3
Function: Hau was worked with strong pressure. The action was transverse. Only area 2 was employed with a uni-directional motion.
Evaluation: This tool was meant to be employed to medium-hard contact material, unidirectional. Area 2 was recognized to be the only transversely used edge.
Points: Action: 1 Contact material: 0 Direction: 1 Area: 1

Tool: 4
Function: Tool No. 4 was used to cut and rip pig flesh and sinew with medium pressure. Area 2 was bi-directionally employed. The tool edge broke once at section A2/A3.
Evaluation: The broken edge aspect was realized. Area 2 showed denticulation characteristically for tools used to cut flesh and rip it against the tool edge. The denticulation and the retouch on both sides of the tool edge made it impossible to conclude the direction of the motion.
Points: Action: 1 Contact material: 1 Direction: 0 Area: 1

Tool: 5
Function: The tool was used longitudinally to deflesh fish with soft pressure. Area 3 was bi-directionally employed.
Evaluation: This tool showed nearly no signs of use-wear. There was one small retouch, that could be natural, but also a microflake scar on area 3. No part of the tool showed the slightest polish. Experience with the experimentally produced flakes showed that soft material, especially fish, displays nearly no use-wear by defleshing. The single microflake scar was decisive to assign this tool to cutting up of soft material.
Points: Action: 1 Contact material: 1 Direction: 0 Area: 1

Test: B
Subject: C       ( male, 21 )
Tool: 1
Function: This tool was used to whittle koa uni-directional. Area 2 was used in a longitudinal action. Parts of the edge broke due to use with strong pressure.
Evaluation: The broken edge of area two was observed, the area itself assigned to transverse action on medium-hard material. The hardness of the contact material was figured through a comparative study of use pattern intensity on the experimentally produced flakes. Four microflake scars pointed to uni--directional motion.
Points: Action: 1 Contact material: 1 Direction: 1 Area: 1

Tool: 2
Tool No. 2 was used transversely to scrape kukui with strong pressure. Area 2 was uni-directional employed.
Evaluation: The tool was meant to be used transversely on medium-soft to medium-hard material. Area 2 was recognized to be the only used one. Three microflake scars pointed to uni-directional motion.
Points: Action: 1 Contact material: 1/2 Direction: 1 Area: 1

Tool: 3
Function: This tool was used for boring of kukui with medium pressure. The tool was drilled bi-directionally. Only the tip of area A2/A3 was engaged. This use was against the prescribed probable application.
Evaluation: Tool edge 3 showed two retouches and crushing on area A2/A3. Some aspects of area A2/A3 were rounded, so that it was recognized that this area was mainly used. Cutting of medium-hard material was concluded. Uni- or bi-directional motion could not be seen.
Points: Action: 0 Contact material: 0 Direction: 0 Area: 1

Tool: 4
Function: The tool was not used.
Evaluation: The tool was definitely found not to be used. Feather termination was all around the tool. Not a single disturbance in the surface structure of the dorsal as well as ventral side could be determined.
Points: Action: 1 Contact material: 1 Direction: 1 Area: 1

Tool: 5
Function: This tool was used transversely with area 1 with medium pressure, uni-directional. The contact material was koa. A second use of area 3 was pig bone sawing with strong pressure. The motion was bi-directional.
Evaluation: The tool was meant to be used on three sides. Area 1 was assigned to transverse action on medium soft material. Two microflake scars pointed to uni-directional motion. Area 2 was meant to be used on soft material, probably fish, with a longitudinal action. There were no scars that would indicate uni- or bi-directional motion. Finally, area 3 was meant to be used longitudinally on hard material.

The characteristic sawing denticulation was visible and pointed to bi-directional motion.
Points: Action: 1/2 Contact material: 0 Direction: 1/2 Area: 1/2

Total accumulated points: 30
   Action: 8 1/2 Contact material: 6 Direction: 6 Area: 9 1/2
Total possible points: 40
   Action: 10 Contact material: 10 Direction: 10 Area: 10

Even though one tool was not used in the prescribed way, great accuracy was achieved. 75 % of the total possible point amount was interpreted correctly. Several factors that rendered the analysis more difficult were found out and shall be mentioned here. If medium-soft material was used with extremely strong pressure or, on the other hand, medium-hard material with extremely soft pressure, a distinction between them was almost impossible. The absence of microflake scars is another disadvantage in the investigation of the direction of the motion. Without them, a direction can not be clearly stated, only implied. When soft material was used as contact material, especially fish flesh, the border between an unused tool and this tool was hardly discernible. As the result of the investigation of tool 3, used by subject C, shows, the investigator was presupposed with the idea of finding the kind of use-wear he was supposed to find. If the preconditions like in this example changed, the investigator was unable to state the usage of the tool. Knowing this, it seems to be appropriate to adjust the accuracy to a lower percentage, in addition it seems advisable that other researchers do the same experiments with a greater variety of possible uses.

## IX. SUMMARY AND CONCLUSION

The careful reader will undoubtedly have observed a discrepancy between some initially intended research projects and the outcome of the experiments. Even though the most convenient and most possible angle of use /skew could have been established for the tools, the use-wear investigation of the Waikalua flakes shows that those angles must not inevitably lead to special tool use. ( Compare section VI. ) At the beginning, the author expressed the supposition that flakes that may display use-wear or edge damage, associated with special tasks, but whose edge angle were inconvenient for this purpose must be covered or hafted. Contrary to these arguments, the author assumes the use of the tools with steeper or flatter angles towards the contact material, when it would hurt the user, even though this angle would result in worse cutting, scraping, etc. This conclusion resulted from the fact that absolutely no evidence for hafting was found on the tools. Evidence could have been friction patterns on the tool surface caused by the haft or plant material that was pressed in the indentions of the tool surface assuming that a freshly cut haft was used.

In the beginning of the present work, the author explained in full the weaknesses of purely statistical methods and why he did not use the computer for this purpose. The measurements of the Waikalua flakes established the necessary preconditions to compare them with the experimentally produced ones and to sort out 34 possibly used flakes. Since Riford's previous classification proved to be useless for the present study, Sullivan's and Rosen's flake attribute key was employed to establish another classifactional system. Additionally, the tool number, the size class, and the present polish and cortex were recorded. Weighing and counting differences in regards to the previous examination were observed. In a second step, the weight, length, width, and thickness of the 34 selected flakes were measured, the relative and absolute edge angle was established, as well as the edge curvature was recorded. First observations were also noted.

The sorting of the Waikalua flakes showed that these flakes were waste products commonly observed on traditional Hawaiian adze manufacturing places. Consequently, the following tool manufacturing experiments were restricted to adze manufacturing in order to produce equivalent flakes. Since the originally used basalt material source was not accessible any more, Mauna Kea basalt was chosen to be worked with in the experiments. Although the pedrological analysis displayed a slightly different structure of both basaltic materials, the hardness according Mohs's scale was the same. Generally, the adze manufacturing experiments confirmed Williams 1989 proposed model of adze manufacture reduction phases. The primary, as well as the secondary reduction ,mainly involved percussion flaking with the use of freehand percussion and on-anvil bipolar flaking technique. The purpose of these experiments was 4-fold. First it should test Williams reduction model, secondly it should establish the best manufacturing technique, thirdly it should develop a density variation of the " waste flakes ", and finally a flake scatter pattern should be drawn and analyzed. The breakage of the basaltic material could be controlled as long as the extreme edge of the anvil was used to support the working block. A flat cortex side of the block seemed to be desirable to use as a base for the working preform. The cortex will be taken off in the secondary reduction. Most of the chipped off flakes will be accumulated along and on the sides of the working edge of the anvil in a radius of 50 cm. Only a few flakes will fall outside of a 2 x 3 meter unit. Close to the anvil edge, there will be over 30 flakes per 5 x 5 cm unit, while more distant parts display 15, 5, or 0 - 2 flakes per 5 x 5 cm unit.

The carefully collected and screened flake material was sorted in the same way as the already finished Waikalua material. Even though a detailed, comparative analysis would be unlikely ( finding conditions ), general traits in size, number, and quantity were recognizable. Most of the flakes were small in size and fell under the debris category. Only few high quality flakes were present, due to the hardly controllable working of basaltic material. The lack of core or block fragments at the Waikalua site pointed to a preform refinement phase, or if polished flakes occurred, to the rejuvenation or the resharpening phase of polished adzes. In the following, the experimentally produced flakes were applied to supposedly worked contact material in prehistoric Hawaii. Wood, fish, pig, and bird were selected for the experiments while sometimes only soft, hard, or both parts should be contacted by the tools. A preliminary investigation of the tools should detect and record eventual edge damage prior to use. A variety of data was recorded in the ongoing use-experiments. These data included the angle the tool was held towards the object, the worked material, the tool use, the direction of usage, the elapsed time, the number of strokes, and the pressure that was applied to the tools. Additionally, several remarks about the cutting abilities of the tools and the experimental peculiarities and modifications were made. The evaluation of the quality and suitability of the flakes in terms of sawing, scraping, etc. can be summarized as follows: (Table G )

The high and low power analysis of the experimental tools brought amazing results, as almost every single tool displayed use-wear. In addition to the description of the use-wear, general traits could be seen when cutting special contact material. It was found that cutting fish will leave no recognizable use-wear on the tools, while flesh cutting usually develops a characteristic denticulation of the cutting edge due to ripping of the flake against the tool edge. This work also developed criteria to distinguish several tool uses through the careful observation of the use-wear. When, for example, only the dorsal side of the supposedly used cutting edge showed definite use-wear in form of microflake scars, polish, and perhaps striation, then a scraping or planing motion seemed to be most possible. The occurrence of snap, feather, step, and hinge terminated microflake scars, and their possible arrangement, were assigned to respective contact material that caused them, in order to determine the tool use of the Waikalua material. A deliberate photographic documentation, the enumeration of comparative analysis, and blind tests support the statements made about use-wear characteristics. The observation of highly adhesive plant residues to the tool surface of the experimental tools gave hope for the detection of similar residues on the Waikalua material.

| Action | Contact Material | Most appropriate edge angle in degrees | Most convenient edge angle in degrees | Size | Thickness | Pressure | Bluntness after Minutes / Strokes |
|---|---|---|---|---|---|---|---|
| Sawing/ Cutting | Bone | 40 - 90 | 90 for dividing | Medium to large | Cutting edge constantly small Grip thickened | Medium | 3 - 5 / 180 - 240 |
| Cutting | Flesh | 5 - 50 | Various angles | Small and sharp | Thin | Soft/Medium | 4 - 5 / 300 - 350 |
| Whittling | Wood | 30 - 55 | 50 - 60 | Small to medium and sharp | Thin but sturdy | Medium | 2 - 3 / 250 - 300 |
| Sawing | Wood | --- | 90 for dividing | Medium to large | Cutting edge constantly small Grip thickened | Medium | 1.5 / 150 - 215 |
| Scraping | Wood | 35 - 90 | 40 - 50 | Medium to large | Triangular shape | Med/Strong | 3 - 4 / 350 - 400 |
| Planing | Wood | 35 - 90 | 0 - 20 | Medium to large | Triangular shape | Med/Strong | 5 - 7 / 500 - 600 |

Table G: Evaluation of the flakes in tabular form

( Page 70 )

The investigation of the use-wear of the Waikalua material showed once again that theory and practice might differ immensely. Even though 14 of the 34 tools had been established as being used only eight times, a reliable conclusion could be ascertained. This could be explained through post-depositional damage or alteration of the tool surface. This would draw a dismal perspective for future use-wear analysis with material that might be even older then the presently used material, as alteration processes would have more time to work. The theory of a most convenient angle of use as an indicator for special tool use, proved to be insignificant as mentioned earlier.

Unfortunately, no sickle sheen or corn gloss that could point to phytolith, could be observed adhering to the tool's surface. It is remarkable that also the experimentally used flakes showed no signs of phytolith presence. The explanation for this phenomenon could be the extremely fine texture of the basalt material that would not allow the build up of phyto-lithic material. More successful were the botanical - chemical experiments using chemicals to show proof of lignin. Special methods had to be worked out in order to exfoliate the residues from the cutting edge and mount them on slides. Saline solution and CSP cleanser were the demonstrably best exfoliating agents. Four residues were observed, described and analyzed. The latter was done by the Department of Botany in Hawaii. Sclerenchyma, fiber, and xylem elements showed proof of use of the tools for cutting and scraping purposes, at least on wood. A blood test was negative, so that meat cutting can only be implied through use-wear analysis.

To wrap up this report, it is time to inquire if the previously asked questions might be able to be answered through analysis. The analysis of the edge outline and margin regions of the Waikalua flakes pointed to adze manufacturing using the on-anvil bipolar flaking technique and perhaps sometimes the freehand percussion technique. The latter technique was implied because proportionally not enough flakes showed crushing on the proximal or the distal ends. Since not the whole chipping floor was excavated, and as such the extension of the flake scatter was not measured, a final answer is impossible. Free hand percussion flaking would result in a wider flake dispersement than the on-anvil bipolar method.

The use wear analysis of the experimentally used flakes, established criteria to assign the Waikalua ones to special tasks. The appearance and arrangement of microflake scars, definite or lacking denticulation as well as dorsal and/or ventral use-wear patterns, were ascribed to particular tool actions and contact material. Unfortunately, post depositional alterations seem to negatively influence the tool surface in terms of discernible striation and/or denticulation.

The Waikalua site has always been a secondary reduction and rejuvenation place rather then a manufacturing one. This could be determined through the analysis of all the flakes found at the site. Considering the present results as well as Williams 1989, proposed reduction model the material worked at the Waikalua site had been pretreated at another location. This especially, seems to be especially true when someone tries to transport only the blocks that will be needed for the adze production over a longer distance.

The use of flakes for agricultural purposes was proven through botanical-chemical experiments. Aquacultural use could not be determined, as this task would leave no discernible use-wear on the tools. The negative blood test results indicate that the flakes were not used to cut up diverse animals. Other explanations would be the selection of the wrong flakes, others might have shown blood residues, the possibility that the Waikalua site was a pure agricultural site ( so no animals were cut ), or the tool surface does not allow the built-up of blood residues. The analysis of other sites in the above shown manner might solve this problem.

Additionally, the present study shows that the ancient Hawaiians did not always work specialized tools to fulfill minor cutting, scraping, etc. purposes, but selected waste flakes from the adze manufacturing for this task. The used flakes were unmodified, never resharpened, and fastly discarded.

**Summary In German:**
Zu Beginn der vorliegenden Arbeit stellte der Autor die Schwächen von einzig statistisch geleiteten Methoden heraus und erklärte, warum er den Computer für derartige Zwecke nicht verwendete. Die Messungen der Waikalua Abschläge waren eine der notwendigen Voraussetzungen, um diese mit den experimentell produzierten zu vergleichen, und 34 wahrscheinlich benutzte Abschläge auszusortieren. Da sich Rifords vorherige Klassifikation als unbrauchbar herausstellte, wurde Sullivans und Rosens Abschlagsattributschlüssel benutzt, um ein anderes klassifikatorisches System zu erstellen. Zusätzlich wurde die Werkzeugzahl, die Größenklassen und vorhandene Politur oder Rinde vermerkt. Unterschiede in Gewicht und Anzahl der Abschläge zu vorherigen Untersuchungen wurden beobachtet. In einem zweiten Schritt wurden das Gewicht, Länge und Dicke der 34 ausgewählten Abschläge gemessen, der relative, wie absolute Kantenwinkel ermittelt als auch die Kantenbiegung vermerkt. Erste, aufschlußreiche Beobachtungen wurden niedergeschrieben.

Das Sortieren der Waikalua Abschläge zeigte, daß jene Abschläge als Abfallprodukte anzusehen waren, generell anfallend bei der traditionellen hawaiianischen Beilherstellung. Folglich wurde die experimentelle Werkzeugherstellung auf die der Beilanfertigung beschränkt, um vergleichbare Abschläge zu erhalten. Da der ursprünglich genutzte Steinbruch für Basaltmaterial nicht mehr zugänglich war, wurde Mauna Kea Basalt in den Experimenten verarbeitet. Obgleich die pedrologische Analyse geringfügige, strukturelle Unterschiede der beiden Materialien widerspiegelte, so war wenigstens die Härte der Basalte gleich nach Mohs. Im Allgemeinen bestätigten die Beilherstellungsexperimente die von Williams 1989 vorgeschlagenen Reduktionsphasen in der Beilherstellung. Die erste wie auch die zweite Reduktion wurde hauptsächlich durch Abschlagtechniken wie die Freihandschlagtechnik und die Amboß-bipolar Abschlagtechnik ausgeführt. Das Ziel dieser Experimente war viergeteilt. Erstens sollten sie Williams Reduktionsmodel überprüfen, zweitens die besten Herstellungstechniken ermitteln, drittens eine Dichtevariation der Abfallabschläge aufzeigen und schließlich sollte ein Abschlagsverbreitungsmuster gezeichnet und analysiert werden. Der Bruch des Basaltmaterials konnte insofern kontrolliert werden, als die äußerste Kante des Ambosses zur Auflage des zu bearbeitenden Materials benutzt wurde. Die flache Cortexseite des Blockes schien wünschenswert zu sein als Ausgangsfläche für die Arbeitsplatform. Die Cortex wird erst in einem zweiten Bearbeitungsschritt abgeschlagen. Die meisten der abgesplitterten Abschläge sammelten sich entlang den genutzten Amboßseiten an in einem Radius von 50 cm. Nur wenige Abschläge fielen außerhalb einer vorher abgesteckten 2 x 3 Meter Fläche. Nahe der Amboßkante sammelten sich 30 Abschläge pro 5 x 5 cm Fläche, während weiter entfernt gelegene Teile 15, 5 oder 0 - 2 Abschläge pro 5 x 5 cm Fläche zeigten.

Das sorgsam gesammelte und gesiebte Abschlagsmaterial wurde in gleicher Weise sortiert wie das bereits bearbeitete Waikalua Material. Auch wenn eine detaillierte Vergleichsanalyse zu weit gegriffen wäre (Fundbedingungen), so waren allgemeine Merkmale in Größe, Anzahl und Menge erkennbar. Die meisten Abschläge waren klein, und in die Splitterkategorie einzuordnen. Nur wenige ‚hochwertige Abschläge waren vorhanden, zurückzuführen auf die schwerlich kontrollierbare Bearbeitung von Basalt. Das Fehlen von Kernsteinen oder Ausgangsmaterialfragmenten bei der Waikalua Ausgrabung deutete auf eine Verfeinerung von Beilen im ersten Bearbeitungsstadium hin oder, wenn polierte Abschläge vorhanden waren, auf eine Erneuerungs- oder Nachschärfphase. In einem nächsten methodischen Schritt wurden die experimentell hergestellten Abschläge für die Bearbeitung von wahrscheinlich auch prähistorisch genutzten Materialien verwendet. Holz, Fisch, Schwein und Vogel wurden für die Experimente ausgewählt, wobei nur weiche, harte oder beiderlei Teile mit den Steingeräten bearbeitet werden sollten. Eine vorhergehende Untersuchung der Steingeräte ermittelte alle Kantenbeschädigungen der Geräte vor ihrer Nutzung.

Eine Vielzahl von Daten wurde während der Experimente zusammengetragen. So wurde zum Beispiel der Anstellwinkel des Steingerätes ermittelt, das Kontaktmaterial, der Steingerätegebrauch, die Führungsrichtung, die verstrichene Zeit, die Anzahl der Striche und die Andruckstärke. Zusätzlich wurden einzelne Bemerkungen zu den Schneideigenschaften der Geräte gemacht, wie auch über experimentelle Besonderheiten und Abänderungen. Die Auswertung der Qualität und Nutzbarkeit der Abschläge im Hinblick auf Säge-, Schabeigenschaften, etc. kann folgendermaßen zusammengefaßt werden. (Tabelle G)

Die mikroskopische high and low power Analyse der experimentell hergestellten Geräte zeigte erstaunliche Resultate, da nahezu jedes einzelne Gerät Gebrauchsspuren aufwies. Zusätzlich zur reinen Beschreibung der Gebrauchsspuren konnten allgemeingültige Erscheinungen ermittelt werden. Es wurde herausgefunden, daß das Zerlegen von Fisch keine

erkennbaren Gebrauchsspuren am Steingerät hinterläßt, während Fleisch gewöhnlicherweise eine Zähnung der Gebrauchskante hervorruft dadurch daß das Gerät oft ruckartig seitlich bewegt wird, um den Schneideprozeß zu erleichtern.

Diese Arbeit ermittelte ebenso Kriterien zur Unterscheidung von Gerätegebräuchen durch die sorgsame Beobachtung von Gebrauchsspuren. Wenn zum Beispiel nur die dorsale Seite der wahrscheinlich genutzten Gebrauchskante eindeutige Gebrauchsspuren in Form von Mikroretuschen, Politur und eventuell Ritzungen aufweist, scheint eine Schab- oder Hobelbewegung höchst wahrscheinlich. Das Auftauchen von snap, feather, step und hinge geformten Mikroretuschen und deren mögliche Anordnung wurden den jeweilig verursachenden Kontaktmaterialien zugeordnet, um den Gebrauch der Waikalua Geräte festzustellen. Die sorgsame fotografische Dokumentation, die Erwähnung von vergleichbaren Analysen und blind tests unterstützen die Aussagen über Gebrauchsspurencharakteristika. Die Beobachtung von hochgradig anhaftenden Pflanzenresten an der Geräteoberfläche der experimentell hergestellten Steingeräte machte Hoffnung auf ein ebensolches Vorhandensein bei den Waikalua Abschlägen.

Die Gebrauchsspurenanalyse des Waikalua Materials zeigte einmal mehr das Theorie und Praxis stark variieren können. Auch wenn bei 14 von 34 Geräten eine Nutzung angedeutet werden konnte, so war dieses nur 8x sicher möglich. Mögliche Erklärungsvarianten könnten Umlagerungsschäden oder Oberflächenveränderungen sein. Für zukünftige Gebrauchsspurenanalysen von wesentlich älterem Material als das von Waikalua ergeben sich sehr negative Voraussetzungen, da Veränderungsprozesse proportional zum Alter des Fundes zunehmen.

Die anfängliche Theorie des günstigen Gebrauchswinkels als Anzeiger für einen speziellen Gerätegebrauch zeigte sich als unbedeutend. Unglücklicherweise konnte kein Sichel- oder Kornglanz, untrüglicher Hinweis auf Phytolith, an der Geräteoberfläche entdeckt werden. Interessanterweise zeigten auch die experimentell genutzten Abschläge kein solches Phänomen. Eine mögliche Erklärung könnte die äußerst feine Textur des Basaltes sein, welche eine Anlagerung von Phytolithen verhindert. Wesentlich erfolgreicher waren die botanisch-chemischen Experimente, welche Chemikalien zur Feststellung von Lignin verwendeten. Spezielle Methoden wurden erarbeitet um die organischen Reste von der Gebrauchskante abzulösen. Salzlösung und Sodium-Phosphat Reiniger stellten sich als die besten Ablösungsmittel heraus. Vier unterschiedliche organische Reste wurden beobachtet, beschrieben und analysiert. Die Analyse wurde freundlicherweise vom Department of Botany auf Hawaii durchgeführt. Sclerenchym, Fasern und Xylemelemente bewiesen die Anwendung von Geräten für Schneide- und Schabvorgänge zumindest von Holz. Ein Bluttest war negativ, so daß das Schneiden von Fleisch nur durch die Gebrauchsspurenanalyse angedeutet werden kann.

Um diesen Bericht zu einem befriedigenden Ende zu führen, scheint es angebracht herauszufinden, ob eingangs gestellte Fragen durch die Analysen beantwortet wurden. Die Untersuchung der Kantenformen und Außenregionen der Waikalua Abschläge deuteten auf Beilherstellung unter Verwendung der Amboß-, wie auch zeitweilig der Freihandtechnik hin. Die letztere Technik wird angenommen, da proportional nicht genug Abschläge eine Zerbröselung der proximalen oder distalen Enden zeigten. Da jedoch nicht der gesamte Abschlagsplatz ergraben wurde und als solches die Ausdehnung der Abschlagsstreuung nicht gemessen wurde, ist eine endgültige Aussage unmöglich. Die Freihandschlagtechnik würde eine wesentlich weitere Verteilung der Abschläge zur Folge haben als dieses bei der Amboßtechnik der Fall wäre.

Die Gebrauchsspurenanalyse der experimentell genutzten Abschläge erbrachte Kriterien, welche die Waikalua Geräte zu speziellen Arbeiten zuteilen ließ. Das Vorhandensein und die Anordnung von Mikroretuschen, definitiver oder fehlender Zahnung, wie auch dorsaler und/oder ventraler Gebrauchsspurenmuster wurden zu bestimmten Gerätegebräuchen und Kontaktmaterialien zugeordnet. Unglücklicherweise scheinen Umlagerungs- und chemische Prozesse die Erkennbarkeit von Ritzungen und/oder Zahnungen auf der Geräteoberfläche negativ beeinflußt zu haben.

Der Waikalua Platz war immer ein Zweitreduktions- und Gerätereparaturplatz, weniger ein Gesamtherstellungsplatz. Dieses konnte ausgesagt werden durch die Analyse aller gefundenen Abschläge. In Anbetracht der vorliegenden Resultate, wie auch Williams (1989) Reduktionsmodel, wurde das Verarbeitungsmaterial von Waikalua an anderer Stelle vorgearbeitet. Diese Aussage bestätigt sich um so mehr, wenn jemand auch nur versucht ähnliche Gesteinsmassen zu transportieren, welche für die Gesamtbeilherstellung notwendig wären.

Der Gebrauch von Abschlägen für landwirtschaftliche Zwecke wurde bewiesen durch botanisch-chemische Experimente. Aquakultureller Gebrauch konnte nicht nachgewiesen werden, da keine Gebrauchsspuren nachweisbar wären. Die negativen Bluttests zeigen an, daß die Abschläge nicht zum Zerlegen diverser Tiere genutzt wurden. Andere Erklärungen wären die Auswahl der falschen Abschläge, da andere Blutreste aufgewiesen haben könnten, die Möglichkeit, daß Waikalua ein nur landwirtschaftlich genutzter Platz war, oder die Geräteoberfläche eine Anlagerung von Blutresten nicht fördert. Die Analyse anderer Plätze in ähnlicher Weise könnte dieses Problem zur Lösung führen.

Zusätzlich zeigt die vorliegende Studie, daß die prähistorischen Hawaiianer nicht immer spezialisierte Steingeräte herstellten, um kleinere Schneide-, Schabaufgaben, etc. zu erfüllen, sondern Abschläge, anfallend zum Beispiel bei der Beilherstellung, für solche Arbeiten nutzten. Die genutzten Abschläge waren unbearbeitet, wurden niemals geschärft und nach ihrer Nutzung wieder weggeworfen.

# X. RECOMMENDATIONS

A few recommendations might be allowed at this point, as they can make future research in this field more effective and successful. The stone tool manufacturing experiments should be done with basaltic material that has been soaked for several days. This procedure would make the work on the material easier and more accurate results would be obtained.

It also seems advisable to conduct similar flake analysis with volcanic glass flakes. The obtained use-wear results would have more expressiveness, as volcanic glass seems to be more useful for minor cutting, whittling, etc. purposes. Moreover, volcanic glass would display more obvious use-wear.

Furthermore the author suggests an investigation of the plant and animal residue adherence properties of roughly structured material. The outcome of these experiments would support or disprove the theory that the fine texture of the presently used basaltic material adversely affects the residue adherence properties.

A more careful faunal and floral analysis of the respectively investigated sites is desirable. The results are a precondition for the successful comparison of the residues found on the tools. The development of a Phytolith key for Hawaii should go along with this analysis. Plant and animal residue and use-wear analysis for prehistoric tools should be compulsory in order to determine the tool use more properly.

Since this study showed the importance of flakes to solve prehistoric questions, the flakes should be bagged and handled more careful in the future.

Own experience shows that a little more support of researchers would be desirable, even when they work independently. This could clearly enhance the outcome of interdisciplinary and intercultural research.

The working areas of field and laboratory archaeologists should be more professional, especially regarding the equipment. Here the State of Hawaii should be asked to invest more in the Bishop Museum as this institution is not only a tourist attraction, but the investigator and preserver of prehistoric Hawaii.

# XI. BIBLIOGRAPHY

Allen, J. Archaeological excavations in Kawainui marsh, Island of O'ahu. Typescript in library, BPBM,1981

Anderson, P.C. A testimony of prehistoric tasks. Diagnostic residues on stone tool working edges. In World Archaeology 2:181-96, 1980

Ascher, R. Experimental Archaeology. In American Anthropologist 63(4), 793-816, 1961

Athens, J.S. Prehistoric pondfield agriculture in Hawaii. Typescript in library, BPBM, 1983

Atlas of Hawaii Department of Geography, University of Hawaii Press, Honolulu 1973 ( sec. edition 1883 )

Bamforth, D. A comment on "Functional variability in an assemblage of endscrapers". In Lithic Technology 15:61-4, 1986

Barrera, W.Jr. and Kirch, P.V Basaltic glass artifacts from Hawaii: Their dating and prehistoric uses. In Journal of Polynesian Society 82:176-87, 1973

Barrera, W. Kaho'olawe archaeology. In Hawaiian Archaeology 1:31-43, Honolulu 1984

Beggerly, P.P. Edge damage on experimentally used scrapers of Hawaiian basalt. In Newsletter of Lithic Technology 5(3):22-24, 1976

Benfer,R.A. Sampling and classification. In Mueller,J.ed. "Sampling in archaeology". The University of Arizona Press, Tucson, Arizona 1975:226-247

Best, M.G. Out of igneous and metamorphic petrology. Freeman and Company New York, 1982:62-196

Binford, L.R. Stone tools and human behaviour. In Scientific American 220:70-84, 1969

(the same) An archaeological perspective, Pt.IV, New York: Seminar Press 1972

(the same) Sampling, judgement, and the archaeological record. In Mueller,J. ed. "Sampling in archaeology". The University of Arizona Press, Tucson, Arizona 1975:250-257

Bohmers,A. Statistics and graphs in the study of flint assemblages. In Palaeohistoria 5, 1956:1ff

(the same) A statistical analysis of flint artifacts. In Brothwell,D. and Higgs,E. ed."Science in Archaeology" London: Thames and Hudson 1969

Bonk, W.J. Archaeological excavations on West Molokai, M.A. Thesis, University of Hawaii, 1954

Bordaz, J. Tools of the old and new stone age. New York: American Museum of Natural History, 1971

Bordes, F. A propos d'une rieille querelle: peut on utiliser les silex taillés comme fossiles directeurs ? In Bulletin de la Société Préhistorique Francaise 47:242-6, 1950

(the same) Typologie du paleolithique ancien et moyen. CNRS, Paris 1961a

(the same) Reflections on typology and techniques in the palaeolithic. In Artic Anthropology 6, No.1, 1969:1-29

Borofsky, R. Making history, Cambridge University Press, Cambridge 1987

Bradley, B.A. Lithic reduction sequences: A glossary and discussion. In Earl Swanson, ed. "Lithic technology. Making and using stone tools" Mouton Publishers, The Hague, Paris 1975

Brainerd, G.W. The place of chronological ordering in archaeological analysis. In American Antiquity 16, No. 4, 1948:301-313

(the same) The use of mathematical formulations in archaeological analysis. In Griffin,T.J., ed. "Essays on archaeological methods", University of Michigan Press, Ann Arbor 1951

Brigham, W.T. Stone implements and stone work of the ancient Hawaiians. Kraus reprint Co. New York. Originally published as BPBM Memoirs 1(4), 1974

Briuer, F. New clues to stone tool function. Plant and animal residues. American Antiquity 41(4), 1976:478-483

Brown, P.A. Prospects and limits of a phytolith key for grasses in the central United States. In Journal of Archaeological Science 11:345-368

Buck, P. Arts and crafts of Hawaii, BPBM Press 1964

Buckland,P. An experiment in the use of a computer for on-site recording of finds. In Scientific Archaeologist 9, Jan 1973:22-24

Burgess, R.J. and Kvamme, K.C. A. new technique for the measurement of artifact angles. In American Antiquity 43, 1978:482-486

Burton, J. Making sense of waste flakes: New methods for investigating the technology and economics behind chipped stone assemblages. In Journal of Archaeological Science 7, 1980:131-148

Callahan, E. The Pamunkey project, phase I and II. In The Ape, Experimental Archaeology Papers, Vol.4, Virginia Commonwealth University, Richmond 1976

Chapman, P.S. and Kirch, P.V. Archaeological excavations at seven sites, southeast Maui, Hawaiian Islands. In Department of Anthropology Report Series 79-1, BPBM 1979

Chenhall, R.G. The description of archaeological data in computer language. In American Antiquity 32, No.2, !967:161-167

(the same) A rationale for archaeological sampling. In Mueller,J.W.,ed. "Sampling in archaeology", University of Arizona Press, Tucson, Arizona 1975:3-25

Clark, J.T. Continuity and change in Hawaiian agriculture. In Argicultural History, Vol. 60 No. 3 University of California Press, 1986

Clark, S.D. An analysis of Hawaiian basalt awls; A replication and use-wear experiment. M.S. in Department of Anthropology, BPBM Honolulu,1979

(the same) and Riford, M. Archaeological salvage excavations at site 50-0a-65-101, Waikalua-Loko Kane'ohe, Ko'olaupoko, O'ahu Island, Hawaii. Typescript in library Ms.102386, Department of Anthropology, BPBM 1986

Cleghorn, P.L. Survey and savage escavations in specified areas of Wailea Lands, Maui typescript in Department of Anthropology, BPBM 1974

(the same) Phase II, part 2 archaeological salvage operations at site 50-Ma-B10-1, Wailea, Kihei, Maui, Ms 061075, BPBM 1975 (the same) The Mauna Kea adze quarry: Technnological analysis and experimental test. P.H.D. dissertation. University of Hawaii 1982

Cleghorn/Dye and Weisler/Sinton A preliminary pedrographic study of Hawaiian stone adze Quarries. In Journal of the Polynesian Society 94(3), 1985:235-251

Coles, J.M. Archaeology by experiment, Charles Scribner's son, New York, 1973

(the same) Experimental archaeology. Academic Press, Inc. New York, 1979

Collins, D. Stone artifact analysis and the recognition of culture traditions. In World Archaeology, Vol. 2 1970:17-27

Cooley, W. and Lohnes, P. Multivariate data analysis, New York: Wiley, 1971

Cordy, R. Sampling prolblems in regional interpretation in Hawaiian archaeology. 1982

Crabtree, D. An introduction to flint-working. In Idaho State Museum Occasional Papers No. 28 1973a

(the same) The obtuse angle as functional edge. Tebiwa 16:46-53 1973b

Cowgill, G.L. Sampling and reliability problems in archae ology. In "Archeologie et Calculateurs" Paris: Editions du Centre National du la Rercherche Scientifique, 1970

Croxton, F.E. and Cowdon, D.J. Applied general statistics. Englewood Cliff: Prentice Hall 1955

Culbert, T.P. The ceramic history of the Central Highlands of Chiupas, Mexico. In Papers of the New World Archaeological Foundation, Publication 14, No. 19, Provo 1965

Dempsey, P. and Baumhoff, M.A. The statistical use of artifact distributions to establish chronological sequences. In American Antiquity 28, 1963:496-509

Dibble, H.L. The interpretation of middle paleolithic scraper morphology. In American Antiquity 52(1), 1987:109-117

(the same) and Whittaker, J.C. New experimental evidence on the relation between percussion flaking and flake variation. In Journal of Archaeological Science 8/3, 1981:283-296

Donahue, R.E. Microwear analysis and site function of Paglicci Cave, level 48. In World Archaeology, Vol. 19(3). Feb. 1984:357-375

Doran, J. and Hodson, F.R. Mathematics and computers in archaeology. Cambridge, Harvard University Press, 1975

Dragoo, D.W. Some aspects of eastern north American prehistory. A review 1975. In American Antiquity 41, 1976:3-27

Dumond, D.E. A reexamination of Eskimo-Aleut prehistory. In American Anthropologist 89, 1987:32-56

Dunnell, R.C. Seriation method and its evaluation. In American Antiquity 35(3), 1970:305-19

(the same) Systematics in prehistory. New York Free Press, 1971

Ehrich, R.W. Some reflections on archaeological interpretation. In American Anthropologist 52, 1950:456-82

(the same) Further reflections In American Anthropologist 65, 1963:16-31

Emory, K.P. and Sinoto, Y.H Hawaiian archaeology: O'ahu excavations, BPBM Special Publications 49,1961

Epstein, J.F. Towards the systematic description of chipped stone. In Actas y Memorias XXXV Congreso International de Americanistas 1, 1964:155-69

Evens, J. The ancient stone implements, weapons, and ornaments of Great Britan. Longmans, Green, Reader and Dyer: London 1872

Faulkner, A. Mechanical principles of flintworking. P.H.D. dissertation. Washington State University 1972

Fedje, D. Scanning electron microscopy, analysis of usestriae. In Hayden,B. "Lithic use-wear analysis", Academic Press New York 1979:179-18

Ferguson, T.A. Lithic analysis and the discovery of prehistoric man - land relationships in uplands of Big South Fork of the Tennessee Cumberland Plateau. P.H.D. dissertation, University of Tennessee 1988 Order No. DA8904051

Fish, P.R. Beyond tools: Middle paleolithic debitage analysis and cultural inference. In Journal of Anthropological Research 37, 1981:374-86

Flintknapper's Exchange Laboratory of Archaeology, Department ofAnthropology,Catholic University of America, Washington, D.C. 20064 ( a newsletter for lithic technologists published three times a year )

Folan, W.J.and Rick/Zacharchuck The mechanization of artifact processing. In American Antiquity 33(1), 1968:86-89

Fonton de E.M. and Lumeley de H. Les civilisations de la Meditérranée septentrionale et leurs intercurrences. Le complexe Montadien. In Bulletin de la Société Prehistorique Francaise 52, 1955:379-94

Ford, J.A. Comment on A.C.Spaulding's "Statistical techniques for the discovery of artifact types". In American Antiquity 19, 1954:390-91

(the same) A quantitative method for deriving cultural chronology, Pan American Union, Technical Manual 1, 1962

Frayer, D.W. Body size, weapon use, and natural selection in the European Upper Paleolithic and Mesolithic. In American Anthropologist 83, 1981:57-73

Frison, G. Functional analysis of certain chipped stone tools. In American Antiquity 33, 1968:149-55

Gardin, JC. Four codes for the description of artifacts. In American Anthropolgist 60, 1958:335-357

Gelfand, A.E. Seriation methods for archaeological materials. In American Antiquity 36, 1971:263-74

Gendel, P. and Pirnay, L. Microwear analysis of experimental stone tools: further test results. In Studia Prehistoria Belgica 2, 1982:251-65

Gibson, E.C. Diachronic patterns of lithic production, use and exchange in the southern Maya lowlands. P.H.D. Dissertation, University Microfilm, An Arbor, Harvard University 1986

Gladwin, T. East is a big bird. Havard University Press 1970

Goodwin, A.J.H. Chemical alteration ( patination ) of stone. In VFPA 28, 1960:300-12

Gould, R.A. Chipping stones in the Outback. In Natural History 77, 1968:42-49 (the same)   The anthropology of residues. In American Anthropologist 80, 1978:815-35

Graham, F. and Galloway/Schollar   Model studies in computer seriationIn Journal of Archaeological Science 1, March 1976:1-30

Grimes, J. and Grimes, B.   Flakeshavers: Morphometric. Functional and life-cycle analysis of a paleoindian unifacial tool class. In Archaeology of Eastern North America 13, 1985:35-57

Guire Mc, R. Whittaker, H. A., and McCarthy/McSwain   A consideration of observational error in lithic use-wear analysis. In Newsletter of Lithic Technology, Vol.11(3), Dec. 1982:59-63

Handy,E/Craighill   Native planters in old Hawaii. BPBM Museum Bulletin 233, Honolulu 1972

Hansen, H.O.   Some main trends in the development of the Lejre Center, Lejre, Denmark 1974

(the same)   The prehistoric village at Lejre. Historical-Archaeological Research Centre, Lejre 1977

Hayden, B.   Lithic use-wear analysis. Academic Press, Inc. New York 1979

Heider, K.G.   Archaeological assumptions and ethnographical facts: A cautionary tale from New Guinea. In Southwestern Journal of Anthropology 23, 1967:52-64

Heinzelin de, J.   Manuel de typologie des industries lithiques. L'Institut Royal des Sciences Naturelles de Belgique. Brussels 1962

Hester, T.R. and Heizer, R.F.   Problems in the functional interpretation of artifacts: Scraper planes from Mitla and Yugul, Oaseaca, University of California ( Berkeley ) Archaeological Research Facility, Contribution No.14, 1972:107-23

Hodges, H.W.   Artifacts: An introduction to early materials and technology. London: J.Baker, 1964

(the same)   Technology in the ancient world. New York: Knopf 1970

Hole, F.   Approaching typology rationally. In The Record, Dallas, Archaeological Society 27(3), 1971:11-16

(the same) and Flannery/Neeley   Prehistory and human ecology of the Deh LuranPlain. An early village sequence from Khuzistan, Iran. Memoirs of the Museum of Anthropology, University of Michigan No.1, 1969

Hole, F. and Shaw, M.   Computer analysis of chronological seriation. Houston, Texas: Rice University Studies 53(3), 1967

Hunt, T. and Kirch, P.V.   An archaeological survey of the Manu'a Islands, American Samoa. In Journal of Polynesian Society, Vol.97(2), June 1988

Hurcombe, L.   Residue studies on obsidian tools. In Unrath,G. "An evaluation of use-wear studies: a multi-analyst approach." Early Man News 9/10/11, Tübingen 1984/85/86:83-92

Ilkjaer, J.   A new method for observation and recording of use-wear. In Hayden,B. "Lithic use-wear analysis." Academic Press, New York 1979:345-50

Ingersoll, D. and Yellen/MacDonald Experimental archaeology. Columbia University Press. New York 1977

Jelinek, A.J.   The production of secondary multiple flakes. In American Antiquity 36(2), 1971:198-200

(the same)   Form, function and style in lithic analysis. In Cleland,C.B. ed. "Cultural change and continuity" Academic Press, New York 1976:19-33

Jeter, M.D.   Analysis of flaked stone artifacts and debitage. n Doyel,D.E. and Debowski,S.S. ed. "Prehistory in Dead Valley, east-central Arizona: The TG+E Springerville report", Arizona State Museum Archaeological Series 144, Tucson 1980:235-305

Kaeppler, A.L.   Cook voyage artifacts. Bishop Museum Press, Honolulu 1978

Kamminga, J.   The nature of use-polish and abrasive smoothing on stone tools. In Hayden,B. ed. "Lithic use-wear analysis", Academic Press, New York 1979:143-158

Keeley, L.H.   Technique and methodology in microwear studies: a critical review. In World Archaeology 5(3), 1974:323-336

(the same)   The function of paleolithic flint tools. In Scientific American 237(5), 1977:108-27

(the same)   Experimental determination of stone tool uses: A microwear analysis. Chicago University Press 1980

(the same) and Newcomber, M.   Microwear analysis on experimental flint tools: A test case. In Journal of Archaeological Science 4, 1977:29-64

Keller, C.   The development of edge damage patterns on stone tools. In Man 1(4), 1966:501-11

Kelly, R.L.   The three sides of a biface. In American Antiquity 53, 1988:717-34

Kerhof, F. and Müller-Beck, H.   Zur bruchmechanischen Deutung der Schlagmarken an Steingeräten. In Glastechnische Berichte 42, 1969:439-48

Kirch, P.V.   Marine exploitation in prehistoric Hawai'i: Archaeological excavations at Kalahuipua'a, Hawai'i Island. In Pacific Anthropological Records 29. Department of Anthropology BPBM 1979

(the same)   Feathered gods and fishhooks. An introduction to Hawaiian archaeology and prehistory. University of Hawaii Press, Honolulu 1985

Kirch, P.V. and Kelly, M.   Prehistory and ecology in a windward Hawaiian valley: Halawa Valley Molokai. In Pacific Anthropological Record 24, Department of Anthropology BPBM 1975

Kluckhohn, C.   The use of typology in anthropological theory. In Wallace,A.F.C. ed. "Man and Cultures", Philadelphia, University of Rennsylvania Press 1960

Knudson, S.J.   Culture in retrospect. An introduction to archaeology. Rand MC Nally, Chicago 1978

Krauss, B.   Syllabus - Ethnobotany of Hawaii - 105. University of Hawaii 1972

Krieger, A.D.   The typological concept. In American Antiquity 9, 1944:271-88

(the same)   Archaeological typology in theory and practice. In Selected Papers of the Fifth International Congress of Anthropology and Ethnological Science 1960:271-88

Laplace, G.   Essai de typologie systématiqe. In Annali dell'Universià de Ferrara (Nuova Serie). Lezione XV Paleontologia umana e Plaetnologia: supplemento II at volume I 1964

Lawrence, R.A.  Experimental evidence for the significance of attributes used in edge-damage analysis. In Hayden,B. "Lithic use-wear analysis" Academic Press New York 1979:113-22

Leach, F. and Davidson, J.  Archaeological studies of Pacific stone recources.BAR International Series 104,1981

Lenoir, M.  Les grattoirs - burins du Morin et du Roc de Marcamps. In Bulletin de la Société Préhistorique Française 75, 1978:73-82

Lewenstein, S.M.  Stone tool use at Cerros: The ethnoarchaeological and use-wear evidence. Austin, University of Texas Press 1987

Loy, T.  Prehistoric blood residues: Detection on tool surfaces and identification of species of origin. In Science 220. 1983:1269-1271

Macdonald, G.A. and Abbot/Peterson  Volcanoes in the sea. University of Hawaii Press, Honolulu 1970

Mc Coy, P.C.  The Mauna Kea adz quarry project: A summary of the 1975 field investigation. Typescript in the Department of Anthropology. Ms 051276, 1976

(the same)  The BPBM Mauna Kea adz quarry project. Typescript in the Department of Anthropology Ms 012778, 1978

Mc Lean, R.C. and Cook, W.R.J.  Plant science formulae; a reference book for plant science laboratories. Macmillan, London 1941, Review 1952

Minzoni-Deroche, A.  Typologies en Préhistoire. P.H.D. thesis. University of Paris, 1981

(the same)  Lithic artifact interpretation. An empirical approach. In World Archaeology 11(1), 1985:19-31

Morris, G.  Microwear and organic residue studies on sweet track flint. In Sommerset Levels Papers 10, 1984:97-106

Moss, E.  The functional analysis of flint implements: Prinevent and Pont d'Ambon, two case studies from the French final paleolithic. In BAR International Series 177, 1983

Mueller, J.W. ed. Sampling in archaeology. In Society of American Archaeology Memoirs 28, 1974, second edition The University of Arizona Press, Tucson, Arizona 1975

(the same)  Archaeological research as cluster sampling. In Mueller,J.W. ed. "Sampling in Archaeology", The University of Arizona Press, Tucson, Arizona 1975:33-41

Muto, G.R.  A stage analysis of the manufacture of stone tools. In Ackens,M. ed. "Great Basin anthropological conference 1970", Selected Papers, University of Oregon Anthropological Papers 1, 1971a

(the same)  A technological analysis of the early stages in manufacture of lithic artifacts. Unpublished M.A. thesis, Idaho State University, 1971b

Myers, O.H.  Some applications of statistics to archaeology. In Service des Antiques de l'Egypte, 1950

Nagata, K.M.  Early plant introduction in Hawaii. In The Hawaiian Journal of History 19, Hong Kong 1985

Nance, J.D.  Lithic analysis: Implications for the prehistory of central California. University of California, Los Angeles, Department of Anthropology, Archaeological Survey Annual Report 12, 1970:62-103

(the same)  Functional interpretation from microscopic analysis. In American Antiquity 36, 1971:361-66

Newcomer, M.H. and Sieveking, G.  Experimental flake scatter - patterns: A new interpretive technique. In Journal of Field Archaeology 7, 1980:345-52

Nissen, K. and Dittemore, M.  Ethnographic data and wear pattern analysis: A study of socketed Eskimo scrapers. In Tebiwa 17, 1974:67-87

Nowatzyk, G.  Die Funktionsinterpretation von Steinartefakten. In BAR International Series 429, 1988

Oakley, K.P.  Man the tool-maker. British Museum of Natural History, London 1967

Odell, G.H.  The application of microwear analysis to lithic components of an entire prehistoric settlement: Methods, problems, and functional reconstructions. P.H.D. dissertation, Department of Anthropology, Harvard University 1977

(the same)  A new and improved system for the retrieval of functional information from microscopic observations of chipped stone tools. In Hayden,B. ed. "Lithic use-wear analysis", Academic Press New York 1979:329-44

(the same)  Verifying the reliability of lithic use-wear assessments by "blind tests": The low power approach. In Journal of Field Archaeology 7, 1980:87-120

Parson, L.A.  Bilbao, Guatemala: An archaeological study of the Pacific coast Cotzumalhuape region. Milwaukee Public Museum Publications in Anthropology 11(1), Milwaukee 1967

Patterson, T.C.  The last sixty years: Towards a social history of American archaeology in the USA. In American Anthropologist 88,1986:7-26

Pearson, R.J. and Kirch, P.V  An early prehistoric site at Bellows Beach, Waimanalo, O'ahu, Hawaiian Islands. In Pietrusewsky, M.  Archaeology and Physical Anthropology in Oceania 6, 1971:204-34

Phillips, P.  Traceology (Microwear) studies in the USSR. In World Archaeology 19(3), Feb. 1984:349-56

Piperno, D.  A comparison and differentiation of phytoliths from maize and wild grasses: Use of morphological criteria. In American Antiquity 49, 1984:361-83

Pryor, F.L.  The adoption of agriculture. In American Anthropologist 88, 1986:879-97

Purdy, B.A.  Fractures of the archaeologist. In Swanson,E. ed. "Lithic Technology. Making and using stone tools", Mouton Publishers, The Haque, Paris 1975

Rawlins, T.E. and Takahashi, W.N.  Techniques of plant histochemie and virology. National Press, Milbrae,Los Angeles 1952

Read, D.W. Sampling procedures for regional surveys: A problem of representativeness and effectiveness. In Journal of Field Archaeology 13(4), Winter 1986:477-91

Redman, C.  Multistage fieldwork and analytical techniques. In American Antiquity 38, 1973:61-79

Reynolds, P.J.  Experimental archaeology and the Buster ancient farm research project: In Collis,J. ed. "The iron age in Britain - a review" University of Sheffield 1977a:32-40 (the same) Archaeology by experiment: A research tool for tomorrow.In Darvill,T.C.,Pearson,M.P., Smith,R.W., and Thomas,R.M. eds."New aproaches to our past. An archaeological forum", University of Southampton 1978

Richards, T.H. Microwear patterns on experimental basalt tools. In BAR International Series 460, 1980

Rouse, I. On the typological method. In American Anthropologist 10, 1944:202-204

(the same) The classification of artifacts in archaeology. In American Antiquity 25, 1960:313-23

(the same) Prehistory, typology and the study of society. In Chang,K.C. ed. "Settlement archaeology", Palo Alto, California: National Press Books 1968

(the same) Classification for what ? In Norwegian Archaeological Review 3, 1970:4-34

Rowe, J.H. Stratigraphy and seriation. In American Antiquity 26(3), 1961:324-30

Rovner,I. Plant opal phytolith analysis. In Advances on Archaeological Method and Theory 6, 1983:225-66

Sackett, J.R. Quantitative analysis of upper palaeolithic stone tools. In American Anthropologist 68(2), 1966:356-94

Schousboe, R. and Riford/Kirch Volcanic-glass flaked stone artifacts. In Clark,J.T. and Kirch,P.V. eds. "Archaeological investigations of the Mudlane-Waimea-Kawaihae road corridor", Department of Anthropology Report Series 83-1, BPBM 1983:348-70

Schiffer, M.B. Behavioral archaeology. Academic Press New York 1976

Schofield, A.J, The interprtation of surface lithic collections. Case studies from southern England. P.H.D. dissertation, University of Southampton 1988, Order No. BRDX84127

Scurfield, G. and Anderson/Segnit Silica in wooden stems Australian Journal of Botany 22,1974:211-29

Semenov, S.A. Prehistoric technology, Thompson M.W. translation. London: Cory, Adams and Mac Kay 1964

Shafer, H.J. and Holloway, R.G. Organic residue analysis in determining stone tool function. In Hayden,B. ed. "Lithic use-wear analysis", Academic Press New York 1979

Shea, J.J. On accuracy and relevance in lithic use-wear analysis. In Lithic Technology 16(2-3), 1987:44-51

Sheets, P. Edge abrasion during biface manufacture. In American Antiquity 38, 1973:215-18

Shott, M.J. On tool-class use lives and the formation of archaeological assemblages. In American Antiquity 54, 1989:9-30

Shutler, R. and Kess, C.A. A lithic industry from New Britain, Territoryof NewGuinea, with possible real and chronological relationships. In Bulletin of the Institute of Ethnology, Academia Sinica 27, 1969:129-140

Siegel, S. Nonparametric statistics for the behavioral science. Mc Graw-Hill, New York 1956

Siegel, P.E. Functional variability within an assemblage of endscrapers. In Lithic Technology 13(2), 1984:35-51

Siegel, P.E. Edge angle as a functional indicator: A test. In Lithic Technology 14(2), 1985:90-94

Sieveking, A. The palaeoloithic industry of Kota Tampan, Perak, Northwestern. In Asian Perspectives 2, 1958:91-102

Sinoto, Y.H. Chronology of Hawaiian fishhooks. In Journal of the Polynesian Society 71, 1962:162-66

(the same) Hawaiian fishhook classification and coding system (revised 1979). Typescript in Department of Anthropology, BPBM, 1979

Soehren, L.J. Hawaii excavations: 1965. Typescript in library BPBM, 1966

Sonnenfeld, J. Interpreting the function of primitive imple ments. In American Antiquity 28, 1962:56-65

Sonneville-Bordes D. de Statistical techniques for the dis covery of artifact types. In American Antiquity 18,1953:305-13,391-393

(the same) Le paléolithique supérieur en Péregord. Delmas, Bordeaux 1960

(the same) and Perrot, J. Lexique typologique du Paléolithique supérieur.Outillage lithique: I Grat-toirs - II Outils solutréens. In Bulletin de la Société Prehistorique Française 51:327-33
Outillage lithique: III Outils composites. In BSPF 52:76-9
Outillage lithique: IV Burins. In BSPF 53:408-12

Spaulding, A.C. The concept of artifact type in archaeol-ogy. In Plateau 45, 1973:149-63

Spaulding, A.C. Multifactor analysis of association (Ceramics). In Cleland,C.E. ed. "Cultural change and continuity", Academic Press New York 1975

Speth, J. The mechanical basis of percussion flaking. In American Antiquity 37, 1972:34-60

(the same) Experimental investigations of hard-hammer percussion flaking. In Tebiwa 17, 1974:7-36

(the same) Miscellaneous studies in hard-hammer percus-sion flaking: The effects of oblique impact. In American Antiquity 40, 1975:203-207

(the same) The role of platform angle and core size in hard-hammer percussion flaking. In Lithic Technol-ogy 10, 1981:16-21

Stahle, D.W. and Dunn, J.E. An analysis and application of size distribution of waste flakes from the manufac-ture of bifacial stone tools. In World Archaeology 14(1), June 1982:84-97

Stevens, W.C. Plant anatomy. Fourth edition. P.Blakiston's, Philadelphia 1924

Sullivan, A.P. and Rozen, K.C. Debitage analysis and ar-chaeological interpretation. In American Antiquity 50(4), 1985:755-79

Swanson, E. Lithic technology: Making and using stone tools. Mouton Publishers, The Hague, Paris 1975

Sabloff, J.A. and Smith, R. The importance of both analytic and taxonomicclassification in the type-variety system. In American Antiquity 34(3), 1969:278-85

Thomas, D.H. Archaeology Holt, Rinhart and Winston, New York 1979

Thomson, D. Some wood and stone implements of the Bindibu tribe of central western Australia. In PPS 30, 1964:400-422

Tomenchuk, J.   The calculation of edge loss on chipped stone tools resulting from use. In Hayden,B. "Lithic use-wear analysis", Academic Press New York 1979

Toth, N.   The Oldowan reassessed: A close look at early stone artifacts. In Journal of Archaeological Science 12, 1985:101-20

Tringham, R.et al   Experimentation in the formation of edge damage: A new approach to lithic analysis. In Journal of Field Archaeology 1, 1974:171-96

Troike, R.C.   Time and types in archaeological analysis: The Brainerd-Robinson technique. In TASB 28, 1957:269-84

Tugby, D.J.   A typological analysis of axes and choppers from southeast Australia. In American Antiquity 24, 1958:24-33

Tuoky, D.R.   Salvage excavations at City of Refuge National Historical Park, Honaunau, Kona, Hawaii. Typescript in library BPBM 1965

Unrath, G.   An evaluation of use-wear studies: A multi-analyst approach. In Early Man News 9/10/11, Tübingen 1984/85/86:117-76

Van Horn, D.M.   The archaeological survey: Chipped stone.In Expedition 19(1), 1976:50-54

Vaughn, P.   Use-wear analysis of flaked stone tools. University of Arizona Press, Tucson 1985

Wallis, F.S.   Petrology as an aid to prehistoric and medieval archaeology. In Endeavour 14, 1955:146-51

Wallrath, M.   Excavations in the Tehuantepec region, Mexico. In Translations of the American Philosophical Society 57(2), Philadelphia 1967

Ward, G.K.   A systematic approach to the definition of sources of raw material. In Archaeometry 16, 1974:41-53

Weisler/Marshall and Kirch   The structure of settlement space in a Polynesian chiefdom: Kawela, Moloka'i, Hawaiian Islands. In New Zealand Journal of Archaeology 7, 1985:129-58

Wentworth, C.K. and Mac Donald, G.A.   Structures and forms of basaltic rocks in Hawaii. In Geological Survey Bulletin 994, Washington 1953

Whallon, R.Jr.   The computer in archaeology: A critical survey. In Computers and the Humanities 7(1), Sept.1972:29-45

White, E.M. and Hannus, L.A.   Chemical wearing of bones in archaeological soils. In American Antiquity 48(2),1983:316-46

Willcock, J.D.   A general survey of computer applications in archaeology. In Scientific Archaeologist 9, Jan.1973:17-21

Williams, S.S.   A technological analysis of the debitage assemblage from Ko'oho'olau rockshelter No.1, Mauna Kea Adze Quarry, Hawaii. M.A. Washington State University 1989

Wilmsen, E.   Functional analysis of flaked stone artifacts. In American Antiquity 33, 1968:156-61

Wilmsen, E.   Lithic analysis and cultural inference: A Paleo-Indian case. In Anthropological Papers of the University of Arizona 16, 1970

(the same)   Lithic analysis in palaeoanthropology. In Leone,M.P. ed."Contemporary Archaeology", Carbondale III, Southern Illinois University Press, 1975

Wyant, J.R.   An experimental study of lithic use-wear. In Doelle,W.H. ed."Desert resources and Hohokam subsistence. The Conoco Florence Project", Arizona State Museum Archaeological Series 103, 1976:231-43

Yerkes, R.   Prehistoric life on the Mississippi floodplain: Stone tool use, settlement organization, and subsistence practices at the Labras Lake Site, Illinois. University of Chicago Press 1987

Ziegert, H.   Objektorientierte und problemorientierte Forschungsansätze in der Archäologie. In Hephaistos 2, 1980:57-65.

(the same)   Wissenschaftliche Arbeitstechniken in den Kulturwissenschaften. In Reihe Kulturwissenschaften 12, 1986

# Abbreviation Key for Appendix A to D

D= Dorsal ; V= Ventral

Configuration: SC= Scattered ; CO= Continuous ; OV= Overlapping ; SU= Superposed

Edge Rounding: SL= Slight ; UN= Unmodified ; ST= Strong

Denticulation: U= Unintermitted ; I= Intermitted ; D= Deep ; S= Shallow

Termination: Snap, Feather, Step, Hinge

Action: Sli= Slicing ; Cut= Cuting ; Deflesh= Defleshing ; Srap= Scraping ; Plan= Planing

Tool: CF= Complete Flake ; BF= Broken Flake ; FF= Flake Fragment

COa= Flakes from the Primary Reduction ; COb= Flakes from the Secondary Reduction

SP= Flakes produced with special angles

Contact Material: *Italics= Cooked ; Italics= Grilled*

80

| Flake | Weight in gr | Length in cm | Width in cm | Thickness in cm | Relative Angle in degrees | Absolute Angle in degrees | Edge Curvature | Retouch / Comments |
|---|---|---|---|---|---|---|---|---|
| FF COa 1 | 48.92 | 6.6 | 4.6 | 2.3 | 50 - 55 | 55 - 60 | Slightly concave ; Even | * |
| CF COb 2 | 9.87 | 2.7 | 4.3 | 1.0 | 30 - 35 | 20 - 25 | Slightly convex ; Rough | Crushing of the forward edge |
| CF COa 3 | 13.39 | 3.7 | 3.9 | 0.9 | 30 | 30 | Straight ; Rough | |
| BF COb 4 | 4.40 | 3.6 | 2.7 | 0.6 | 35 - 40 | 40 - 45 | Irregular ; Even | Heavy damage ; Cracks |
| FF COb 5 | 22.14 | 5.6 | 3.5 | 1.8 | 40 - 50 | 55 - 65 | Strongly convex ; Rough | |
| CF COa 6 | 7.03 | 2.7 | 5.2 | 0.7 | 20 - 25 | 15 - 20 | Slightly convex ; Rough | |
| FF COa 7 | 8.38 | 3.9 | 4.1 | 0.6 | 35 - 40 | 30 | Strongly concave ; Rough | |
| FF COa 8 | 6.21 | 2.2 | 3.7 | 0.9 | 30 | 40 - 45 | Straight ; Rough | |
| FF COa 9 | 41.97 | 6.3 | 3.4 | 2.1 | 50 | 55 | Straight ; Rough | |
| FF COa 10 | 45.64 | 5.6 | 4.9 | 2.0 | 50 - 55 | 55 | Slightly convex ; Rough | Heavy edge damage ; Crushing |
| FF COa 11 | 111.89 | 10.9 | 6.2 | 2.1 | 50 | 55 - 60 | Irregular ; Rough | |
| FF COa 12 | 102.08 | 8.4 | 4.5 | 3.0 | 70 - 75 | 70 - 75 | Slightly concave ; Even | |
| CF COa 13 | 44.80 | 5.7 | 6.1 | 1.6 | 40 - 45 | 20 - 25 | Strongly concave ; Rough | |
| CF COa 14 | 28.48 | 5.8 | 4.4 | 0.8 | 40 - 45 | 50 - 55 | Straight ; Rough | |
| CF COa 15 | 46.28 | 6.3 | 5.3 | 1.4 | 30 - 35 | 40 | Strongly concave ; Rough | 1 natural retouch |
| CF COa 16 | 25.55 | 7.3 | 3.8 | 0.9 | 20 - 25 | 30 - 35 | Slightly convex ; Rough | |
| FF COa 17 | 8.48 | 5.5 | 2.1 | 1.0 | 45 | 50 | Irregular ; Rough | |
| FF COa 18 | 17.18 | 4.5 | 3.5 | 1.1 | 40 - 45 | 35 - 40 | Slightly convex ; Rough | |
| CF COa 19 | 57.98 | 3.8 | 7.9 | 1.7 | 50 - 55 | 50 - 55 | Slightly convex ; Rough | |
| FF COa 20 | 6.49 | 5.7 | 2.3 | 0.7 | 35 | 35 | Strongly convex ; Rough | |
| FF COa 21 | 5.58 | 5.3 | 2.3 | 0.4 | 30 | 35 - 40 | Slightly concave ; Rough | |
| FF COa 22 | 11.54 | 5.2 | 2.9 | 0.9 | 40 | 40 | Slightly concave ; Rough | |
| BF COa 23 | 10.33 | 4.7 | 2.6 | 0.9 | 45 - 50 | 50 | Slightly concave ; Rough | |
| BF COa 24 | 8.36 | 3.7 | 3.1 | 0.7 | 35 | 40 - 45 | Straight ; Rough | |
| BF COa 25 | 17.18 | 5.7 | 2.9 | 1.0 | 30 | 25 - 30 | Slightly convex ; Rough | 1 natural retouch |
| CF COa 26 | 99.39 | 5.5 | 7.5 | 2.7 | 40 - 45 | 50 - 55 | Slightly concave ; Rough | |
| FF SP 27 | 32.12 | 4.2 | 4.0 | 2.4 | 45 | 45 | Straight ; Rough | |
| BF SP 28 | 8.45 | 4.7 | 2.8 | 0.8 | 20 - 25 | 25 - 30 | Irregular ; Rough | 1 natural retouch |
| FF SP 29 | 15.60 | 5.8 | 2.3 | 1.3 | 40 - 50 | 45 - 50 | Straight ; Rough | |
| BF SP 30 | 2.84 | 3.7 | 2.3 | 0.4 | 10 - 15 | 10 | Slightly concave ; Rough | |
| FF SP 31 | 47.57 | 4.8 | 4.7 | 1.4 | 60 - 70 | 75 | Straight ; Rough | 1 natural retouch |
| BF SP 32 | 29.80 | 4.2 | 7.0 | 1.3 | 40 - 45 | 45 | Straight ; Even | |
| FF SP 33 | 41.54 | 5.5 | 4.2 | 1.6 | 30 - 40 | 35 - 40 | Straight ; Rough | 1 natural retouch |
| CF SP 34 | 21.03 | 3.3 | 7.7 | 0.7 | 10 - 15 | 15 - 20 | Straight ; Rough | |
| FF SP 35 | 75.76 | 6.4 | 5.1 | 3.1 | 70 - 75 | 70 - 75 | Straight ; Even | |

Appendix A: Measurements and first observations of the experimentally produces flakes

( Page 81 )

| Flake | Weight in gr | Length in cm | Width in cm | Thickness in cm | Relative Angle in degrees | Absolute Angle in degrees | Edge Curvature | Retouch / Comments |
|---|---|---|---|---|---|---|---|---|
| BF SP 36 | 4.33 | 2.6 | 2.4 | 1.0 | 30 - 35 | 40 | Straight ; Even | |
| BF SP 37 | 13.35 | 3.0 | 4.6 | 0.8 | 40 - 45 | 55 - 60 | Slightly convex ; Rough | |
| FF SP 38 | 62.29 | 5.3 | 4.3 | 2.2 | 80 - 85 | 80 - 85 | Straight ; Even | |
| FF SP 39 | 6.87 | 1.9 | 3.4 | 0.9 | 60 - 65 | 70 | Irregular ; Rough | |
| FF SP 40 | 17.44 | 2.7 | 3.8 | 1.1 | 50 - 55 | 55 | Slightly convex ; Rough | Edge crushing |
| CF SP 41 | 2.98 | 2.3 | 3.4 | 0.4 | 10 | 20 - 25 | Strongly convex ; Even | |
| FF SP 42 | 9.84 | 4.1 | 2.7 | 1.0 | 30 - 35 | 25 - 30 | Slightly convex ; Rough | |
| FF SP 43 | 31.15 | 4.2 | 3.3 | 2.4 | 50 | 50 | Strongly convex ; Rough | |
| FF SP 44 | 24.68 | 5.5 | 4.1 | 1.2 | 45 | 50 - 55 | Strongly convex ; Rough | |
| FF SP 45 | 33.39 | 6.7 | 3.9 | 1.5 | 55 - 60 | 60 - 70 | Strongly convex ; Even | |
| FF SP 46 | 6.41 | 5.4 | 1.6 | 0.9 | 55 | 55 - 65 | Strongly concave ; Even | |
| FF SP 47 | 39.79 | 4.4 | 5.0 | 2.1 | 50 | 50 | Straight ; Rough | |
| FF SP 48 | 11.75 | 4.4 | 2.0 | 1.7 | 45 - 50 | 45 - 50 | Slightly convex ; Rough | |
| FF SP 49 | 28.59 | 4.5 | 4.9 | 1.6 | 40 - 50 | 55 - 65 | Straight ; Rough | |
| BF SP 50 | 53.09 | 6.8 | 5.7 | 1.7 | 35 - 45 | 60 - 65 | Irregular ; Rough | |
| FF SP 51 | 7.98 | 4.7 | 2.7 | 0.7 | 55 - 60 | 35 - 40 | Irregular ; Rough | |
| FF SP 52 | 15.73 | 6.4 | 2.5 | 1.1 | 65 - 70 | 55 - 60 | Straight ; Rough | |
| BF SP 53 | 8.14 | 2.7 | 3.9 | 0.7 | 40 | 45 - 55 | Straight ; Even | |
| FF SP 54 | 91.93 | 6.3 | 3.6 | 3.4 | 85 | 85 | Straight ; Rough | Several notches |
| FF SP 55 | 50.44 | 6.0 | 4.5 | 2.9 | 65 - 70 | 75 - 80 | Straight ; Even | |
| FF SP 56 | 6.14 | 4.6 | 2.7 | 0.7 | 70 | 70 | Slightly concave ; Even | |
| FF SP 57 | 137.2 | 7.0 | 5.6 | 4.2 | 55 - 60 | 60 | Slightly convex ; Rough | |
| CF SP 58 | 89.05 | 8.6 | 5.0 | 1.9 | 45 - 55 | 40 - 50 | Strongly convex ; Rough | |
| BF SP 59 | 11.71 | 4.3 | 4.3 | 0.7 | 20 - 25 | 30 | Strongly convex ; Even | 1 natural retouch |
| CF SP 60 | 2.40 | 1.7 | 3.6 | 0.4 | 20 | 35 - 40 | Irregular ; Rough | 1 natural retouch |
| FF SP 61 | 9.71 | 3.4 | 2.3 | 0.9 | 30 - 40 | 45 | Straight ; Even | |
| FF SP 62 | 6.43 | 3.7 | 2.1 | 0.7 | 40 - 50 | 50 - 55 | Slightly concave ; Rough | |
| FF SP 63 | 32.12 | 3.9 | 4.6 | 1.4 | 70 - 80 | 70 - 80 | Straight ; Rough | |
| BF SP 64 | 59.25 | 7.2 | 6.0 | 2.3 | 55 - 60 | 55 - 60 | Straight ; Rough | |
| CF SP 65 | 6.95 | 3.2 | 3.9 | 0.6 | 35 - 40 | 45 - 50 | Straight ; Even | |
| BF SP 66 | 7.64 | 3.9 | 3.6 | 0.7 | 40 - 45 | 50 - 55 | Straight ; Rough | |
| FF SP 67 | 87.19 | 9.5 | 4.6 | 2.0 | 25 - 30 | 35 | Irregular ; Rough | 1 natural retouch |
| FF SP 68 | 10.71 | 2.9 | 3.1 | 1.4 | 45 | 45 | Slightly concave ; Rough | |
| FF SP 69 | 15.42 | 6.0 | 2.5 | 1.7 | 50 | 55 - 60 | Strongly concave ; Rough | |
| FF SP 70 | 8.87 | 4.9 | 2.3 | 1.0 | 60 - 65 | 65 | Slightly concave ; Rough | |

Appendix A; Continued

| Flake | Weight in gr | Length in cm | Width in cm | Thickness in cm | Relative Angle in degrees | Absolute Angle in degrees | Edge Curvature | Retouch / Comments |
|---|---|---|---|---|---|---|---|---|
| FF SP 71 | 10.03 | 4.7 | 2.5 | 0.8 | 25 - 35 | 20 - 30 | Strongly concave ; Even | Several notches |
| FF SP 72 | 5.86 | 4.7 | 2.4 | 0.7 | 25 - 35 | 35 - 40 | Slightly convex ; Even | 1 natural retouch |
| FF SP 73 | 6.24 | 3.6 | 2.3 | 0.8 | 30 - 35 | 40 | Irregular ; Rough | 1 natural retouch |
| FF SP 74 | 5.69 | 4.4 | 1.7 | 0.8 | 40 | 40 | Straight ; Rough | |
| FF SP 75 | 9.08 | 4.5 | 2.5 | 0.9 | 50 - 55 | 55 - 65 | Strongly concave ; Rough | |
| FF SP 76 | 16.40 | 4.9 | 2.6 | 2.0 | 40 - 50 | 45 - 55 | Strongly concave ; Rough | Heavy edge damage ; Crushing |
| BF SP 77 | 55.88 | 4.4 | 8.0 | 1.7 | 55 - 60 | 55 - 60 | Irregular ; Rough | |
| FF SP 78 | 24.01 | 4.9 | 3.3 | 1.7 | 40 | 40 | Slightly convex ; Rough | |
| FF SP 79 | 18.17 | 2.3 | 5.7 | 1.5 | 65 | 65 | Straight ; Rough | |
| FF SP 80 | 61.90 | 6.4 | 5.5 | 2.0 | 75 - 85 | 80 - 85 | Slightly concave ; Rough | 1 natural retouch |
| CF SP 81 | 47.33 | 5.7 | 7.9 | 1.3 | 30 - 35 | 40 - 45 | Irregular ; Rough | |
| FF SP 82 | 23.09 | 4.8 | 6.3 | 0.9 | 50 - 55 | 55 | Irregular ; Rough | |
| CF SP 83 | 25.88 | 5.5 | 4.0 | 2.3 | 60 | 65 - 70 | Straight ; Even | |
| CF SP 84 | 12.68 | 3.1 | 5.5 | 0.8 | 30 - 40 | 45 - 50 | Strongly convex ; Rough | |
| FF SP 85 | 22.25 | 5.5 | 2.4 | 1.8 | 30 - 35 | 40 | Slightly convex ; Rough | |
| FF SP 86 | 27.03 | 5.6 | 4.4 | 1.3 | 40 | 35 - 45 | Straight ; Even | |
| CF SP 87 | 12.65 | 4.1 | 3.3 | 1.0 | 45 | 45 | Strongly convex ; Rough | |
| FF SP 88 | 9.36 | 6.3 | 2.1 | 0.7 | 25 - 30 | 35 - 40 | Irregular ; Rough | 1 natural retouch |
| FF SP 89 | 8.35 | 4.6 | 2.9 | 0.8 | 60 | 65 - 70 | Strongly convex ; Even | |
| FF SP 90 | 12.00 | 4.2 | 3.4 | 1.1 | 40 - 45 | 40 - 50 | Straight ; Rough | 1 natural retouch |
| BF SP 91 | 17.34 | 3.7 | 4.5 | 0.9 | 40 - 50 | 55 - 60 | Straight ; Rough | |
| FF SP 92 | 6.60 | 5.4 | 2.1 | 0.5 | 20 - 25 | 20 - 25 | Irregular ; Rough | 1 natural retouch |
| FF SP 93 | 239.2 | 8.4 | 6.9 | 4.9 | 90 | 90 | Straight ; Even | |
| FF SP 94 | 136.4 | 7.7 | 4.5 | 3.5 | 80 - 85 | 85 | Irregular ; Rough | |
| FF SP 95 | 268.2 | 7.7 | 7.1 | 3.6 | 45 - 50 | 50 - 55 | Slightly convex ; Rough | 1 natural retouch |
| FF SP 96 | 55.95 | 7.2 | 5.5 | 1.6 | 50 | 55 - 60 | Straight ; Rough | |
| FF SP 97 | 125.9 | 9.1 | 5.7 | 3.5 | 60 | 60 - 65 | Slightly concave ; Even | |
| FF SP 98 | 158.8 | 8.8 | 5.8 | 3.7 | 65 - 70 | 70 - 75 | Straight ; Even | |
| FF SP 99 | 41.27 | 4.8 | 4.3 | 1.6 | 70 - 75 | 70 - 75 | Slightly concave ; Even | |
| FF SP 100 | 91.95 | 9.2 | 5.3 | 1.4 | 45 - 50 | 55 - 60 | Strongly concave ; Even | |
| BF SP 101 | 93.84 | 6.1 | 7.9 | 1.9 | 60 - 65 | 65 - 75 | Strongly concave ; Rough | |
| FF SP 102 | 22.84 | 6.5 | 3.2 | 1.0 | 45 - 50 | 35 - 40 | Slightly concave ; Rough | |
| FF SP 103 | 76.19 | 6.4 | 4.0 | 2.3 | 80 | 80 | Slightly concave ; Even | |

Appendix A: Continued

( Page 83 )

| Tool | Contact Material | Action | Total Micro-flake Scars D / V | Snap D/V | Feather D / V | Step D/V | Hinge D/V | Configuration D / V | Edge Rounding D / V | Polish/Smoothing D / V | Striation D / V | Denticulation |
|---|---|---|---|---|---|---|---|---|---|---|---|---|
| FF SP100 | Leaves;Ohiaå-lehua | Saw / Cut | 1 / 3 | 1/1 | -- / 2 | --/-- | --/-- | SC / SC | SL;UN / SL;UN | Yes / Yes | -- /Yes | I / S |
| FF SP 45 | Leaves ; Hau | Saw / Cut | 2 / 2 | 2/-- | 1 / 1 | --/-- | --/-- | SC / SC | SL;UN / SL;UN | Yes / Yes | -- / -- | I / S |
| FFCOa 1 | Pig Bone | Sawing | 7 / 5 | 1/1 | -- / 1 | 3/2 | 3/1 | SC / SC | ST / ST | Yes / Yes | Yes/Yes | None |
| CFCOa15 | Pig Bone | Sawing | 3 / 4 | --/1 | -- / -- | 1/1 | 2/2 | SC / SC | ST / ST | Yes / Yes | Yes/Yes | None |
| FFCOa18 | Pig Bone | Sawing | 5 / 5 | 1/-- | 1 / -- | 2/3 | 1/2 | SC / SC | ST / ST | Yes / Yes | Yes/Yes | None |
| FFCOa 8 | Manini Bone | Sawing | 3 / 2 | --/-- | -- / 1 | 1/1 | 2/1 | SC / SC | ST / ST | Yes / Yes | -- /Yes | None |
| FF SP 73 | Alaihi Bone | Cutting | 2 / 3 | --/1 | 1 / 1 | 1/1 | 1/-- | SC / SC | SL;ST / SL;ST | Yes / Yes | -- / -- | None |
| CFCOb 2 | Alaihi Bone | Sawing | 3 / 1 | --/-- | 1 / 1 | 2/-- | --/1 | SC / SC | SL;ST / SL;ST | Yes / Yes | Yes / -- | None |
| FF SP102 | Manini Bone | Sawing | 1 / 2 | --/-- | 1 / -- | 1/2 | --/-- | SC / SC | SL / SL | Yes / Yes | -- / -- | None |
| FF SP 46 | Manini Bone | Sawing | 4 / 1 | 1/-- | 1 / -- | --/-- | 2/1 | SC / SC | SL / SL | Yes / Yes | -- / -- | None |
| FF SP 78 | Chicken;Flesh/Bone | Saw / Cut | 5 / 3 | --/-- | 1 / -- | 2/2 | 1/3 | SC / SC | ST / ST | Yes / Yes | -- /Yes | None |
| CF SP 58 | Chicken;Flesh/Bone | Saw / Cut | 4 / 7 | --/-- | 1 / -- | 3/1 | 4/2 | SC / SC | ST / ST | Yes / Yes | Yes / -- | None |
| FF SP 57 | Chicken;Flesh/Bone | Saw / Cut | 6 / 6 | --/2 | 1 / -- | 2/4 | 1/3 | SC / SC | ST / ST | Yes / Yes | Yes/Yes | None |
| FF SP 98 | Chicken;Flesh/Bone | Saw / Cut | 3 / 2 | --/-- | 1 / -- | --/2 | 2/-- | SC / SC | ST / ST | Yes / Yes | -- /Yes | None |
| FF SP 90 | Awcowco;Flesh/Bn. | Saw / Cut | 3 / 2 | 1/1 | -- / 1 | --/-- | 2/1 | SC / SC | SL / SL | Yes / Yes | -- / -- | I / S |
| BF SP101 | Pig Bone | Sawing | 4 / 6 | 2/1 | -- / 1 | 1/3 | 1/1 | SC / SC | ST / ST | Yes / Yes | Yes/Yes | None |
| FF SP 49 | Awcowco;Flesh/Bn. | Saw / Cut | 2 / 2 | 1/1 | -- / 1 | --/-- | 1/-- | SC / SC | SL / SL | Yes / Yes | -- / -- | None |
| CFCOa19 | Manini;Flesh/Bone | Slicing | 2 / 3 | 1/2 | -- / 1 | --/-- | 1/1 | OV;SC / SC | SL / SL | Yes / Yes | -- / -- | None |
| BFCOa23 | Manini Flesh | Cut / Sli | -- / -- | --/-- | -- / -- | --/-- | --/-- | -- / -- | -- / -- | -- / -- | -- / -- | None |
| FF SP 43 | Manini Flesh | Cut / Sli | -- / 1 | --/-- | 1 / -- | --/-- | --/-- | -- / -- | -- / -- | -- / -- | -- / -- | None |
| BF SP 77 | Manini Flesh | Cut / Sli | -- / 1 | --/-- | -- / 1 | --/-- | --/-- | -- / SC | -- / -- | -- / -- | -- / -- | None |
| FF SP 52 | Manini Flesh | Cut / Sli | -- / -- | --/-- | -- / -- | --/-- | --/-- | -- / SC | -- / -- | -- / -- | -- / -- | None |
| CFCOa 6 | Manini;Flesh/Bone | Deflesh. | 4 / 3 | --/-- | 2 / 1 | 2/2 | --/-- | SC / SC | SL / SL | Yes / Yes | -- / -- | I / S |
| CFCOa 3 | Alaihi Flesh | Deflesh. | 2 / 3 | --/-- | 2 / -- | --/2 | --/1 | SC / SC | SL / SL | Yes / -- | -- / -- | I / S |
| BF SP 66 | Awcowco Flesh | Cut / Sli | -- / -- | --/-- | -- / -- | --/-- | --/-- | -- / -- | -- / -- | -- / -- | -- / -- | None |
| CF SP 41 | Chicken Flesh | Cut / Sli | 3 / 2 | 1/1 | 1 / -- | 1/1 | 1/-- | SC / SC | SL / SL | Yes / -- | -- / -- | I / S |
| CF SP 81 | Chicken Flesh | Cut / Sli | 2 / 3 | --/1 | 1 / -- | 2/1 | --/-- | SC / SC | SL / SL | Yes / -- | -- / -- | U / S |
| FF SP 33 | Pig Flesh | Cut / Sli | 3 / 2 | --/-- | 2 / 1 | 1/1 | --/-- | SC / SC | SL / SL | Yes / Yes | -- / -- | U / D |
| FF SP 55 | Pig Flesh | Cut / Sli | 4 / 5 | --/1 | 2 / 3 | 2/1 | --/-- | SC / SC | SL / SL | Yes / Yes | -- / -- | U / D |
| FF SP 79 | Pig Flesh | Cut / Scra | 5 / 6 | --/-- | 3 / 1 | 2/4 | --/1 | SC / SC | SL;ST / SL;ST | Yes / Yes | -- / -- | U / D |
| FFCOa17 | Pig Flesh | Cut / Sli | 6 / 3 | 2/-- | 2 / 2 | 1/1 | 1/-- | SC / SC | SL / SL | Yes / Yes | -- /Yes | U/D |
| FFCOa10 | Pig Flesh | Cut / Sli | 2 / 2 | --/1 | -- / 1 | 1/1 | --/1 | SC / SC | SI / SL | Yes / Yes | -- / -- | I / S |
| FF SP 92 | Chicken;Fl./Sinews | Cut / Sli | 2 / 3 | --/-- | 1 / 1 | 1/1 | --/1 | SC / SC | SL;ST / SL;ST | Yes / Yes | -- / -- | I / S |
| FF SP 27 | Chicken;Flesh/Bone | Cut / Sli | 5 / 4 | --/-- | 3 / 2 | 2/2 | --/-- | SC;CO/SC;CO | ST / ST | Yes / Yes | Yes/Yes | None |

Appendix B: Results of the microscopic investigation of the experimentally used flakes

| Tool | Contact Material | Action | Total Micro-flake Scars D / V | Snap D/V | Feather D / V | Step D/V | Hinge D/V | Configuration D / V | Edge Rounding D / V | Polish/Smoothing D / V | Striation D / V | Denticulation |
|---|---|---|---|---|---|---|---|---|---|---|---|---|
| BF SP 36 | Chicken;Fl/Sinews | Cut / Sli | 4 / 7 | --/1 | 2 / 3 | 2/3 | --/-- | SC;CO/SC;CO | SL;ST / SL;ST | Yes / Yes | -- / Yes | None |
| FF SP 67 | Pig;Flesh/Sinews | Cut / Sli | 4 / 3 | --/-- | 1 / 2 | 2/1 | 1/-- | SC / SC | SL;ST / SL;ST | Yes / Yes | -- / -- | I / S |
| BFCOa25 | Pig;Flesh/Sinews | Cut / Sli | 3 / 3 | 1/-- | 1 / 1 | 1/2 | --/-- | SC / SC | SL;ST / SL;ST | Yes / Yes | -- / -- | I / S |
| FF SP 72 | Pig;Flesh/Bone | Cut / Sli | 4 / 7 | --/-- | 2 / 3 | 2/4 | --/-- | OV;SC/OV;SC | ST / ST | Yes / Yes | Yes / Yes | None |
| FFCOa 7 | Pig;Flesh/Sinews | Cut / Sli | 4 / 3 | --/-- | 1 / 1 | 3/1 | --/1 | SC / SC | SL;ST / SL;ST | Yes / Yes | Yes / -- | I / S |
| FF SP 95 | *Chicken;Fl/Sinews* | Cut / Sli | 3 / 3 | --/-- | 2 / 2 | 1/1 | --/-- | SC / SC | SL / SL | -- / -- | -- / -- | I / S |
| FF SP 62 | *Pig;Fl/Sinews/Bone* | Cut / Sli | 3 / 4 | --/-- | 2 / 1 | 1/2 | --/1 | SC / SC | SL;ST / SL;ST | Yes / -- | -- / -- | None |
| FFCOa21 | Chicken;Fl/Sinews | Cut / Sli | 5 / 4 | --/-- | 2 / 2 | 3/1 | --/1 | SC / SC | SL / SL | Yes / -- | -- / -- | I / S |
| FF SP 74 | Pig;Fl/Sinews/Bone | Cut / Sli | 9 / 9 | --/1 | 4 / 3 | 3/5 | 2/-- | CO / CO;OV | ST / ST | Yes / Yes | Yes/Yes | I / S |
| FF SP 83 | Pig;Flesh/Sinews | Cut / Sli | 3 / 4 | --/-- | 2 / 2 | 1/2 | --/-- | SC / SC | SL / SL | Yes / Yes | -- / -- | I / S |
| CFCOa26 | Koa | Scraping | 4 / -- | --/-- | 1 / -- | 3/-- | --/-- | SC / -- | SL / SL | Yes / -- | -- / -- | None |
| FF SP 63 | Koa | Scraping | 4 / 1 | --/-- | 2 / -- | 2/-- | --/1 | SC / SC | SL / UN | -- / -- | -- / -- | None |
| BF SP 32 | Ohia-a'lehua | Scraping | 7 / 1 | --/-- | 3 / 1 | 4/-- | --/-- | CO/OV / SC | ST / SL | -- / -- | -- / -- | None |
| FF SP 96 | Hau | Scraping | 4 / -- | --/-- | 2 / -- | 2/-- | --/-- | SC / -- | SL / UN | Yes / -- | -- / -- | None |
| FF SP 68 | Kukui | Scraping | 2 / -- | --/-- | 2 / -- | --/-- | --/-- | SC / -- | SL / -- | -- / -- | -- / -- | None |
| BF SP 64 | Kukui | Scraping | 3 / -- | --/-- | 1 / -- | 2/-- | --/-- | SC / -- | SL / -- | Yes / -- | -- / -- | None |
| FF SP 89 | Ohia-a'lehua | Scraping | 3 / -- | --/-- | 1 / -- | 2/-- | --/-- | SC / -- | SL / UN | -- / -- | -- / -- | None |
| FF SP 56 | Hau | Scraping | 2 / -- | --/-- | 2 / -- | --/-- | --/-- | SC / -- | SL / UN | -- / -- | -- / -- | None |
| FF SP 94 | Kukui | Scraping | 3 / -- | --/-- | 2 / -- | 1/-- | --/-- | SC / -- | SL / UN | -- / -- | -- / -- | None |
| FF SP 80 | Ohia-a'lehua | Scraping | 2 / -- | --/-- | 2 / -- | 1/-- | --/-- | SC / -- | SL / UN | -- / -- | -- / -- | None |
| CFCOa13 | Kukui | Scraping | 3 / -- | --/-- | 2 / -- | 1/-- | --/-- | SC / -- | SL / UN | Yes / -- | -- / -- | None |
| FF SP 86 | Hau | Scraping | 3 / -- | --/-- | 2 / -- | 1/-- | --/-- | SC / SC | SL / UN | -- / -- | -- / -- | None |
| FF SP 48 | Koa | Planing | 5 / 1 | --/-- | 3 / 1 | 2/-- | --/-- | SC / -- | SL / SL | Yes / Yes | Yes / -- | None |
| FF SP 39 | Koa | Planing | 4 / -- | --/-- | 3 / -- | 1/-- | --/-- | SC / -- | SL / SL | Yes / -- | Yes / -- | None |
| FF SP 38 | Koa | Planing | 7 / 2 | --/-- | 3 / 2 | 2/-- | 2/-- | SC / SC | SL / UN | Yes / Yes | -- / -- | None |
| BFCOa24 | Ohia-a'lehua | Planing | 8 / -- | 1/-- | 4 / -- | 3/-- | --/-- | CO / -- | ST / SL | Yes / Yes | -- / -- | None |
| FFCOa22 | Hau | Planing | 3 / -- | --/-- | 1 / -- | 2/-- | --/-- | SC / -- | SL / SL | Yes / -- | -- / -- | None |
| BF SP 91 | Kukui | Planing | 2 / -- | --/-- | 2 / -- | --/-- | --/-- | SC / -- | SL / SL | Yes / -- | -- / -- | None |
| FF SP 75 | Kukui | Planing | 3 / -- | --/-- | 2 / -- | 1/-- | --/-- | SC / -- | SL / SL | Yes / -- | -- / -- | None |
| FF SP 97 | Kukui | Planing | 12 / 2 | 1/-- | 6 / 1 | 4/-- | 1/1 | CO;OV / SC | ST / SL | Yes / Yes | Yes / -- | None |
| FFCOa12 | Ohia-a'lehua | Planing | 5 / -- | --/-- | 3 / -- | 2/-- | --/1 | SC / -- | ST / -- | Yes / -- | -- / -- | None |
| FF SP 93 | Hau | Planing | 7 / 1 | --/-- | 5 / -- | 2/-- | --/-- | SC / SC | SL / SL | Yes / Yes | Yes / -- | None |
| CFCOa14 | Ohia-a'lehua | Sawing | 3 / 5 | --/1 | 2 / 2 | 1/2 | --/-- | SC / SC | ST / ST | -- / Yes | -- / -- | None |
| FF SP 29 | Kukui | Sawing | 8 / 8 | 1/2 | 4 / 3 | 3/2 | --/1 | COOV/COOV | ST / ST | Yes / Yes | -- / -- | None |

( Page 85 )

Appendix B: Continued

| Tool | Contact Material | Action | Total Micro-flake Scars D / V | Snap D/V | Feather D / V | Step D/V | Hinge D/V | Configuration D / V | Edge Rounding D / V | Polish/Smoothing D / V | Striation D / V | Denticulation |
|---|---|---|---|---|---|---|---|---|---|---|---|---|
| FFCOa20 | Hau | Sawing | 2 / 2 | 1/- | 1 / 1 | -/1 | -/- | SC / SC | ST / ST | -- / -- | -- / -- | None |
| FFCOa 9 | Hau | Sawing | 5 / 4 | -/1 | 3 / 1 | 2/2 | -/- | SC / SC | ST / ST | Yes / -- | -- / -- | None |
| CF SP 87 | Kukui | Sawing | 5 / 7 | 2/1 | 1 / 3 | 2/3 | -/- | SC / SC | ST / ST | Yes / Yes | Yes/Yes | None |
| FF SP 54 | Kukui | Sawing | 3 / 3 | 1/1 | 1 / 1 | 1/1 | -/- | SC / SC | ST / ST | -- / -- | -- / -- | None |
| CFCOa16 | Ohia-a'lehua | Sawing | 2 / 4 | -/- | 1 / 2 | -/2 | 1/- | SC / SC | ST / ST | -- / -- | -- / -- | None |
| BF SP 59 | Kukui | Sawing | 1 / - | 1/- | - / - | -/- | -/- | SC / -- | SL / -- | -- / -- | -- / -- | None |
| FF SP 61 | Kukui | Sawing | 3 / 2 | -/- | 1 / 1 | 2/1 | -/- | SC / SC | ST / ST | Yes / -- | -- / -- | None |
| CF SP 84 | Kukui | Sawing | 6 / 5 | -/1 | 3 / 3 | 3/1 | -/- | SC / SC | ST / ST | Yes / Yes | -- / -- | None |
| CF SP 65 | Koa | Sawing | 2 / 1 | -/- | 1 / 1 | 1/- | -/- | SC / SC | SL / SL | -- / -- | -- / -- | None |
| FF SP 35 | Koa | Sawing | 2 / 3 | -/1 | 1 / 2 | 1/- | -/- | SC / SC | ST / ST | Yes / -- | -- / -- | None |
| CF SP 34 | Koa | Sawing | 6 / 5 | 1/1 | 2 / 2 | 2/2 | 1/- | SC / SC | ST / ST | Yes / Yes | Yes/Yes | None |
| FF SP 88 | Koa | Sawing | 2 / 2 | -/- | 1 / 2 | 1/- | -/- | SC / SC | SL / SL | -- / -- | -- / -- | None |
| BF SP 30 | Kukui | Whittling | 5 / 5 | 1/1 | 2 / 2 | 2/2 | -/- | SC / SC | ST / ST | Yes / Yes | -- / -- | None |
| BF SP 28 | Kukui | Whittling | 3 / 2 | -/- | 2 / 1 | 1/1 | -/- | SC / SC | SL / SL | -- / -- | -- / -- | None |
| FF SP 85 | Ohia-a'lehua | Whittling | 2 / 4 | -/1 | - / 2 | 2/1 | -/- | SC / SC | ST / ST | Yes / -- | -- / -- | None |
| FF SP 71 | Hau | Whittling | 2 / 1 | -/- | 2 / 1 | -/- | -/- | SC / SC | SL / SL | -- / -- | -- / -- | None |
| FF SP 42 | Kukui | Whittling | 3 / 1 | -/- | 1 / - | 2/1 | -/- | SC / SC | ST / ST | -- / Yes | -- / -- | None |
| FFCOb 5 | Hau | Whittling | 2 / 3 | -/- | 2 / 2 | -/1 | -/- | SC / SC | SL / SL | -- / -- | -- / -- | None |
| BF SP 53 | Hau | Whittling | 4 / 1 | 1/- | 2 / 1 | 1/- | -/- | SC / SC | SL / SL | Yes / -- | -- / -- | None |
| BF Sp 37 | Ohia-a'lehua | Whittling | 2 / 2 | -/- | 1 / 1 | 1/1 | -/- | SC / SC | ST / ST | -- / Yes | -- / -- | None |
| FF SP 44 | Kukui | Whittling | 3 / 3 | 1/1 | 2 / 1 | -/1 | -/- | SC / SC | SL / SL | -- / -- | -- / -- | None |
| CF SP 82 | Kukui | Whittling | 2 / 2 | -/- | 2 / - | -/2 | -/- | SC / SC | ST / ST | Yes / -- | -- / -- | None |
| FF SP 47 | Ohia-a'lehua | Whittling | 2 / 3 | -/1 | 1 / 1 | 1/1 | -/1 | CO / CO | SL / SL | -- / Yes | Yes / -- | None |
| FF SP 69 | Ohia-a'lehua | Whittling | 6 / 5 | 1/- | 3 / 2 | 2/2 | -/- | SC / SC | ST / ST | Yes / Yes | -- / -- | None |
| FF SP 31 | Kukui | Whittling | 3 / 2 | -/- | 2 / 1 | 1/1 | -/- | SC / SC | SL / SL | -- / -- | -- / -- | None |
| FF SP 51 | Ohia-a'lehua | Whittling | 1 / 4 | -/1 | - / 2 | 1/1 | -/- | SC / SC | SL / SL | -- / -- | -- / -- | None |
| FF SP 99 | Kukui | Whittling | 4 / 3 | -/- | 2 / 1 | 2/2 | -/- | SC / SC | SL / SL | -- / Yes | -- / -- | None |
| FF SP103 | Kukui | Whittling | 2 / 2 | -/1 | 2 / - | -/1 | -/- | SC / SC | SL / SL | -- / -- | -- / -- | None |
| CF SP 60 | Koa | Whittling | 3 / 3 | -/- | 2 / 2 | 1/1 | -/- | SC / SC | ST / ST | Yes / Yes | -- / -- | None |
| BF SP 50 | Koa | Whittling | 4 / 3 | -/- | 2 / 1 | 2/2 | -/- | SC / SC | ST / ST | Yes / Yes | -- / -- | None |

Appendix B: Continued

( Page 86 )

| Flake | Weight in gr | Length in cm | Width in cm | Thickness in cm | Relative Angle in degrees | Absolute Angle in degrees | Edge Curvature | Retouch / Comments |
|---|---|---|---|---|---|---|---|---|
| FFW 1 | 12.104 | 6.7 | 3.7 | 0.4 | 10 - 20 | 15 - 25 | Straight ; Rough - Even | 1 new breakage ; Polish and rounded edges |
| CFW 2 | 53.066 | 6.7 | 4.7 | 1.5 | 45 - 50 | 55 - 60 | Irregular ; Rough | 1 Retouch (natural ?) ; 6 microflake scars |
| CFW 3 | 67.296 | 7.9 | 4.8 | 2.0 | 50 - 60 | 35 - 45 | Slightly concave ; Rough | 1 retouch could be natural |
| CFW 4 | 20.258 | 4.7 | 4.4 | 0.9 | 25 - 30 | 25 - 30 | Strongly convex ; Even | Edge smoothing/rounding ; 4 microflake scars |
| FFW 5 | 20.985 | 5.8 | 4.4 | 1.4 | 35 - 40 | 40 - 50 | Slightly convex ; Even | Micro-denticulation ; Scarring ; Microflaking ; Polish |
| FFW 6 | 17.514 | 5.2 | 3.9 | 0.9 | 30 | 30 | Irregular ; Rough | 2 retouches ; maybe natural |
| FFW 7 | 24.611 | 6.1 | 4.6 | 0.7 | 30 - 35 | 35 - 45 | Irregular ; Rough | New breakage ; Not used |
| FFW 8 | 7.247 | 3.9 | 2.9 | 0.6 | 25 - 30 | 25 | Straight ; Rough | 1 natural retouch |
| CFW 9 | 6.451 | 3.9 | 3.1 | 0.5 | 25 - 30 | 40 | Slightly convex ; Even | Definite edge rounding ; 2 microflake scars |
| FFW 10 | 3.762 | 3.2 | 2.5 | 0.6 | 20 - 25 | 30 - 35 | Irregular ; Rough | 1 notch seems to be recent |
| CFW 11 | 45.092 | 6.4 | 5.1 | 1.2 | 35 - 40/30 - 40 | 45 / 30 - 40 | Straight/StronglyConcave | Probable2-sided use;Denticul;Notch;Retouch;Scarring |
| CFW 12 | 2.459 | 3.1 | 2.2 | 0.4 | 10 - 15 | 15 - 20 | Strongly convex ; Rough | Even though suitable no use-wear was detectable |
| BFW 13 | 16.376 | 5.6 | 4.5 | 0.9 | 25 - 30 | 35 - 40 | Slightly concave ; Rough | No use-wear discernable |
| CFW 14 | 21.824 | 4.3 | 4.2 | 1.0 | 40 - 45 | 40 - 45 | Strongly convex ; Even | Definite edge rounding ; 2 microflake scars |
| BFW 15 | 5.518 | 3.2 | 3.3 | 0.6 | 25 | 30 - 35 | Straight ; Rough | Micro-denticulation;but no hint what caused it |
| BFW 16 | 11.734 | 5.2 | 2.9 | 0.7 | 15 - 30 | 25 | Strongly concave ; Even | Edge rounding;7 microflake scars;Crushing;Denticul. |
| FFW 17 | 16.690 | 4.8 | 3.1 | 1.2 | 35 | 35 | Irregular ; Rough | 1 retouch supposedly natural |
| FFW 18 | 69.055 | 7.0 | 6.1 | 1.4 | 45 - 50 | 55 - 60 | Straight ; Rough | Strongly patinated ; 1 new retouch ; No use-wear |
| CFW 19 | 9.852 | 3.7 | 3.3 | 0.7 | 20 - 25 | 20 - 30 | Slightly concave ; Rough | No use-wear discernable |
| CFW 20 | 9.737 | 4.5 | 2.5 | 0.7 | 35 - 40 | 35 - 40 | Slightly convex ; Even | Smooth edge looks like waterworn |
| FFW 21 | 24.675 | 5.9 | 3.5 | 1.3 | 35 | 40 - 50 | Straight ; Rough | 1 retouch ; Patinated ; No indication of use |
| BFW 22 | 8.274 | 4.2 | 3.4 | 0.7 | 20 - 25 | 25 | Straight ; Even | Definite edge rounding ; Polish of the dorsal side |
| BFW 23 | 8.660 | 4.0 | 3.9 | 0.4 | 15 - 20 | 20 - 30 | Slightly convex ; Even | Definite edge rounding |
| FFW 24 | 9.097 | 5.1 | 2.9 | 0.7 | 45 | 45 | Slightly concave ; Rough | Sharp edge ; No use-wear present |
| CFW 25 | 12.246 | 4.3 | 3.2 | 1.0 | 30 - 35 | 35 - 40 | Irregular ; Rough | No use-wear |
| CFW 26 | 8.514 | 4.4 | 2.7 | 0.7 | 25 - 30 | 35 | Straight ; Rough | Strongly patinated ; 1 natural retouch |
| FFW 27 | 8.468 | 4.9 | 1.7 | 0.7 | 30 | 30 | Straight ; Rough | Crushing ; 7 Microflake scars |
| BFW 28 | 11.377 | 4.7 | 3.0 | 0.9 | 35 | 35 - 40 | Straight ; Even | Mat. seems not suitable; but edge round.6microfl.scrs. |
| FFW 29 | 16.700 | 3.9 | 2.6 | 1.5 | 70 - 75 | 80 | Straight ; Rough | No use-wear |
| CFW 30 | 34.821 | 6.3 | 4.2 | 1.2 | 40 - 50 | 45 - 50 | Irregular ; Rough | Shows crushing at the point where it laid on the anvil |
| CFW 31 | 9.279 | 4.3 | 3.4 | 0.5 | 20 | 20 | Slightly convex ; Even | Edge rounding ; Scarring ; 2 microflake scars |
| CFW 32 | 18.655 | 5.3 | 3.7 | 1.0 | 40 | 20 | Irregular ; Rough | Even though suitable no use-wear was discernable |
| FFW 33 | 26.836 | 5.3 | 3.6 | 1.3 | 50 - 55 | 45 - 55 | Straight ; Even | 4 microflake scars ; Edge rounding ; Definite use |
| BFW 34 | 24.463 | 6.7 | 3.4 | 1.1 | 40 - 45 | 50 - 55 | Straight ; Rough | No use-wear |

( Page 87 )

Appendix C: Measurements and first observations of the Waikalua flakes

Appendix D: Results of the microscopic investigation of the Waikalua Flakes

| Tool | Total Micro-flake Scars D / V | Snap D/V | Feather D / V | Step D/V | Hinge D/V | Configuration D / V | Edge Rounding D / V | Polish/Smoothing D / V | Striation D / V | Denticulation | Action | Contact Material |
|---|---|---|---|---|---|---|---|---|---|---|---|---|
| FFW 1 | None | -/- | - / - | -/- | -/- | None | SL / SL;UN | Yes / Yes | -- / -- | None | Cutting | Soft (Fish?) |
| CFW 2 | 6 / - | -/- | 4 / - | 2/- | -/- | SC / - | SL / UN | Yes / - | - / - | None | Scraping | Md-Hd (Wood) |
| CFW 3 | - / - | -/- | - / - | -/- | -/- | - / - | - / - | - / - | - / - | One Notch | Not used | Not used |
| CFW 4 | 1 / 3 | -/- | 1 / 1 | -/1 | -/1 | SC / SC | SL / SL | Yes / Yes | - / - | Interm/Shallow | Cut / Sli | Soft Flesh |
| FFW 5 | 4 / 5 | 1/0 | 2 / 2 | 1/2 | -/1 | SC / SC | SL / SL | Yes / Yes | - / - | Uninter/Deep | Cut / Sli | Soft Flesh |
| FFW 6 | 1 / - | -/- | 1 / - | -/- | -/- | SC / - | - / - | - / - | - / - | None | Not used | (Fish?) |
| FFW 7 | - / - | -/- | - / - | -/- | -/- | - / - | - / - | - / - | - / - | None | Not used | Not used |
| FFW 8 | - / - | -/- | - / - | -/- | -/- | - / - | - / - | - / - | - / - | None | Not used | Not used |
| CFW 9 | 2 / - | -/- | 1 / - | 1/- | -/- | SC / - | SL / UN | - / - | - / - | None | Scraping | Soft |
| FFW 10 | - / - | -/- | - / - | -/- | -/- | - / - | - / - | - / - | - / - | One Notch | Not used | Not used |
| CFW 11 | 5 / 5 | -/- | 2 / 2 | 3/2 | -/1 | SC / SC | SL;ST / SL;ST | Yes / Yes | Yes / -- | Interm/Shallow | Cut / Sli | Soft-Medium |
| CFW 12 | - / - | -/- | - / - | -/- | -/- | - / - | - / - | - / - | - / - | None | Not used | Not used |
| BFW 13 | - / - | -/- | - / - | -/- | -/- | - / - | - / - | - / - | - / - | None | Not used | Not used |
| CFW 14 | 2 / - | -/- | 2 / - | -/- | -/- | SC / - | SL / SL;UN | - / - | - / - | None | Scraping | Soft |
| BFW 15 | - / - | -/- | - / - | -/- | -/- | - / - | - / - | - / - | - / - | Interm/Shallow | Not used | Not used |
| FFW 16 | 4 / 3 | -/- | 2 / 1 | 1/2 | 1/- | SC / SC | SL;ST / SL;ST | Yes / Yes | - / - | Interm/Shallow | Cut / Sli | Soft Flesh |
| FFW 17 | - / - | -/- | - / - | -/- | -/- | - / - | - / - | - / - | - / - | None | Not used | Not used |
| FFW 18 | - / - | -/- | - / - | -/- | -/- | - / - | - / - | - / - | - / - | None | Not used | Not used |
| CFW 19 | - / - | -/- | - / - | -/- | -/- | - / - | - / - | - / - | - / - | None | Not used | Not used |
| CFW 20 | - / - | -/- | - / - | -/- | -/- | - / - | - / - | - / - | - / - | None | Not used | Not used |
| FFW 21 | - / - | -/- | - / - | -/- | -/- | - / - | - / - | - / - | - / - | None | Not used | Not used |
| BFW 22 | 5 / 3 | 1/- | 2 / 1 | 2/2 | -/- | SC / SC | ST / ST | Yes / Yes | - / - | None | Whittling | Medium-Hard |
| BFW 23 | 2 / 2 | -/- | 2 / 1 | -/1 | -/- | SC / SC | SL / SL | - / - | - / - | None | Whittling | Medium-Soft |
| FFW 24 | - / - | -/- | - / - | -/- | -/- | - / - | - / - | - / - | - / - | None | Not used | Not used |
| CFW 25 | - / - | -/- | - / - | -/- | -/- | - / - | - / - | - / - | - / - | None | Not used | Not used |
| CFW 26 | - / - | -/- | - / - | -/- | -/- | - / - | - / - | - / - | - / - | None | Not used | Not used |
| FFW 27 | 4 / 3 | -/- | 3 / 2 | 1/1 | 1/- | SC / SC | ST / ST | Yes / Yes | -- / Yes | None | Sawing | Medium-Hard |
| BFW 28 | 6 / - | 1/- | 2 / - | 3/- | -/- | SC / - | ST / Sl;UN | Yes / - | - / - | None | Scra / Pla | Medium-Soft |
| FFW 29 | - / - | -/- | - / - | -/- | -/- | - / - | - / - | - / - | - / - | None | Not used | Not used |
| CFW 30 | - / - | -/- | - / - | -/- | -/- | - / - | - / - | - / - | - / - | None | Not used | Not used |
| CFW 31 | 1 / 1 | -/- | - / - | -/1 | 1/- | SC / SC | SL / SL | - / - | - / - | None | Whittling | Soft |
| CFW 32 | - / - | -/- | - / - | -/- | -/- | - / - | - / - | - / - | - / - | None | Not used | Not used |
| FFW 33 | 4 / - | 1/- | 2 / - | 1/- | -/- | SC / - | ST / UN | Yes / - | - / - | None | Scraping | Medium-Soft |
| FFW 34 | - / - | -/- | - / - | -/- | -/- | - / - | - / - | - / - | - / - | None | Not used | Not used |

# University of Hawaii at Manoa

**Department of Botany**
St. John Plant Science Laboratory
Room 101 • 3190 Maile Way • Honolulu, Hawaii 96822
Telephone (808) 948-8369 • Cable Address: UNIHAW
(808) 956-8369

12. September 1990

Dear Boris,

we examined your samples under the light microscope and did histochemical tests for lignification.

The samples were found to contain plant material. The following photo slides of plant tissue were taken on a Zeiss Photomicroscope II.

Slide 16        Sclerenchyma (sclereids)
                   stain reaction (red) with Phloroglucinol-HCl

Slide 17        fiber
                   no stain reaction with Phloroglucinol-HCl

Slide 18, 19 Xylem elements

Good luck for your dissertation.

Sincerely,

(Dr. Karin Ruth Jacobsen) (Gail Murakami)

( Appendix E: Results of histochemical tests for lignification )

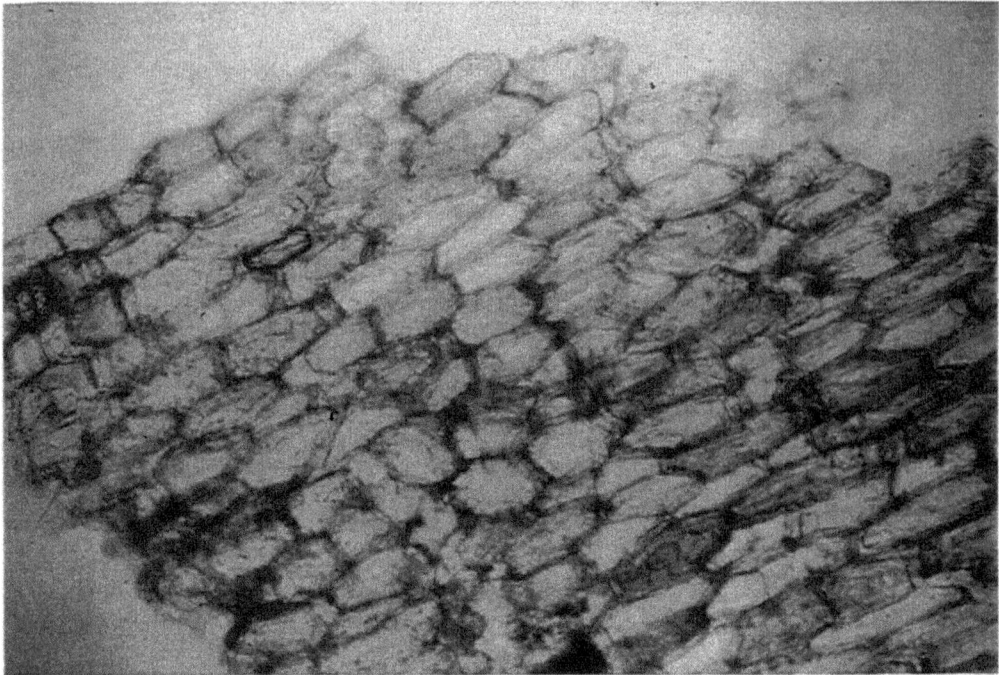

( Appendix E: Slide 16 Sclerenchyma )

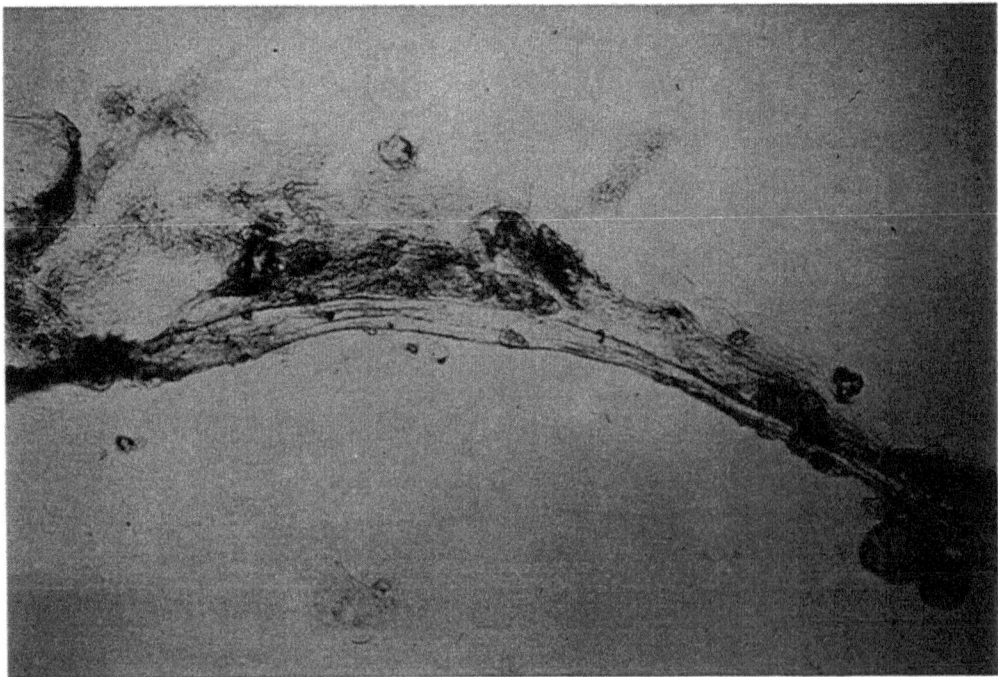

( Appendix E: Slide 17 Fiber )

( Appendix E: Slide 19 Xylem elements )

( Appendix E: Slide 20 Fiber )

91

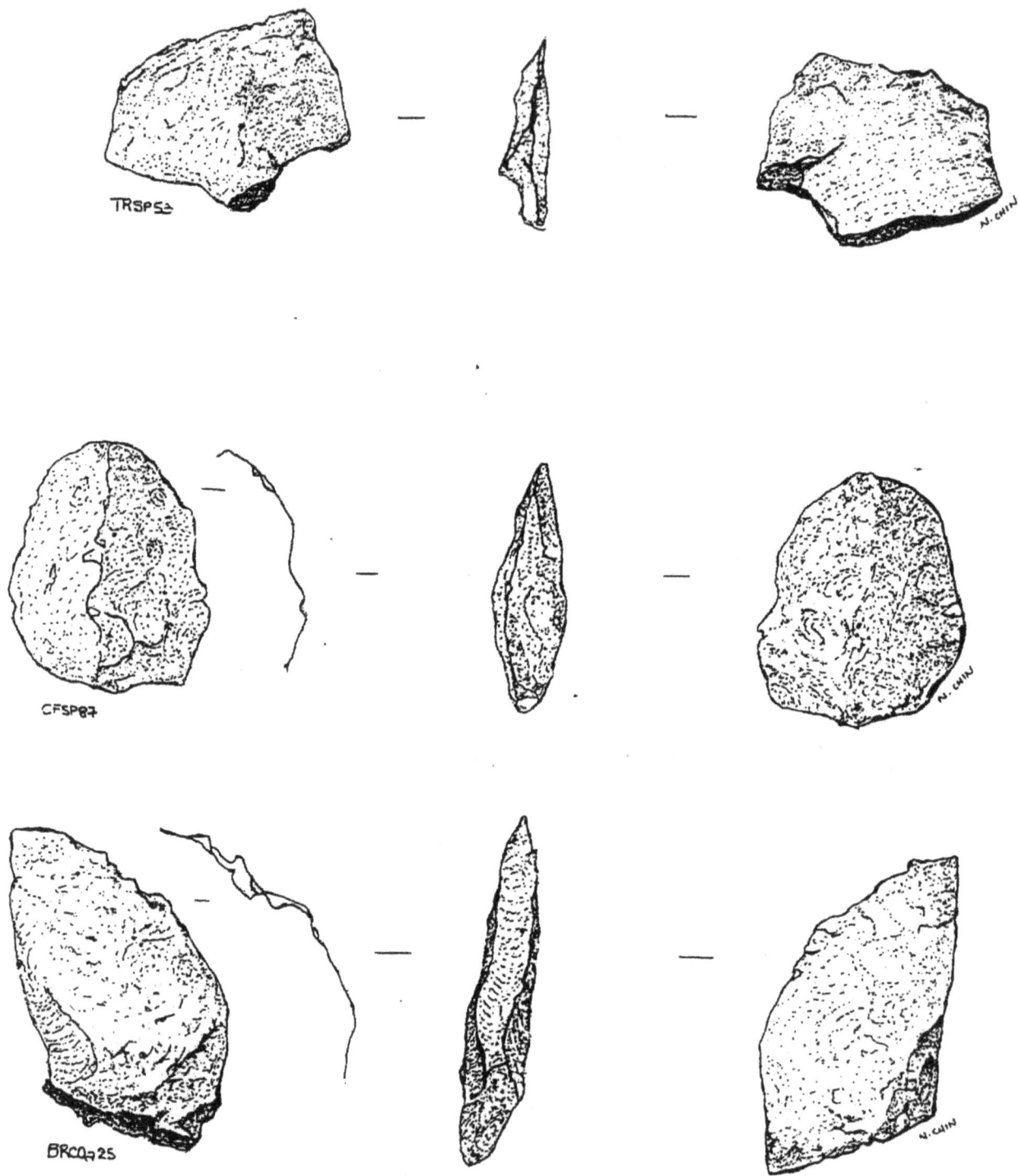

TRSPS3

CFSP87

BRCO725

( Appendix F: Some basalt flakes used for experiments )

( Drawing by Nancy Chin )

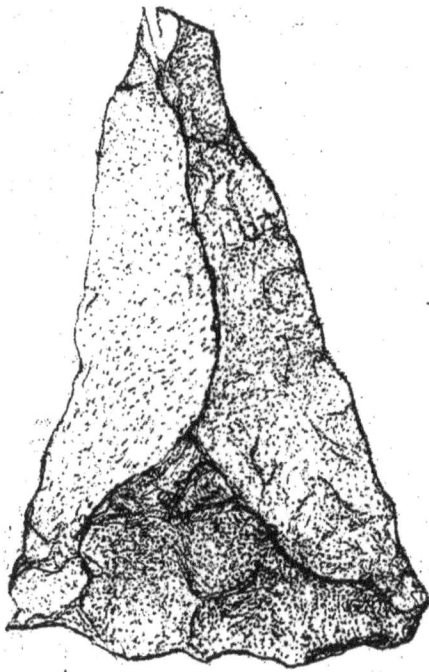
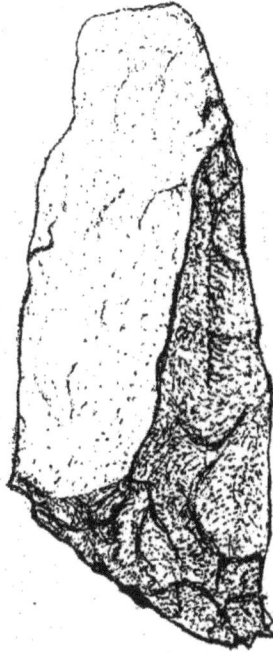
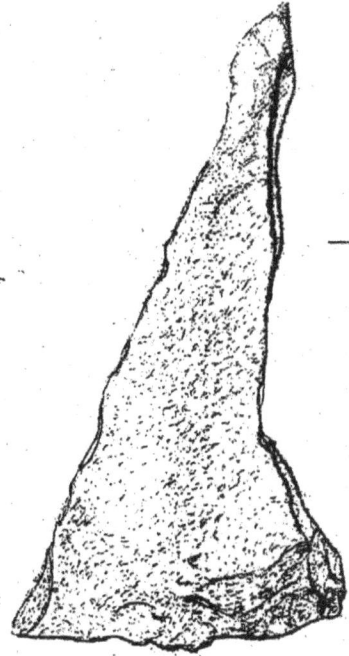

FFSP97

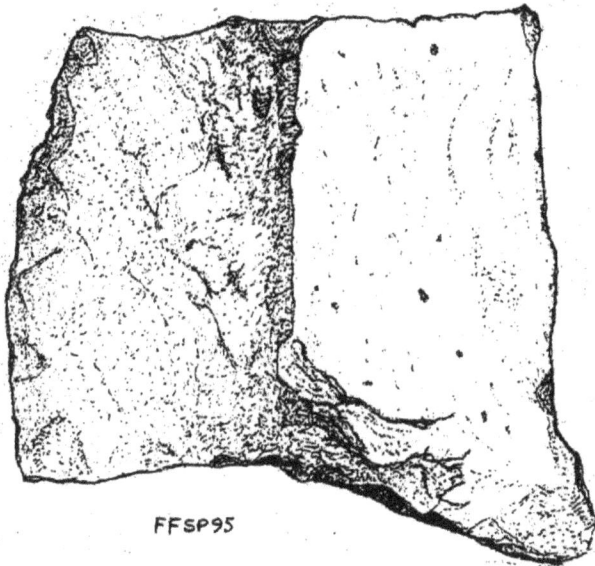

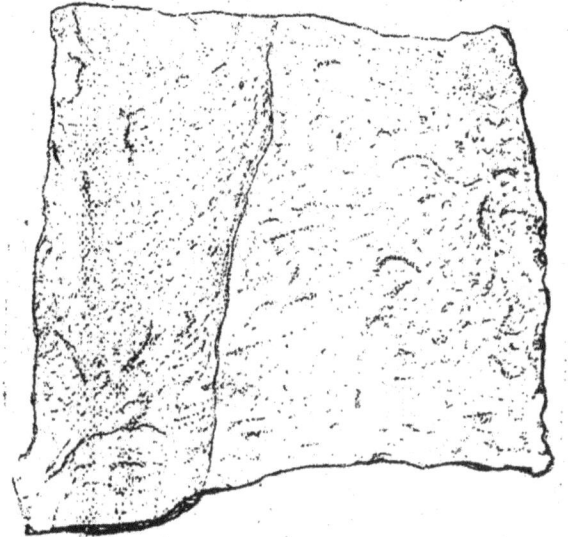

FFSP95

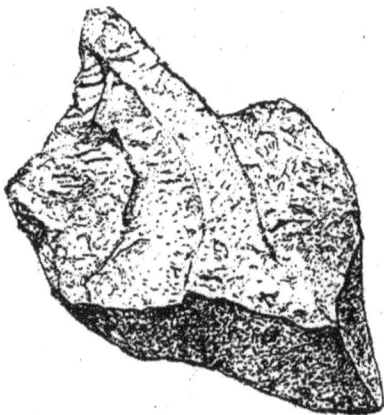
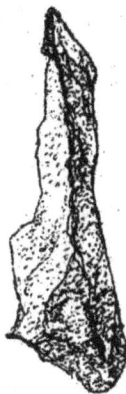

BRSP32

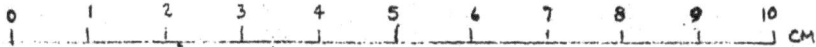

0  1  2  3  4  5  6  7  8  9  10  CM

( Appendix F: Some basalt flakes used for experiments )

( Drawing by Nancy Chin )

93

( Appendix G: Waikalua flake FF W 27 showing polish and striation at 200x magnification )

( Appendix G: Waikalua flake FF W 16 displaying edge rounding at 100x magnification )

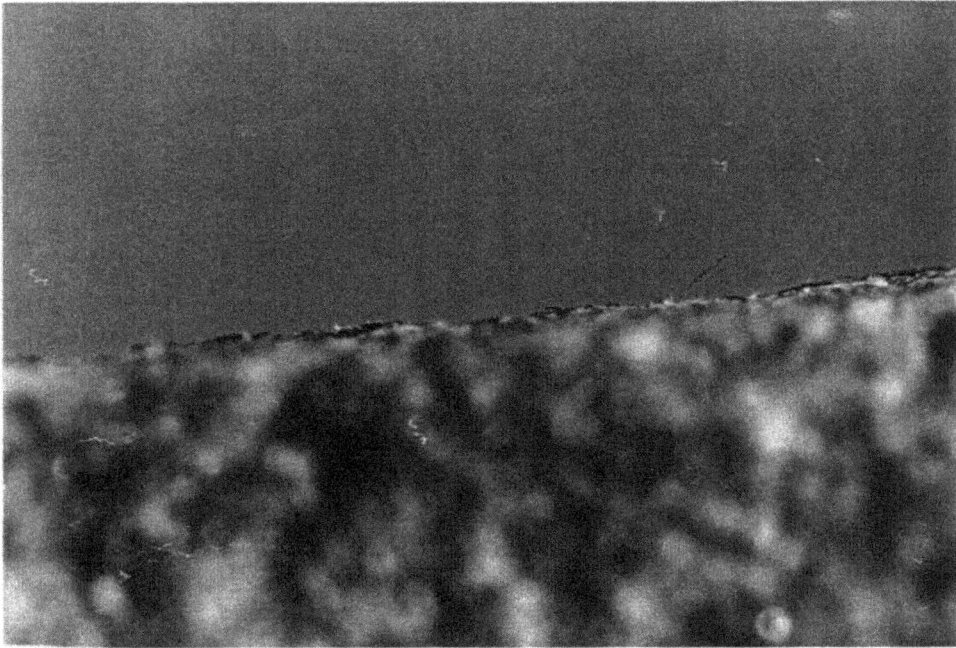

( Appendix G: Waikalua flake FF W 5 showing edge rounding at 100x magnification )

( Appendix G: Waikalua flake BF W 22 displaying polish at 350x magnification )

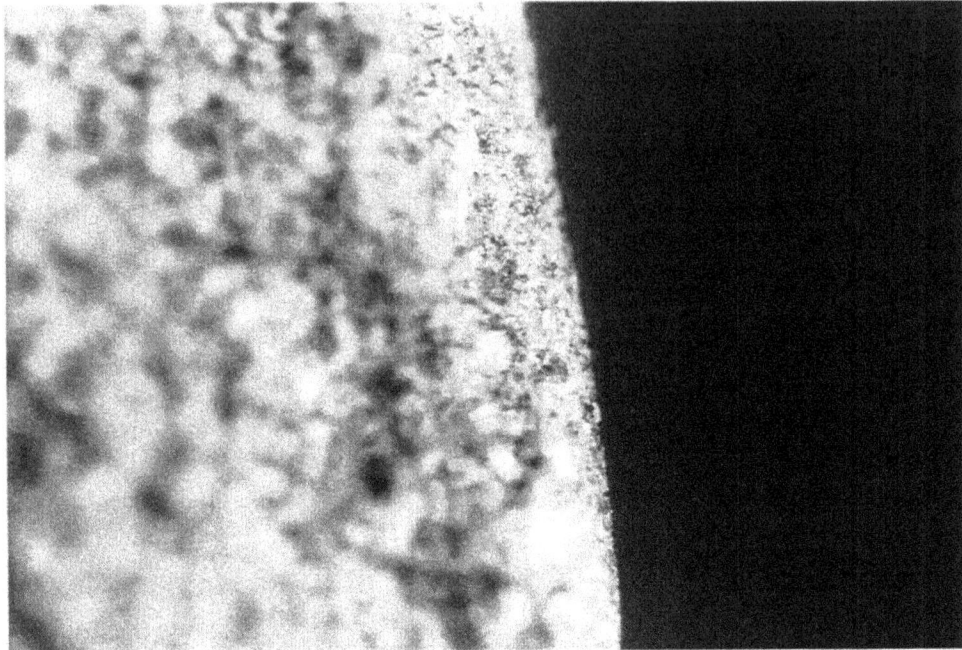

( Appendix H: Flake BF SP 30 displaying a polished edge at 200x magnification )

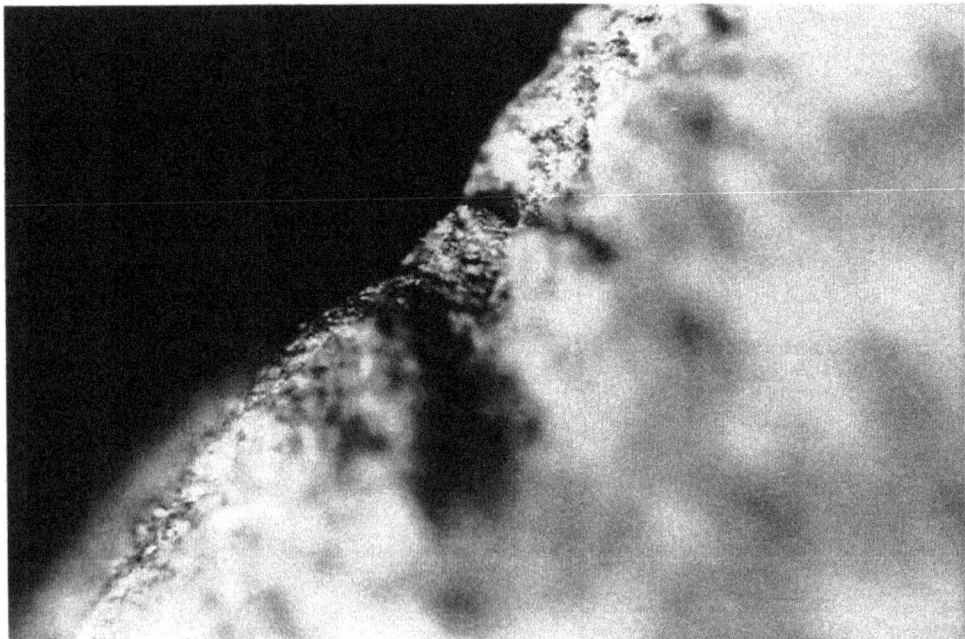

( Appendix H: Flake FF COa 7 showing retouch at 200x magnification )

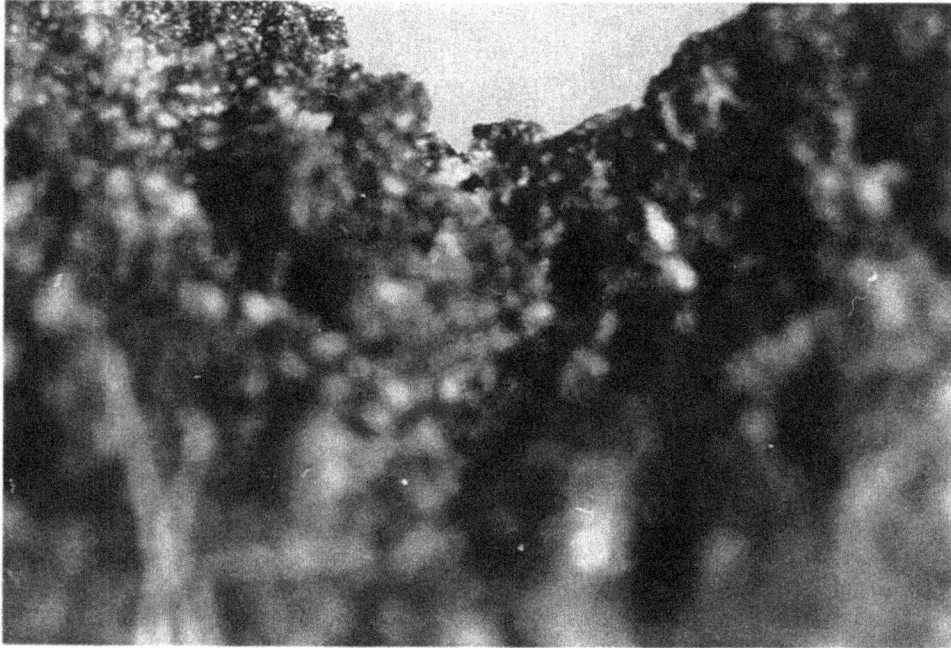

( Appendix H: Flake CF SP 81 showing scarring and denticulation at 200x magnification )

( Appendix H: Flake FF COa 1 displaying polish and striation at 350x magnification )

( Appendix H: Flake FF SP 55 displaying denticulation at 350x magnification )

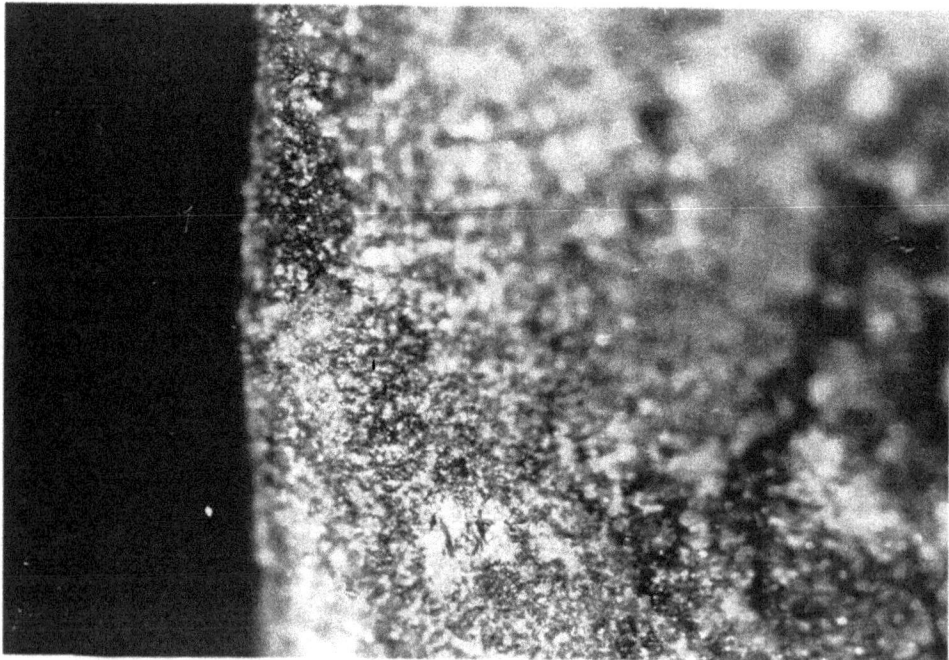

( Appendix H: Flake BF SP 64 showing polish at 200x magnification )

( Appendix H: Flake FF SP 85 displaying microflake scars with plant material adherent )

( Appendix H: Flake CF SP 87 showing polish and striation at 350x magnification )

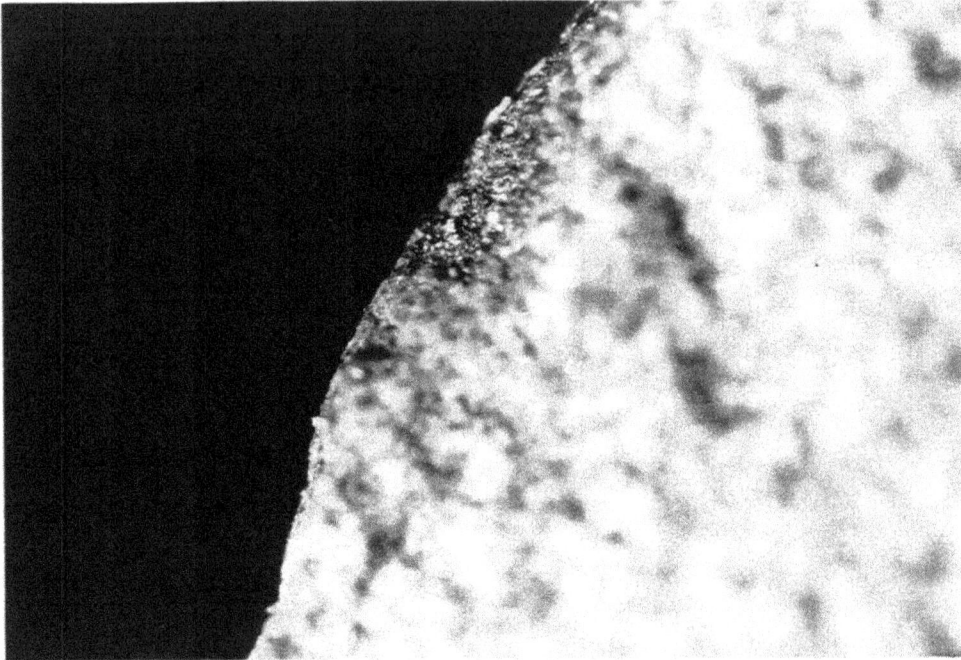

( Appendix H: Flake FF SP 93 displaying rounding and polish at 100x magnification )

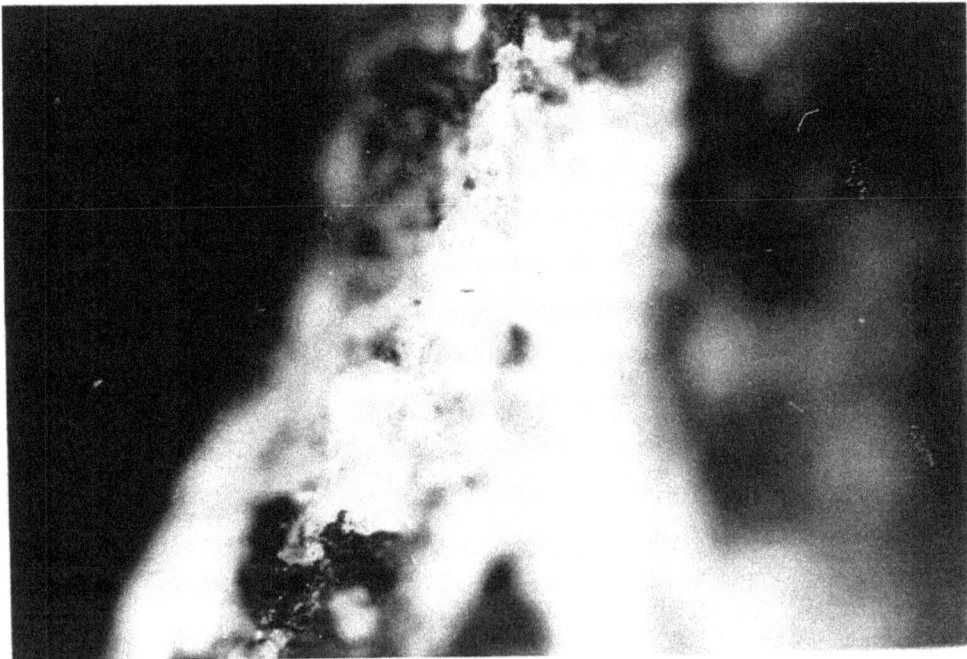

( Appendix H: Flake FF Coa 18 showing crushing at 350x magnification )

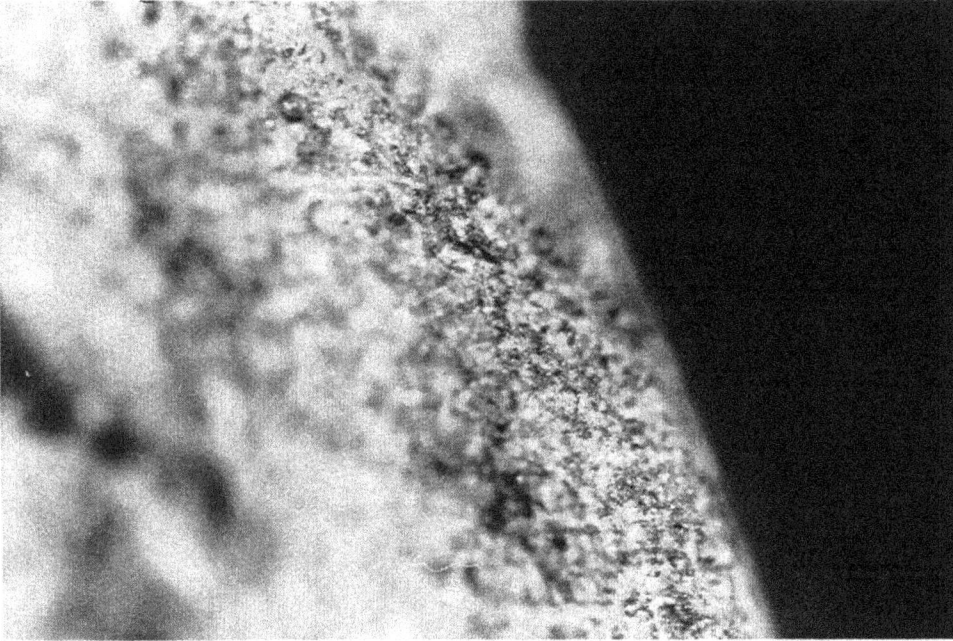

( Appendix H: Flake FF SP102 showing polish at 100x magnification )

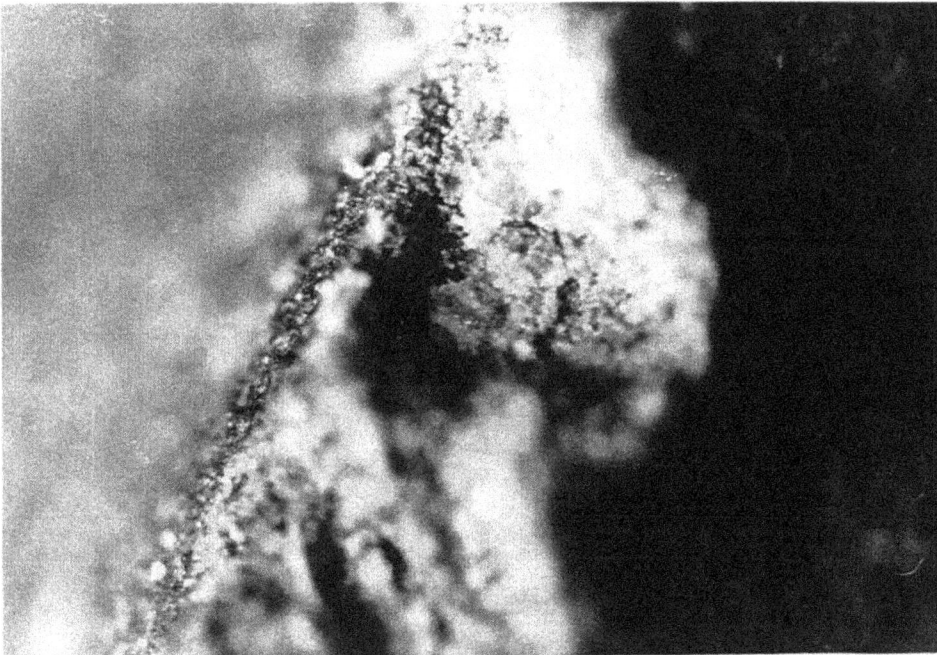

( Appendix H: Flake BF SP 36 displaying a microflake scar at 350x magnification )

( Appendix H: Flake BF SP 37 displaying egde smoothing at 100x magnification )

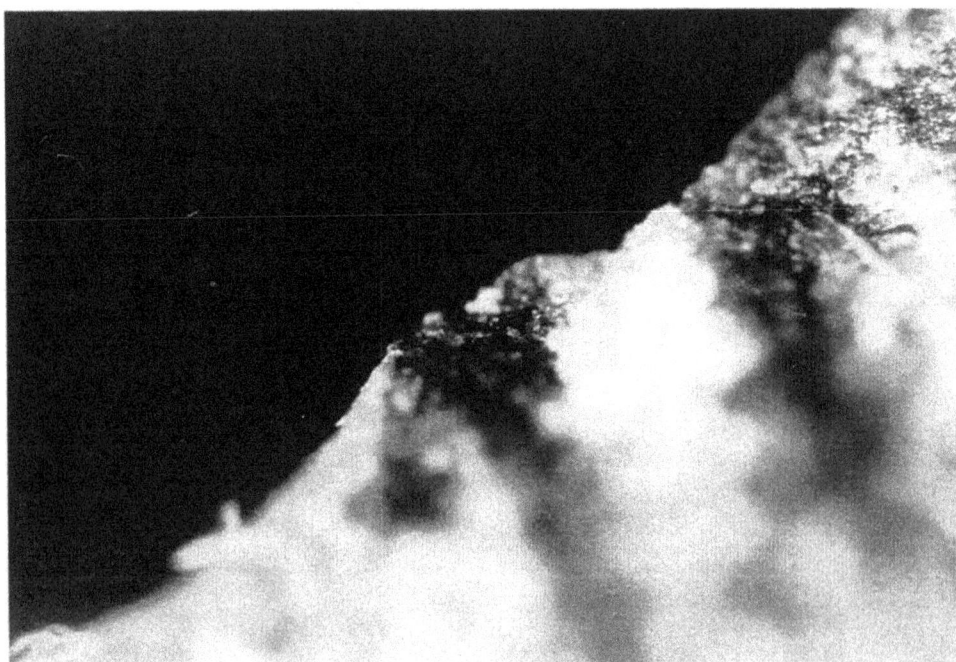

( Appendix H: Flake BF SP 50 showing crushing and flaking at 200x magnification )

( Appendix H: Flake FF SP 74 displaying polish and striation at 200x magnification )

( Appendix H: Flake FF SP 92 showing edge rounding at 100x magnification )

www.ingramcontent.com/pod-product-compliance
Lightning Source LLC
Chambersburg PA
CBHW061300270326
41932CB00029B/3419